Crimen Exceptum

The English Witch Prosecution in Context

Gregory J Durston

❦ WATERSIDE PRESS

Crimen Exceptum: The English Witch Prosecution in Context
Gregory J Durston

ISBN 978-1-909976-65-8 (Paperback)
ISBN 978-1-910979-75-4 (Epub ebook)
ISBN 978-1-910979-76-1 (Adobe ebook)

Copyright © 2019 This work is the copyright of Gregory J Durston. All intellectual property and associated rights are hereby asserted and reserved by the author in full compliance with UK, European and international law. No part of this book may be copied, reproduced, stored in any retrieval system or transmitted in any form or by any means, including in hard copy or via the internet, without the prior written permission of the publishers to whom all such rights have been assigned worldwide.

Cover design © 2019 Waterside Press by www.gibgob.com

Printed and bound in Poland by BookPress.eu

Main UK distributor Gardners Books, 1 Whittle Drive, Eastbourne, East Sussex, BN23 6QH. Tel: +44 (0)1323 521777; sales@gardners.com; www.gardners.com

North American distribution Ingram Book Company, One Ingram Blvd, La Vergne, TN 37086, USA. Tel: (+1) 615 793 5000; inquiry@ingramcontent.com

Cataloguing-In-Publication Data A catalogue record for this book can be obtained from the British Library.

Ebook *Crimen Exceptum: The English Witch Prosecution in Context* is available as an ebook and also to subscribers of Ebrary, Ebsco, Myilibrary and Dawsonera.

Published 2019 by
Waterside Press Ltd.
Sherfield Gables, Sherfield on Loddon,
Hook, Hampshire, RG27 0JG.

Online catalogue WatersidePress.co.uk

Table of Contents

About the author *vii*
Acknowledgements *viii*
Frequently Used Acronyms *ix*

1 **Historical Background** 11
      Preliminary Matters *11*
      Sources of Information *12*
      A Legal Phenomenon *14*
      Criminal Procedure *18*
      The Medieval Background *19*
      From Sorcery to Witchcraft *23*
      Cunning Folk and Benign Magic *26*
      The Identification of Black Witches *29*
      From Credulity to Scepticism *34*
      Counterfeit and Fraud *37*
      Extent of Witch Persecution *39*
      The Wider British Isles *44*
      Meta-Narratives *48*
      Female Involvement *52*
      Urban Witches *53*

2 **Candidates for Witch-hood** 55
      Introduction *55*
      Gender *59*
      Familial Connections *62*
      Previous Allegations *63*
      Age and Marital Status *64*
      Character and Social Status *66*

3 **A Witch's Career** 69
      Introduction *69*

　　　　　Familiars　*73*

　　　　　Alternative Forms of Enchantment　*77*

4　**Living With the Witch** 79

　　　　　Introduction　*79*

　　　　　The Dangers of Prosecution　*81*

　　　　　Appeasing the Witch　*82*

　　　　　Passive Defence　*83*

　　　　　Active Defence　*85*

　　　　　Scratching　*85*

　　　　　Use of Ecclesiastical Courts　*87*

　　　　　Vagabond Actions　*89*

5　**The Witchcraft Statutes** 91

　　　　　Introduction　*91*

　　　　　The 1542 Act　*92*

　　　　　The 1563 Act　*95*

　　　　　Elizabethan Prosecutions: A County Profile　*100*

　　　　　The 1604 Statute　*101*

　　　　　Jacobean Prosecutions: A County Profile　*108*

6　**Entering the Criminal Justice System** 111

　　　　　Introduction　*111*

　　　　　Triggering Event　*112*

　　　　　Supporting Allegations　*115*

　　　　　Taking Action　*116*

　　　　　Pre-Examination Questioning　*118*

　　　　　Justices of the Peace and the Witch-Hunting Process　*118*

　　　　　The JPs' Examination　*121*

　　　　　The Role of Confessions　*122*

　　　　　Deep Interrogation　*126*

　　　　　Growing Caution About Confessions　*130*

　　　　　The Decision to Prosecute　*131*

　　　　　Bail　*131*

　　　　　Ancillary Orders　*132*

Choice of Forum *133*
Pre-Trial Detention *135*

7 **Specialist Tests for Witchcraft** 137
Introduction *137*
Reciting Scripture *138*
Scratching *139*
The Witch's Teat *139*
Pricking and the Witch's Mark *142*
Natural Blemishes *145*
Swimming *146*

8 **Trial and Punishment** 153
Introduction *153*
The Grand Jury Hearing *153*
Arraignment *155*
The Trial *156*
The Evidence Adduced at Trial *157*
The Witnesses *158*
Expert Evidence *161*
Conviction and Execution Rates for Witchcraft *164*
Post-Conviction Reprieves *165*
Pregnancy *168*
Execution of Witches *169*

9 **Late-Jacobean and Caroline Prosecutions** 173
Introduction *173*
A Turning Point *174*
Caroline Prosecutions *176*

10 **The Civil War and Interregnum** 181
Introduction *181*
Matthew Hopkins and John Stearne *184*
Subsequent Campaigns *188*
Newcastle and Northumberland *188*

Kent *190*
Other Regions *191*
Late-Interregnum *191*

11 **From the Restoration to Abolition** 193
Introduction *193*
The Final Fifty Years *197*
The 1700s *199*
Final Conviction *201*
The Pamphlet War *201*
Final Prosecution *202*
Last Formal Allegations *203*
Repeal and the 1736 Act *203*
Survival of Popular Witch Beliefs *204*
Post-Repeal Incidents *205*

12 **Conclusion** 209

Select Bibliography *211*

Index *229*

About the author

Gregory J Durston is a barrister-at-law who has taught in Law Schools in England and Japan. He was for many years Reader in Law at Kingston University, Surrey and is currently an adjunct professor at Southern Cross University School of Law and Justice, New South Wales, Australia. He is the author of *Fields, Fens and Felonies: Crime and Justice in Eighteenth-Century East Anglia* (Waterside Press, 2016) and *Whores and Highwaymen: Crime and Justice in the Eighteenth-Century Metropolis* (Waterside Press, 2012).

Acknowledgements

I would like to acknowledge the invaluable assistance provided by the staff at Kingston University Library, Southern Cross University Library, and the British Library, as well as those at the county record offices cited. Additionally, I am extremely grateful for assistance from Rhoda Koenig and Judge Nicholas Philpot. Readers should note that abbreviated titles are sometimes used in footnotes; the full versions of these sources can be found on first use in the text and/or in the *Select Bibliography*.

Gregory Durston

London
Easter, 2019

Frequently Used Acronyms

ERO Essex Record Office

NRO Norfolk Record Office

OBSP Old Bailey Sessions Papers

TNA The National Archives

WYRO West Yorkshire Record Office

Crimen Exceptum

CHAPTER 1

Historical Background

Preliminary Matters

This book focuses on English prosecutions for witchcraft during the almost 200 years in which it was a secular felony. As such, it has a predominantly legal focus, covering all stages of the litigation process, from formal accusation, through trial and conviction, to execution. However, to make sense of the law and practice governing such prosecutions, it is also necessary to consider the context in which they occurred, and the years before and after proscription.

A huge amount of research on early-modern witchcraft, in all its aspects, has been published in the past three decades. Indeed, several scholars have argued that historians of the period are excessively preoccupied with the topic, which has received attention that is entirely out of proportion to its significance.[1] Nevertheless, a focus on the legal context of English witch trials can provide invaluable insights into the wider criminal justice system at this time, and raise more general questions about the law, some of which are still germane today. It also opens a window on day-to-day life in early-modern England, and can provide a vehicle for exploring a large range of issues in the period, from the status of women to the professionalisation of the legal process.

Furthermore, the issues raised by witchcraft are not purely of historical interest. Self-described witches still generate law-and-order problems in

---

1. Jan Machielsen, "'Moved and Seduced by the Instigation of the Devil': Witchcraft and the Law, 1450–1701". In *The Research Handbook on Interdisciplinary Approaches to Law and Religion*, Russel Sandberg et al. (ed.) 2016, p. 2.

various parts of the world, with murder (especially of children and albinos) sometimes being committed to secure body parts, with a view to using them for magical charms and rituals. Much more commonly, the banishment and killing of those suspected to be witches, particularly in countries such as India, Nepal, Papua New Guinea, the Congo, Angola, Nigeria, South Africa, Tanzania, and Indonesia, claims or destroys lives. These practices have sometimes become a challenge for developed countries because of their presence amongst migrant communities.[2] For example, in 2001 the mutilated torso of a ritually "sacrificed" West African child was found floating in the River Thames in London.[3]

Sources of Information

English court records are limited for much of the period when witchcraft was proscribed. Only the Home Circuit's gaol calendars for assizes (the highest jury court) have survived for the Elizabethan era, although there were six circuits, while those for Quarter Sessions (the lower jury court) are even thinner. Records for the seventeenth and eighteenth-centuries are better, but far from perfect; for example, on the Western Circuit most records are missing before 1670, apart from some bail books from about 1654. Worst of all, those for the important Midland Circuit are not available until the early-nineteenth century.

Furthermore, even when records produced by the English common law criminal justice system survive in their entirety, they are fairly limited, being largely confined to allegation, plea, verdict and sentence. There is almost no official evidence of what actually went on during the trial except, very occasionally, the sworn written deposition of a witness, taken before an examining justice of the peace (JP), appended to other papers in the case (and even this is not guaranteed to have been repeated in court).[4] In this the system differs from many of its continental counterparts, which adhered to Roman law.

---

2. Miranda Forsyth, "The Regulation of Witchcraft and Sorcery Practices and Beliefs", *Annual Review of Law and Social Science*, v. 12 (2016), p. 342.
3. Martin Bright and Paul Harris, "Thames torso boy was sacrificed", *The Observer*, 2 June 2002.
4. Jonathan Barry, *Witchcraft and Demonology in South-West England, 1640–1789* (Basingstoke: Palgrave Macmillan, 2013), p. 9.

For example, the records for witch trials in sixteenth century Rothenburg include extensive *Urgichtenbücher* or interrogation books. Suspects were held in the city gaol, where two members of the council questioned them, sometimes with the use of torture, about their alleged crimes. Near-verbatim records were made of these interrogations as they took place: these were then read and discussed by the rest of the council. When a trial was over, these records were bound into the interrogation books, along with all other documents pertaining to the case, including witness statements, the opinions of legal, theological, or medical experts, and any letters written to or by the council about the case. In some cases these run to hundreds of pages. This produces a rich source, one that is unmatched in England.[5]

However, supplementing official sources of information are large numbers of tracts and chapbooks on English witch trials. The first of these appears to have been published in 1566; others followed fairly swiftly, but they largely petered out after about 1597, and did not restart on a significant basis until 1612, before declining again between the early-1620s and the onset of the Civil War (which saw a surge in publications). They range in degrees of reliability from the highly accurate (fairly rare) to the extremely fanciful. For example, it seems that a chapbook from the early-eighteenth century, *An account of the tryals examination and condemnation of Elinor Shaw and Mary Phillip's* [sic] *(two notorious witches) at Northampton assizes on Wednesday the 7th of March, 1705*, is entirely fictitious (no witches were executed in England after 1685), and it is not the only such publication. Even those that are based on real trials differ considerably in reliability, especially on legal issues.

There are also a number of published books from the era that focus on, or allude to, the subject. Some books cover felony trials generally, only touching on witch prosecutions tangentially, but are vital to reconstructing the forensic environment for such hearings. Others comment directly on witch trials. Among the most important of the latter is a book by Thomas Potts, published in 1613, and based on his experience as the clerk of assize during the major witch trial that occurred in Lancashire in

---

5. Alison Rowlands, *Witchcraft Narratives in Germany: Rothenburg, 1561–1652* (Manchester: Manchester University Press, 2003), p. 7.

1612 (the largest held in England up to that time).⁶ As a court clerk, his legal expertise meant that his work, which was also formally approved by the trial judge involved, provides a rare professional insight into a Jacobean witch trial.

Together, such publications greatly influenced popular perceptions of witchcraft and, consequently, other witch trials. For example, in the 1650s there was a rash of witch trials in the tiny English colony of Bermuda, although its officials appear to have had no prior experience of identifying witches or conducting hearings into their crimes. It has been noted that the practices and procedures found in these trials are "curiously similar" to those described in English witch trial books of the time, as is the language employed in them.⁷ The inference must be that such books were the source of their "expertise" about such matters.

Nevertheless, it should also be remembered that at least some of the demonologies by contemporary authors were works of polemic, attempts to change commonly held attitudes rather than descriptions of general belief. Their bindings were often flimsy, their sales mixed, and some were not reprinted; they were rarely thought worthy of a permanent place in private libraries.⁸

A Legal Phenomenon

The early-modern European witch-hunts were neither orchestrated massacres nor spontaneous pogroms. Alleged witches, especially those in England, were not rounded up at night and summarily killed extra-judicially or lynched as the victims of mob justice. They were executed after trial and conviction with full legal process.⁹ As the Cambridge divine William Perkins observed in 1608, the identification of witches was not for "every man, but is to be done Judicially by the Magistrate,

---

6. Thomas Potts, *The Wonderfull Discoverie of Witches in the Countie of Lancaster* (London, 1613), p. B1.
7. Virginia Bernhard, "Religion, Politics, and Witchcraft in Bermuda, 1651–1655", *The William and Mary Quarterly*, v. 67, no. 4 (2010), p. 706.
8. Simon Francis Davies, *Witchcraft and the Book Trade in Early Modern England*, Ph.D. thesis, University of Sussex, 2013, p. 175.
9. Peter S. Poland, "A Matter of Life, Death, and Legal Procedure: What every Texas lawyer should know about the European witch hunts", *Texas Bar Journal*, v. 77, no. 9 (2014), p. 785.

according to the forme and order of the Law". The exceptions, where it was alleged that ordinary people had taken the law into their own hands, were noteworthy for their rarity and would, legally, have been classified as murder. Indeed, in 1667 it was claimed that three men had been hanged after the York Assizes for murdering a Wakefield woman suspected of bewitching one Nathan Dodgson.[10]

However, and inevitably, a handful of such cases did occur. For example, during the highly unusual circumstances of the English Civil War, it seems that a witch may have been summarily executed near Newbury. As a contingent of the parliamentary army was marching through the area, some of its soldiers foraged for food; one of them apparently saw a tall, slender woman standing on a very flimsy board on a nearby river. Several of their commanders then came by, and also saw the woman standing on the plank "turning and winding it which way she pleased". When she came ashore they ordered that she be seized. She revealed little in questioning, and the officers debated amongst themselves as to what should be done with her, given that it "so apparently appeared she was a Witch". Being loath to set her free, or to take her with them, they resolved to shoot her. However, this proved pointless, the bullets apparently missing or bouncing off and the witch laughing at the troops. Eventually, one of them, who had heard that drawing blood from the vein on the temple of a witch would break her power, was allowed to cut her. The witch immediately knew that the devil had left her and her power was gone; she began lamenting. The soldiers discharged a pistol beneath her ear, killing her instantly.[11]

It is impossible at this distance in time to know how much, if any, truth to ascribe to this account, although it was reported elsewhere, the troops' conduct being mocked by their royalist counterparts, who felt that they were "so superstitious, you thinke one tooth of such a grave, old woman may be the preservation of Prince Rupert himselfe".[12]

---

10. James Sharpe, *Witchcraft in Seventeenth-Century Yorkshire: Accusations and Counter Measures* (York: University of York, Borthwick Papers, 1992), p. 14.
11. Tract 1643, pp. 1–6.
12. *Mercurius Britanicus Communicating the Affaires of Great Britaine*, 10 October 1643-17 October 1643.

The summary execution of another witch by parliamentary forces near Malmesbury is also mentioned in documents from about the same time.

More generally, it is likely that a few villagers secretly did away with the odd person rumoured to be a witch, after which their neighbours closed ranks and refused to give up potential suspects to the authorities. For example, in May 1562 a maid named Anne Borough informed the Exeter magistrates that three months earlier her master, Thomas Marshall, had gone out one night and carried out a savage physical assault upon a woman in the city. When it was (mistakenly) suggested to the merchant that she had died, his response was merely to say, "It is but an olde wytche gonne". He may have thought she had bewitched him and was attempting to draw her blood and so break her power.[13] In December 1625 Robert Urmeston wrote to Edward Nowell, describing the murder of a reputed female witch that had been committed by a man named Pemberton near Whalley in Lancashire.[14]

Such cases were found in other parts of the British Isles. For example, a witch lynching appears to have occurred in Antrim town in 1698, when the Presbyterian neighbours of an allegedly bewitched young girl murdered an old woman by strangling and burning her after the Scottish manner. A similar case occurred in Scotland itself, in 1704, when a mob dragged the suspected witch Janet Cornfoot from a house and down to the harbour in Pittenweem. There she was beaten and then covered by a door that had heavy stones placed on top of it, until she was crushed to death.[15]

Occasionally, people being "tested" as suspected witches also died as a result of their experiences, even if this had not originally been the aim. For example, in 1699 the elderly Widow Coman, thought to be a witch in Coggeshall, Essex, was repeatedly "swum" by a mob on a cold November day. She subsequently contracted what appears to have been severe influenza and died.[16] Similarly, in September 1730, after a

---

13. Mark Stoyle, "'It Is But an Olde Wytche Gonne': Prosecution and Execution for Witchcraft in Exeter, 1558–1610", *History*, vol. 96, no. 2 (2011), p. 139.
14. John Bruce (ed.) *Calendar of State Papers Domestic: Charles I, 1625–26*, (London: HMSO, 1858), pp. 166–178.
15. Stuart MacDonald, "Torture and the Scottish Witch-hunt: a re-examination", *International Review of Scottish Studies*, v. 27 (2002), p. 100.
16. Tract 1712 (1), p. 21.

child started having fits at Frome in Somerset, a local cunning man was consulted, and a woman named Richards duly identified as the witch responsible. She was dragged from her house, despite having a fever, and swum before almost 200 spectators in a millpond, where she appeared to float. Richards was recovered from the water, albeit already very ill. Brandy was poured down her throat to revive her, but she died an hour later. Subsequently, only three of the 40 people—one of them a local constable—who had been actively involved in swimming her could be identified, as local people closed ranks. A coroner's inquest returned a non-capital manslaughter finding against them.[17]

A tiny number of "witches" were killed *during* such procedures, rather than dying from their after-effects. In 1751, some 15 years after the crime of witchcraft was abolished, two paupers, a man named John Osborne and his wife Ruth, widely reputed among their neighbours in Tring in Hertfordshire to be malefic witches, and who resided in a local workhouse, were seized by a huge mob from the vestry room of a church to which they had fled for sanctuary and dragged to Marston Mere, where they were enclosed in a sheet and thrown in.[18] One of the alleged ringleaders, Thomas Colley, an intoxicated chimney sweep, then waded in and turned them over with a stick so that the woman eventually drowned. He was subsequently convicted of murder and hanged, his body being gibbeted fairly near to the mere to act as a public deterrent to such behaviour. Prior to his death, he appears to have been encouraged or prompted to make a signed confession, partly blaming his actions on strong liquor, and urging others to reject so "absurd & wicked a Conceit" as to believe in witches.[19] Even so, his execution had to be temporarily delayed because local people threatened to rescue him, thinking that he had been unfairly treated, given that his victim was a witch; a guard of soldiers was required to escort him to the gallows.[20] Nevertheless, such cases were the exception. The vast majority of English witches who were

---

17. *Daily Journal*, 15 January 1731.
18. *London Evening Post*, July 30, 1751–August 1, 1751.
19. Hertfordshire Archives, ref: D.ELw.z22.
20. *Read's Weekly Journal Or British Gazetteer* 10 August 1751; *General Evening Post* 17 August 1751- 20 August 1751.

killed met their deaths at the end of a rope, on a properly appointed gallows, after trial and conviction.

Criminal Procedure

In theory, English witches were subject to exactly the same pre-trial and trial procedure as any other felony suspect or defendant. Nevertheless, witchcraft was not like any other crime, not least because, unlike conventional offences, most people in the modern era would view the crimes alleged as inherently impossible. As a result, the prosecution was faced with "proving" something that could not have occurred. This sometimes necessitated recourse to forensic methods that would not have been acceptable for conventional crimes.

Crimen Exceptum

This state of affairs was found throughout Europe. On the Continent witchcraft was often expressly recognised as *crimen exceptum,* a crime that differed from other offences so that normal evidential rules and requirements could be relaxed. As the Burgundian Judge Henri Boguet noted in 1602, it was a "crime apart" because of its enormity, its secrecy, and its nocturnal nature, so that, in witch cases, the "usual legalities and ordinary procedure cannot be strictly observed".[21] Contrary to some modern belief, it was certainly not unique in this. Treason, heresy, counterfeiting and even some forms of murder were often accorded the same status, because witnesses to such crimes were often hard to find, allowing trial judges to move matters along on strong suspicion, even if the normal, strict, rules of evidence were not fully satisfied.[22]

The willingness of courts to do this varied from country to country, but also sometimes within a country, by region. For example, it has been argued that those areas of early-modern France where the judiciary adhered to the letter of the law were less likely to produce prosecutions and convictions for witchcraft than those where magistrates were willing

---

21. Brian P. Levack (ed.), *The Witchcraft Sourcebook* (London: Routledge, 2004), p. 135.
22. Jonathan L. Pearl, *The Crime of Crimes: Demonology and Politics in France, 1560–1620* (Waterloo: Wilfrid Laurier University Press, 1999), p. 33.

to depart from established legal rules. As a result, the presence of witch trials within the country was often indicative of locally weak legal institutions. However, the growth of the "fiscal state" during the early-modern era, one that could collect taxes efficiently, required standardised and properly enforced judicial procedures everywhere; as these expanded, the frequency of French witch trials decreased.[23]

In practice, the same willingness to treat witchcraft as a crime apart prevailed in England, although, because the country was not bound by the formal evidential requirements found in many Roman law states, it was less clearly enunciated. As in parts of the Continent, it was argued that such relaxation was necessary in witch cases because "The Justices of Peace may not always expect direct evidence, seeing all their works are workes of darkenesse, and no witnesses present with them to accuse them".[24] This sometimes had a wider impact on the criminal-justice system. For example, Barbara Shapiro has suggested that the detailed discussion of witch trials found in published material of the time contributed to a sharper understanding and definition of the previously neglected use of circumstantial evidence in English law.[25]

The Medieval Background

Belief in magic has been identified in almost all pre-modern societies, including those dominated by the great monotheistic religions. In medieval Europe, it was woven into the fabric of rural life, sometimes being blended with aspects of orthodox Christianity. This is unsurprising; throughout the sixteenth century, Protestant leaders such as Martin Luther could deplore the incorrigible profanity of the masses, which sometimes appeared almost congenitally incapable of mastering basic Christian doctrine. In England one observer claimed that sermons delivered on the faith usually "went in at the one eare, and out at the other". In the early-seventeenth century, a Kentish clergyman could still complain

---

23. Noel D. Johnson and Mark Koyama, "Taxes, Lawyers, and the Decline of Witch Trials in France", *The Journal of Law and Economics*, v. 57, no. 1 (2014), p. 86.
24. Tract 1645 (1) pp. 1–8.
25. Orna Alyagon Darr, *Marks of an Absolute Witch: Evidentiary Dilemmas in Early Modern England* (Farnham: Ashgate, 2011), pp. 81–82.

that only about one in ten of his parishioners "knew the basics of Protestant doctrine".[26]

As a result, people at all levels of society, in all parts of Europe, might have recourse to magical spells, folk healing, divination, and fertility charms or potions, and this was as marked in England as it was, for example, in France, despite the developing sixteenth century confessional divide.[27] There was a widespread faith in the reality of invisible powers and spirits, both benign and malign, to influence daily life, while a belief in witchcraft was almost endemic.

Nevertheless, for much of the medieval period the secular courts were not very concerned about these phenomena, and even church forums do not normally appear to have been preoccupied with the subject, whether in England or on the Continent.[28] In 1258 Pope Alexander IV even issued a canon expressly discouraging prosecutions for witchcraft. On a very localised basis, and by way of illustration, between the late-fourteenth and late-fifteenth-centuries, nobody found guilty of using sorcery was executed at Rothenburg in Germany. Some people there were banished, whether for several years or permanently, and in 1409, in one of the most extreme disposals, a woman was branded after she had promised to teach other females how to find buried treasure and to work love magic. (It is unclear whether this was imposed for sorcery or fraud). However, in 1435 two women who had used sorcery appear to have escaped any form of punishment.[29]

The situation in late-medieval England was equally benign. In most cases it was left to the lower ecclesiastical courts to deal with those who claimed to perpetrate "magical" activities. The basic forum for witchcraft hearings was the archdeacon's court, although decisions could sometimes be appealed to the bishop's consistory court.[30] Cases would be

---

26. Larry Gragg, "Witchcraft in the Early Modern West", *Comparative Civilizations Review*, v. 72, no. 72 (2015), pp. 138–139.
27. Heidi Breuer, *Crafting the Witch: Gendering Magic in Medieval and Early Modern England* (Abingdon: Routledge, 2009); Suzannah Lipscomb, *The Voices of Nimes: Women, Sex, and Marriage in Reformation Languedoc* (Oxford: Oxford University Press, 2019), p. 131.
28. John Bellamy, *Crime and Public Order in England in the Later Middle Ages* (London: Routledge and Kegan Paul, 1973), pp. 61–63 and p. 156.
29. Alison Rowlands, *Witchcraft Narratives*, p. 7.
30. Karen Rushton, "History of the Ecclesiastical Courts of the Diocese of Canterbury, 1566–86", *Archaeologia Cantiana*, v. 134 (2014), pp. 263–281.

presented after periodic visitations by the archdeacon, usually as a result of a defendant's general reputation in his or her parish. Thus, in Chaucer's *Canterbury Tales*, written about 1390, the friar lists the crimes that come under this jurisdiction; among them, but of no more significance than sexual incontinence, is witchcraft: "An erchedeken, a man of high degree, That boldly dide execucioun, In punisshinge of fornicacioun, Of wicchecraft, and eek of bauderye". Frequently the courts seem to have regarded belief in magic, necromancy, and sorcery as simple superstition and a matter for mild correction (and better lay education), if they were prosecuted at all. [31]

Such attitudes continued to prevail in England during the fifteenth and early-sixteenth centuries so that prosecutions for witchcraft and supernatural offences (of all types) were relatively infrequent, even in the church courts. In the large Canterbury diocese, there may have been an average of just two or three such cases a year. Some defendants, especially those who admitted their crimes, were merely admonished and warned not to repeat them. Others were cleared with assistance from their neighbours, acting as compurgators. Where cases were proved or admitted and punishments imposed, they were often milder than those given out for fornication, let alone for "normal" heresy.[32]

This pattern of very occasional prosecutions and mild punishments was replicated in the Winchester and Norwich dioceses and, it seems, elsewhere in England. For example, in 1499 an ecclesiastical court in Norwich cited Marion Clerk for claiming to be able to cure people of various diseases, to prophesy the future, inform clients of impending misfortunes, and find hidden treasure (fairly standard services provided by "cunning folk"). Admitting her guilt, and indicating a religiously syncretic world-view, Marion told the court she received her abilities from "God and the Blessed Mary and from les Gracyous Fayry". Marion's mother, Agnes, was also accused of practising the "superstitious arts". The court merely ordered them not to do such things again and to perform penance. The women duly renounced their former practices and agreed to

---

31. Kathleen Kamerick, "Shaping Superstition in Late Medieval England", *Magic, Ritual, and Witchcraft*, v. 3, no. 1 (2008), pp. 29–53.
32. Sheila Sweetinburgh (ed.), *Later Medieval Kent, 1220–1540* (Martlesham: Boydell Press, 2010), pp. 194–195.

make public procession and offer candles in four places: Norwich cathedral, their parish church in Ashfield, Bury marketplace, and before the image of Saint Mary in Woolpit (a popular place for local pilgrimages).[33] At the most, such cases might be met by ritual beatings, church courts not being able to order punishments that shed blood.

Very occasional allegations of witchcraft being used to effect extremely serious crimes *were* tried in secular courts during the late medieval period. However, these cases, such as that of Dame Alice Kyteler (who had the misfortune to outlive four wealthy husbands) in Ireland in 1324, and Joan of Arc (accused of heresy, treason, and invoking spirits) in Normandy in 1431, often had political overtones.[34] Similarly, in England, Margery Jourdemayne, apparently a "wise woman" from Eye next Westminster, was found guilty of treasonable witchcraft, committed using wax effigies, and burned at the stake in 1441.

Jourdemayne, a woman in her late twenties, had long been reputed as a witch who could provide spells and potions to deal with domestic problems; indeed, a contemporary chronicler referred to her as "callid the wycch of Eye". During the course of the 1441 trial, it was revealed that she had been held for some months at Windsor Castle ten years earlier for an unspecified offence concerning sorcery. Unfortunately, her clients eventually extended to major figures at court whose interests were not confined to love potions and finding lost property. At some point between July and September 1441, Margery was arrested by the King's men and taken to the Tower of London, along with Eleanor, Duchess of Gloucester. It was alleged that Jourdemayne had assisted the duchess, the wife of the uncle to Henry VI, and three clerics, by attempting to use witchcraft to bring about the death of the King. This was not the first such attempt on the monarch's life. In 1430 seven witches from different parts of England had been arrested in London, accused of plotting the young King Henry's death, and imprisoned in the Fleet.[35] Even so, such cases were rare.

---

33. Kamerick, "Shaping Superstition", pp. 29–53.
34. Machielsen, "'Moved and Seduced'", p. 2.
35. Jessica Freeman, "Sorcery at Court and Manor: Margery Jourdemayne, the Witch of Eye next Westminster", *Journal of Medieval History*, v. 30 (2004), p. 346.

From Sorcery to Witchcraft

It seems that a new concept and fear of witchcraft began to emerge in Europe during the early-fifteenth century, as theologians, philosophers, and lawyers started to believe that it was a powerful and heinous offence in its own right. This crime was normally comprised of acts of harmful magic, or *maleficium* (plural, *maleficia*), and heretical devil worship, or diabolism. The two could, of course, be combined; some European prints show those attending a satanic Sabbath also preparing malign spells and potions. However, they might be prosecuted separately.[36]

The 1420s saw some of the first instances of active witch-hunting. There were several cases in the Pyrenees, especially in the Aneu Valley. At about the same time, two women in Rome were executed for killing babies for diabolical reasons.[37] Much more significant were a series of trials for heresy and sorcery that were conducted in the western Alpine area, particularly in Switzerland, in the same decade. In August 1428 delegates from seven districts in Valais demanded that the authorities initiate an investigation into alleged witches and sorcerers. Within 18 months, more than 100 people had been burned at the stake. A further series of witch trials in the region, lasting until 1447, ensued. The exact number of victims is unknown, but is believed to have amounted to almost 400 people. Accusations against them included killing cattle and abducting and consuming children. It was also claimed that these witches (many of them men) would meet Satan and be taught magical curses if they formally renounced Christianity.[38] Such trials then spread slowly into different parts of the Continent, as a belief in the malefic powers of witches who had made a formal pact with the devil gradually gained ground.

Although largely absent before the 1420s, the roots of this transformation of simple sorcery into the darker crime of satanic witchcraft can be traced back to the early-1300s. In the ensuing century, social changes, heightened clerical concern about harmful magic, and a changing

---

36. Brian P. Levack, *The Witch-Hunt in Early Modern Europe* (London: Pearson Education, 2006), pp. 4–9.
37. Machielsen, "'Moved and Seduced", p. 2.
38. Ronald Hutton, *The Witch: A History of Fear, from Ancient Times to the Present* (New Haven: Yale University Press, 2017), p. 171.

understanding as to how it operated altered the attitude of the authorities, both lay and ecclesiastical, towards the phenomenon. It encouraged them to take allegations of magic more seriously. For example, in 1320 the Cardinal of Santa Sabina wrote from the papal seat at Avignon to inquisitors at Toulouse and Carcassonne ordering them to take action against sorcerers in their areas who were engaged in demonic invocation. Some six years later, Pope John issued a decree condemning sorcerers who would "make a pact with hell" in exchange for material benefits.[39]

The belief system on which this new fear of witches was premised was codified in a series of treatises and letters written during the last two-thirds of the fifteenth century by lay judges and clerics. These gradually added new refinements to the subject. For example, around 1436 the Briançonnais secular judge Claude Tholosan wrote *Ut magorum et maleficiorum errores manifesti ignorantibus fiant*, describing the basic acts of *maleficium* and diabolism he had encountered in his judicial career. The notion of the witches' Sabbath and other cultic activities can also be seen taking shape. In 1437, in a letter to all inquisitors of heresy, Pope Eugene IV (1431–1447) observed that the Prince of Darkness was ensnaring Christians into his sect. These unfortunates reportedly made a written agreement or pact with the devil that empowered them to perform evil deeds. In the same year, the Dominican Johannes Nider discussed the concept in the *Formicarius*, a treatise on theology that was, allegedly, partly based on conversations with a secular judge, Peter of Bern. It was followed by the anonymous *Errores Gazariorum*, probably written by an inquisitor in Savoy around 1440, and the first to mention a pact between witches and demons that was written in blood, and by Nicholas Jacquier's *Flagellum Haereticorum Fascinariorum*, written in about 1458. Alphonso de Spina's demonological tract the *Fortalitium Fidei*, written in 1469 and printed two years later, would also be highly influential.[40] Most important of all, in 1486 a pair of German Dominicans, Jacob Sprenger

---

39. Michael D. Bailey, "From Sorcery to Witchcraft: Clerical Conceptions of Magic in the Later Middle Ages", *Speculum*, v. 76, no. 4 (2001), pp. 966–967.
40. Michael D. Bailey, *Magic and Superstition in Europe: A Concise History from Antiquity to the Present* (Lanham: Rowman & Littlefield, 2006), pp. 131–135.

and Heinrich Krämer, produced a rather extreme, but very widely read, work on witchcraft, the *Malleus Maleficarum*.[41]

It should be noted that none of the fairly numerous fifteenth and early-sixteenth century treatises about witchcraft was written or published in England. Indeed, the country played almost no role in the late medieval discourse about witchcraft that produced such notions as the witches' Sabbath and diabolical pact, possibly helping to explain their reduced significance in both the national consciousness and domestic legislation.[42] One of the earliest general treatises on magic and witchcraft in English, Francis Coxe's *A short treatise declaringe the detestable wickednesse of magicall sciences,* came out as late as 1561.

Nevertheless, although the foundations had been laid, secular prosecutions for witchcraft were relatively rare in most of Europe until the middle of the sixteenth century, when larger-scale witch-hunting started to occur over much of the Continent, albeit that it was still highly localised. This reached a peak in the decades after about 1570. By the start of the seventeenth century, many ordinary people and large elements of Europe's governing elite shared a conviction that those who perpetrated harmful magic had traffic with the devil and participated in an organized cult.[43] This belief remained widespread for the first third of the 1600s. Indeed, it has been suggested that as much as 90 per cent of all European witchcraft trials took place in the 30 years before and after 1600, although in a few places, such as the Dutch Republic, they did not last much beyond the start of the seventeenth century (the last execution there was in 1608).

Thereafter, elite belief in witchcraft, and the need to prosecute witches, declined rapidly, although, as a very general rule, it lasted longer in Eastern than in Western Europe. In Poland, witch trials began and finished late, with most occurring between 1675 and 1720, although there was an

---

41. Alan Charles Kors and Edward Peters, *Witchcraft in Europe 1100–1700: A Documentary History* (Philadelphia: University of Pennsylvania Press, 1972), pp. 98–104 and pp. 109–110.
42. William Monter, "Review: Re-contextualizing British Witchcraft", *Journal of Interdisciplinary History*, v. 35, issue 1 (2004), p. 106.
43. Edward Bever, "Witchcraft Prosecutions and the Decline of Magic", *The Journal of Interdisciplinary History*, v. 40, no. 2 (2009), pp. 263–264.

execution for the crime as late as 1774.⁴⁴ In Hungary, the 1720s proved to be the key decade for prosecution.⁴⁵ As late as 1749, Maria Renata Singer, an elderly nun from a convent near Wurzburg in Germany, was executed as a witch, with her body being burnt to ashes and her head impaled on a post near her religious institution. A Jesuit priest then gave a sermon on the need to punish witches. Nevertheless, the aftermath of this execution prompted a debate amongst German intellectuals, and brought a belated close to such cases in Bavaria.⁴⁶ The last known court-ordered execution for witchcraft in Europe occurred at Glarus in Switzerland in 1782, although an allegation of non-fatal poisoning was appended to this case.⁴⁷ The decision occasioned widespread outrage, even at the time.

Cunning Folk and Benign Magic

Although malign or "hurting" witchcraft emerged from a more general tradition of magic during the late medieval period, it was only one aspect of early-modern witchcraft. Non-malefic or "white" magic, as distinct from its "black" counterpart, continued to be part of everyday life for most people.

Throughout the fourteenth century, cunning men and women had offered to help identify thieves and find lost or stolen property, using a variety of magical techniques, just as they would for more than 400 years to come. ("Cunning" derives from the Anglo-Saxon *cunnan*, to know). Sometimes they were even sued in the civil courts when they failed to keep their end of a bargain. As with other forms of magic (see above), and despite longstanding official disapproval, the secular and ecclesiastical authorities rarely took action against them.⁴⁸ Little had changed a century later. The London Commissary Court registers for the second half of the

---

44. Wanda Wyporska, *Witchcraft in Early Modern Poland, 1500–1800* (Basingstoke: Palgrave MacMillan, 2013), p. 23.
45. Malcolm Gaskill, *Witchcraft: A Very Short Introduction* (Oxford: Oxford University Press, 2010), p. 68.
46. Lyndal Roper, *Witch Craze: Terror and Fantasy in Baroque Germany* (New Haven: Yale University Press, 2006), p. 29.
47. Machielsen, "Moved and Seduced", p. 2.
48. Owen Davies, *Popular Magic: Cunning-folk in English History* (London: Hambledon, 2003), iii and pp. 2–3.

fifteenth century reveal that the ecclesiastical authorities were still very reluctant to prosecute those who were consulted by women wanting to attract a husband or people who sought the recovery of missing items.[49]

This popular separation between good and bad witchcraft survived unabated during the era of witch prosecutions, often to the annoyance of the authorities, and even though the activity of cunning folk was sometimes criminalised. Thus, in 1646 John Gaule was to note that amongst ordinary people, a "distinction is usually made betwixt the White and the Blacke Witch: the Good and the Bad witch".[50]

This distinction was found in most of Europe. In Scotland there was the same separation of "charmers", as cunning folk were often known there, from black witches. The former provided similar services to their English counterparts: love-magic; counter-magic; fortune telling and finding stolen goods, etc. Much of the population continued to value their work, even after the Reformation. Reflecting this, although the draconian Scottish Witchcraft Act of 1563 made providing, or even seeking, such magical assistance a potentially capital offence, it was almost never enforced, charming being treated as an ecclesiastical matter, and left to the kirk and its church courts for punishment (usually public penance), if action was taken at all. As a Scottish observer noted after the North Berwick witch panic of 1590–1591, although the 1563 Act provided that all those found "to consult with sorcerers, witches or suthesayers, thay sall dee the death. Bot this law was never heirto-fore put in practise." The 1563 Act was used against diabolical black witches.[51]

How cunning folk entered their "professions" is uncertain; there was no formal agreement with the devil to empower them, as there was with malefic witches. Seventh sons and daughters were widely believed to have the gift of natural powers of healing, but the great majority did not fall into this category. In practice, some may have learnt their trade as apprentices from those who were already established, as was the case with a Dorset cunning man in the 1560s, but there is only limited evidence for this. Most probably they were usually self-taught, perhaps by

---

49. Freeman, "Sorcery at Court", p. 346.
50. Tract 1646 p. 4.
51. Julian Goodare, "The Scottish Witchcraft Act", *Church History*, v. 74, no. 1 (2005), pp. 54–57.

combining a study of sixteenth and seventeenth century occult manuals with a general knowledge of popular tradition.[52]

A variety of names were given to cunning people, in different parts of England. "Wise" man or woman was also popular, while "conjuror" was sometimes found in southern England for male practitioners of the craft; educated people were disproportionately likely to use "white witches" in the decades immediately prior to 1736. Whatever their titles, early-modern cunning folk provided a similar range of supposed services to their medieval predecessors, being, *inter alia*, an amalgam of fortune teller, physician, veterinarian and witch doctor. Most important, they claimed to be able to detect stolen or lost property; identify black witches, thieves and other locally-based felons; unbewitch or at least relieve the symptoms of the bewitched; promote love or attraction; and cure various illnesses. They also provided charms or amulets that purported to protect their wearers.

The dividing line between cunning folk and popular physicians could be very narrow. For example, in 1597 Paul Eigden and Alexander Violett (a former churchwarden) were presented to the Canterbury Archdeacon's Court for consulting a witch or sorcerer. Eigden partially admitted the matter, stating that his wife had been ill and, being aware of one Mother Chambers' reputation as a healer, he consulted her, but denied that she was a witch. Violett had also consulted Chambers, over a sick child, but claimed that she had merely made a normal diagnosis of "yelow jandis" and provided legitimate medicine.[53]

Similarly, at the Ludlow Court Leet in November 1649, Margaret Bridgens was accused of "exorcising witchcrafts, charmings, sorceries etc". She denied that she had any such skill or had ever practised magic. When asked if neighbours had ever requested her to assist them in finding lost and stolen items, she admitted that they had, but insisted that she had not helped them, and could not do so. She also denied that she placed charms on linen taken from the sick to cure their illnesses. However, she admitted to being a conventional healer and conceded that

---

52. Owen Davies, "Cunning-Folk in England and Wales during the Eighteenth and Nineteenth-centuries", *Rural History*, v. 8, no. 1 (1997), pp. 91–107.
53. Arthur Hussey, "Visitations Of The Archdeacon Of Canterbury", *Archaeologia Cantiana*, v. 26 (1904), p. 31.

she had applied "salves and medicines to mend those that hath diseases when they had sought with her". More damagingly, she also admitted that she had been present on one occasion, long before, when a cunning man used magic.[54]

The Identification of Black Witches

The identification of malefic witches was one the most important services provided by cunning folk, and played a major role in witch prosecutions throughout the era of proscription. For example, in 1564, when Agnes and Edward Baynton's only son died in what they thought were suspicious circumstances, they asked Jane Marsh, a widow who claimed to be able to detect people who employed malign witchcraft using her own special powers, to investigate. Marsh blamed two women, claiming that Dorothy Baynton, the beneficiary of Edward's estate if he died without male issue, had procured Agnes Milles to kill the young boy with witchcraft. Dorothy firmly denied the charge, avoided punishment, and eventually brought a lawsuit against Marsh. However, Milles confessed when questioned and was hanged.[55]

Similarly, at the end of the sixteenth century one of Anne Kirk's female neighbours in Castle Alley, London, with whom she had argued violently, accused her of being a witch after one of her children pined away and died, while another was also apparently afflicted. Her husband went to a cunning woman living at Bankside; she duly confirmed a diagnosis of witchcraft. The afflicted family cut off a piece of Kirk's coat, as instructed by this woman, and burned it with the surviving (but sick) child's underwear. The child recovered, but Kirk was eventually executed.[56]

Almost a century later, in the same area, after his wife sickened and their five-year-old daughter died, another man suspected that they had been bewitched. He went to one Dr Hanks, a cunning man in Spittlefields, who advised him to take a quart of his wife's urine, her nail parings, and some of her hair, and boil them, which he did. Afterwards

---

54. Shropshire Archives, ref: LB11/4/76/16.
55. K. J. Kesselring, "Bodies of Evidence: Sex and Murder (or Gender and Homicide) in Early Modern England, c.1500–1680", *Gender & History*, v. 27, no. 2 (2015), pp. 245–262.
56. Anon, *The Triall of Maist. Dorell* (London, 1599), pp. 1–20.

"he swore he heard the prisoner's voice at his door, and that she screamed out as if she were murdered, and that the next day she appeared to be much swelled and bloated".[57]

In East Anglia, in 1654, John Smithbourne's wife developed a large sore on her breast. In order to find a cure he was persuaded by his sister to visit a shoemaker named Hall who was also a well-regarded cunning man. Hall suggested that a witch was behind his wife's medical problems. To counter the *maleficium* he gave her a powder to be ingested and a paper, covered in circular symbols, to be pinned to her clothes (this still survives in the Norfolk Record Office).[58]

However, the use of magical detection was not confined to supernatural crimes. For example, shortly after Easter 1578, Sybil Browne's master lost various pieces of linen that appear to have been drying in his garden, including a smock, a neckerchief, and a pair of ruffs. Browne asked one Thomas Lynforde to go to a Mr Blumfield, a cunning man in Chelmsford, to find out who had taken the garments. Thomas claimed that he saw the face of a man named Barnes in a glass that Blumfield showed him, and so suspected that this man was the thief.[59] This particular cunning man had a widespread reputation for securing the return of stolen goods. In another case, George Freeman lost a mare and eventually went to Blumfield for assistance. Blumfield advised him to seek his mare in the northeast of Chelmsford and charged Freeman a shilling.[60]

However, providing such services could be illegal under the 1563 Act, albeit not a capital offence, and only rarely indicted. Even so, in 1578 Blumfield was prosecuted, and a tailor named Thomas Lynforde from North Ockendon was bound over to give evidence against him. Perhaps Lynforde was a dissatisfied customer.[61]

Recourse to cunning folk was not limited to the peasantry. In 1621 Edward Fairfax noted that their clients included some of the "best sort" amongst his neighbours in Yorkshire.[62] This might extend to clergymen

---

57. OBSP, Trial of Jane Kent, 1 June 1682: t16820601a-11.
58. NRO C/S 3/box 41a.
59. ERO Q/SR 67/44.
60. ERO Q/SR 67/46.
61. ERO Q/SR 67/43.
62. Tract 1621(1) p. 11.

and their assistants. In 1583 the churchwardens of Thatcham in Berkshire sent for a wise woman to find out who had stolen the communion cloth from their church, despite the church's own strong opposition to such investigative techniques. In a similar vein, in 1608 William Laws, the rector of High Halden in Kent, visited William Childes, a cunning man from Tenterden, after his corn was stolen and his cattle fell sick.[63]

Even magistrates might turn to cunning folk. In September 1600, Joseph Stileman wrote to Sir Robert Cecil, noting that the condition of Israel Amyce, a Hertfordshire JP, was a little improved, and there were some hopes of his recovery. The magistrate had apparently fallen gravely ill after he examined a lewd woman who was also a notorious witch, and then committed her to the gaol at Hertford. His doctors could not explain his illness, but Amyce concluded that the woman he had sent to prison had bewitched him in revenge, so that he was almost consumed to the bone. When Stileman heard of this, he sent to a wise woman who lived some 12 miles from Waltham. She sent Amyce some potions to take before he went to bed that night. Having done so, his health improved, and at dinner he could eat more meat than previously.[64] (He eventually died in 1607).

It is impossible to ascertain the number of cunning people, not least because they manifest different levels of involvement. It was clearly extremely high, so that throughout the period under consideration, most English people had ready access to them. In 1616 John Cotta thought that they "swarmed" throughout the kingdom. Similarly, the clergyman and author Robert Burton (1577–1640) complained that it was possible to find "cunning men, wizards and white witches" in every village in the land.[65]

The personal backgrounds of cunning folk varied, but they were far more likely to be male than were black witches. More than 60 per cent of cunning people in MacFarlane's Essex study were men, while 90 per cent of malefic witches from the same county were female.[66] (The witch

---

63. Patricia Hyde and Michael Zell, "Governing the County". In *Early Modern Kent, 1540–1640*, Michael Zell (ed.) (Woodbridge: Boydell Press, 2000), pp. 7–38.
64. R. A. Roberts (ed.), *Calendar of the Cecil Papers in Hatfield House: Volume 10, 1600* (London: HMSO, 1904), pp. 302–315.
65. Gragg, "Witchcraft", p. 140.
66. Darren Oldridge (ed.), *The Witchcraft Reader*, (Abingdon: Routledge, 2002), p. 290.

finder John Stearne also noted this gender difference).⁶⁷ Cunning folk also tended to be of a somewhat higher average social class than black witches. Many were artisans, such as shoemakers and carpenters, practising their craft as a remunerative sideline. Others were low-grade clergymen or schoolmasters. In his Essex survey, Macfarlane concluded that of 23 cunning men with recorded occupations, seven were connected with the medical profession, three were probably clerics, two were schoolmasters, two astrologers, two yeomen, two labourers, one a churchwarden, one a minor gentleman, and three artisans (a miller, comber, and shoemaker). Cunning women might be herbalists and midwives.⁶⁸

According to John Walsh, a Dorset cunning man examined by the ecclesiastical authorities in 1566, witches would practise only one type of magic, either hurting or curing (black or white).⁶⁹ However, other observers, especially clerics and Puritans, were much less sanguine about the difference. They feared that cunning men and women provided an entrée to malefic witchcraft, and they stressed the indivisibility of magic. If cunning folk were not tricksters but had real powers, these did not come from God, so must necessarily have come from the devil.⁷⁰ Furthermore, seeking assistance from white witches was a violation of the First Commandment, and their presence was especially corrosive, because they appeared to be benign and so were more likely to be trusted. As a result, in 1617, Thomas Cooper even thought that the "*Blesser or good Witch* (as we terme her) is farre more dangerous then the *Badde* or *hurting Witch*".⁷¹

In practice, the two categories of witch were not regarded as hermetically separated. For example, Ursula Kemp (1525–1582), a wise woman from St Osyth in Essex, was accused of being a black witch. As her reputation as a cunning person grew, many of her neighbours sought cures from her. However, several of the same people eventually implicated her in malefic witchcraft. Grace Thurlow testified that when she became lame she asked for Kemp's help. Kemp agreed to heal her for a shilling. Thurlow got better but then refused to pay Kemp her fee, saying she could

---

67. John Stearne, *A Confirmation and Discovery of Witch Craft*, London, 1648, p. 87.
68. O. Davies, "Cunning-Folk", pp. 91–107.
69. Barbara Rosen (ed.), *Witchcraft in England 1558–1618*, (New York: Taplinger, 1972), p. 70.
70. George Gifford, *A dialogue concerning Witches and Witchcraftes*, London, 1593, p. G.1.
71. S. F. Davies, *Witchcraft and the Book Trade*, p. 12.

not afford it. The two women argued and Kemp threatened to get even with Thurlow. The latter testified that she and her son had subsequently suffered ill health, and her baby daughter had died. Thurlow complained to the magistrate and an investigation followed.

Moving up the social scale, in December 1643 Nicholas Culpeper (1616–54), a celebrated Cambridge-educated apothecary, astrologer, physician, and herbalist, was indicted at the Middlesex Sessions for bewitching a Shoreditch widow named Sarah Lynge. He was acquitted. Although little is known about the case, it is likely that Lynge was a client, and that the two had fallen out when he failed to cure her of an illness and she concluded that he bore her malice (a not uncommon scenario in such cases).[72]

Joan Peterson (or Patterson), the "Witch of Wapping", a moderately prosperous healer who lived near Shadwell, in London, was also noted for having a foot in both camps. Some claimed Peterson had helped them or their animals, that she had cured a man suffering from severe migraines that were beyond the ken of conventional doctors, and had assisted a cow keeper whose cattle had been bewitched. However, other local people believed that she was the black witch attacking them. For example, it was claimed that Peterson had afflicted a former client who had refused to pay for his cure, so that he "rots as he lies". Even worse, it was asserted that Peterson had bewitched and "strangely tormented" a local child without any apparent justification. Damningly, Peterson's maid allegedly saw her entertain a familiar in the form of a squirrel, which talked with her at night. She was eventually executed at Tyburn in April 1652, although it was strongly rumoured that she had been framed as part of a property dispute, and that underhand methods had been used to secure her conviction.[73]

Despite such cases, it was an uphill battle to change popular attitudes towards white witches. As Richard Bernard noted, although people were sometimes eager to prosecute black witches "the good witch, all sorts

---

72. Frederick Valletta, *Witchcraft, Magic and Superstition in England, 1640–70* (Farnham: Routledge, 2000), p. 114.
73. Tract 1652 (1) pp. 3–7.

can let alone". Even churchwardens usually failed to present them to the ecclesiastical courts, let alone prosecute them in a secular forum.[74]

From Credulity to Scepticism

Throughout the period in which witchcraft was proscribed, from the Tudors to the Hanoverians, credulity and scepticism about the phenomenon co-existed.[75] In 1621 the Reverend Henry Goodcole freely acknowledged the: "diuersitie of opinions concerning things of this nature [witchcraft], and that not among the ignorant, but among some of the learned".[76] Even when belief in witchcraft was at its peak, during the late Elizabethan period, significant numbers of observers, including judges and JPs, would have been doubtful about important aspects of the phenomenon, its extent, or even (albeit very much more rarely) its very existence. Conversely, in 1736, significant numbers of well-educated men still believed in the reality of witchcraft and its ability to effect malign results in the world. What changed were the relative proportions of these two groups.

The fall in witchcraft prosecution was linked, at least in part, to a gradual alteration in elite attitudes. Both the Scientific Revolution and the Enlightenment engendered intellectual change amongst educated people, if only via a process of cultural transmission. In 1685 George Sinclair expressly attributed the rise in scepticism about witchcraft to the spread of the doctrines of Hobbes, Spinoza, and Descartes.[77] Thomas Hobbes thought that witches were not possessed of special powers, though those that claimed to be witches were properly punished because of their threat to public order. The final years of the seventeenth century even saw the more general emergence of what was termed "sadducism" (alluding to the Sadducees of the New Testament), used to describe those who denied the reality of spiritual beings. This belief particularly alarmed the

---

74. Richard Bernard, *A Guide to Grand-Jury Men*, London, 2nd. edn., 1630, p. A5.
75. Malcolm Gaskill, "Witchcraft Trials in England". In *The Oxford Handbook of Witchcraft in Early Modern Europe and Colonial America*, Brian P. Levack (ed.) (Oxford: Oxford University Press, 2013), p. 284.
76. Tract 1621 pp. 1–10.
77. George Sinclair, *Satan's Invisible World Discovered*, Glasgow, 1685, p. 1325.

proponents of witch trials, even if it was held only by tiny numbers of educated people.[78]

The transformation of attitudes was not a simple process, and should not be exaggerated. For example, even in Restoration England, the number of physicians who practised in a completely materialistic framework was relatively small. Most members of the medical profession held varying degrees of acceptance of a traditional world view in which spiritual maladies could produce physical results.[79]

Nevertheless, a general change in attitudes gradually came about because elites dominated the legal process, even if the justice system saw the involvement of people from many other stations in life. All of the judiciary, many JPs, a significant proportion of grand jurors, and some petty jurors were well-educated men. If they were reluctant to entertain allegations of witchcraft, whether in the pre-trial or trial process, it would inevitably affect the number of prosecutions brought, and convictions obtained, for the crime.

Acute scepticism about witchcraft was a minority position, even amongst educated men, in the period from about 1575 to about 1615, when elite and popular views about the phenomenon overlapped to a significant degree. Of course, it was never absent, even at the very height of anti-witch activism. Reginald Scot (1538–1599), a prosperous Kentish gentleman, had studied at Oxford, albeit leaving without taking a degree (not unusual in that period). He was an MP for New Romney and probably a JP at some point in his career. In his erudite and very lengthy *Discoverie of Witchcraft* of 1584, he referenced 212 authors whose works in Latin he had consulted, and another 23 who wrote in English, as well as citing his personal observation of witch prosecutions in his native county. Scot argued that a belief in witchcraft was both patently unreasonable and contrary to the basic principles of reformed religion. Alleged manifestations were deliberate frauds, illusions due to mental illness on the part of the observers, or the product of coincidence. His *Discoverie* was not only the first extant largescale treatise on witchcraft by

---

78. Michael Hunter, "The Decline Of Magic: Challenge And Response In Early Enlightenment England", *The Historical Journal*, v. 55, no. 2 (2012), p. 401.
79. Garfield Tourney, "The Physician And Witchcraft In Restoration England", *Medical History*, v. 16, no. 2 (1972), p. 149 and p. 154.

an English author, but may also have been the most sceptical work on the subject printed anywhere in Europe during the early-modern period.[80]

Scot was not a voice crying in the wilderness, even when he wrote. He was an influential author whose book was widely read, something that may have been indicative of higher levels of scepticism about witchcraft in the 1580s than has sometimes been suggested.[81] Others shared his views. For example, in 1603, the Reverend Samuel Harsnett (1561–1631) published *A Declaration of Egregious Popish Impostures*, an investigation into the exorcisms performed by Catholic priests at Denham in Buckinghamshire during the 1580s. Harsnett was fairly sceptical about the existence of demons. Even in 1616, the Reverend Alexander Roberts could lament that many people thought witches were "deluded by fantasises, and misled, not effecting those harmes wherewith they bee charged, or themselves acknowledge".[82]

Nevertheless, men like Scot were in a minority in Elizabethan and early-sixteenth century England. Sir Edmund Anderson (1530–1605), who was appointed justice of assize on the Norfolk Circuit in 1581, and viewed himself as a scourge of witches, was even better educated, and generally esteemed as a lawyer, being the author of two well-received legal books in his younger days. His views on witchcraft were slightly extreme, even for the time, but not absurdly so. (He was never blindly credulous of such allegations).

More generally, a belief in magic and witchcraft amongst many educated people is easy to discern in the late sixteenth century. For example, magic appears to have been a fashionable temptation for Elizabethan students. In September 1567, a visitation of New College, Oxford, conducted by ecclesiastical commissioners led by the Bishop of Winchester, focussed on uprooting popery, but also considered other moral failings found in the college. Amongst them was the use of magical practices by its members. Thomas Hopkins admitted owning a book with "written conjurations" or spells. He was one of the college's younger members, probably not more than 19-years-old, and had yet to obtain his BA.

---

80. S. F. Davies, "The Reception of Reginald Scot's Discovery of Witchcraft: Witchcraft, Magic, and Radical Religion", *Journal of the History of Ideas*, v. 74, no. 3 (2013), p. 381.
81. S. F. Davies, *Witchcraft and the Book Trade*, p. 175.
82. Alexander Roberts, *A Treatise of Witchcraft*, London, 1616, p. 15.

Hopkins was warned that henceforth he should apply himself to his studies and "not in any way use the magical art or support it in future". He may have gone on to become a clergyman. John Fisher was probably a little older, and certainly more senior, than Hopkins. He, too, had dabbled in magic. Some years later, he failed to secure an MA from the university, apparently for Catholic leanings.[83] Interestingly, at least a century later, academics at St. John's College, Cambridge, still took care to secrete shoes in the wall of one of their college rooms, a traditional practice to protect against witches and evil spirits and something that was discovered only during rewiring in 2016.[84]

However, it should also be stressed that belief in witchcraft existed on a continuum. Until the late seventeenth century even "sceptics" only rarely challenged the existence of witches rather than their powers, their numbers, and, especially, the possibility of proving their presence and distinguishing fraudsters in any given case.[85] Arguably, such qualified scepticism was to be far more important than outright disbelief in the decline of witchcraft prosecutions.

Counterfeit and Fraud

Even those such as Sir Edmund Anderson, who strongly believed in the reality of witchcraft, appreciated that some allegations were fraudulent. Concern about this issue gradually increased, as notorious cases were exposed and gained publicity. For example, 14-year-old Anne Gunter, from North Moreton in Oxfordshire, became ill in the summer of 1604 and, eventually, her sickness was blamed on witchcraft. She reported a range of symptoms, including fits and trances, being insensible to some forms of pain, and vomiting and defecating pins (a classic sign of being under a witch's spell). She blamed three women for cursing her: Agnes Pepwell, Pepwell's (illegitimate) daughter Mary, and the locally unpopular Elizabeth Gregory. The case was investigated by academics from the nearby university. Agnes fled but her daughter and Elizabeth were tried

---

83. Jan Machielsen, "New College of Magic and Wizardry: A Second Note on the 1566/7 Visitation", *New College Notes*, issue 7 (2016), pp. 1–5.
84. *Washington Post*, 19 August 2016.
85. Richard Bovet, *Pandaemonium or the Devils Cloyster* (London: J. Walthoe, 1684), p. 59.

for witchcraft at the Abingdon Assizes in March 1605, where they were found not guilty. In part this was because a Wiltshire gentleman named Thomas Hinton heard about Anne Gunter, and went to North Moreton. He became suspicious, and conducted some surreptitious tests that convinced him that she was a fraud. He then attended the trial and used his connections to warn the judges that there were suspicious features to the affair. The result was a particularly careful examination of the evidence.

Anne's father, Brian Gunter, did not give up, and when King James I came to Oxford during the summer of 1605 he managed to secure an audience and present Anne to him. James referred the matter to the sceptical Archbishop Richard Bancroft, who in turn involved Samuel Harsnett. Eventually, Anne was placed under the close supervision of Henry Cotton, the Bishop of Salisbury. This cleric discovered a hoax by leaving carefully marked pins about his house, which the girl later pretended to regurgitate. The truth gradually came out. Brian Gunter had induced and bullied Anne to accuse the North Moreton women; he had coached her in spitting pins, and had (allegedly) used drugs to put her into trances and enable her to withstand extreme pain. He had also given her various liquids to drink, including a mixture of sack wine and salad oil, to make her vomit. He was tried before the Star Chamber in 1606 for making vexatious accusations of witchcraft and so subverting the course of justice, although the forum's powers of punishment were necessarily very limited.[86]

These cases, and many others like them, encouraged increased caution without requiring judges, JPs, or grand and petty jurors to formally reject the notion of witchcraft altogether. Significantly, Judge Francis North, on circuit in the 1680s, was to stress that exposing an instance of fraud on the facts of a particular case was far more effective in securing a jury acquittal than "denying authoritatively such power to be given old women".[87]

---

86. James Sharpe, *The Bewitching of Anne Gunter: A Horrible and True Story of Deception, Witchcraft, Murder, and the King of England* (London: Routledge, 2000), pp. xii–xiii and pp. 5–6.
87. Roger North, *The Lives of the Right Hon. Francis North, Volume 1* (London: Henry Colburn, 1826), p. 268.

Extent of Witch Persecution

In the 1960s Professor Hugh Trevor-Roper spoke about an early-modern "witch craze" in Europe. However, in recent decades, scholars such as Robin Briggs and Alison Rowlands have observed that, in many ways, what is noteworthy about the period is not how many people were prosecuted for witchcraft, but how few were accused of the crime, given that belief in witchcraft was widespread, as were the laws proscribing it and the natural misfortunes to which it could attributed. Witch-hunting gained momentum only in exceptional situations. The most extreme cases, such as, *inter alia*, the witch-hunts that took place at Trier between 1587 and 1593 (perhaps the biggest in European history), Fulda between 1603 and 1606, and Wurzburg from 1626 to 1631, in which hundreds of people were executed in what were very small German territories, were in no way typical. Similarly, the intensity of late-seventeenth century witch trials in Finnmark, Norway, where 92 people from a population of significantly less than 4,000 were convicted and sentenced to death, was quite unparalleled in other parts of Scandinavia.[88] Instead, persecution was chronologically and geographically patchy throughout the Continent with genuine witch-crazes touching only the lives of a very small number of Europeans for extremely limited periods.[89]

Active witch-hunting, which had once been considered the engine for producing witch trials, is now seen as their most exceptional cause.[90] Some of the severest persecutions — for example, the panics at Wurzburg — occurred adjacent to broadly similar areas and states that had virtually no trials whatsoever.[91] On a larger scale, for much of the period there were almost no witch prosecutions in southern France (where Protestant sympathies were often strong), even though there is ample evidence of a belief in the existence of malefic witchcraft, with some

---

88. Torbjørn Alm, "The Witch Trials of Finnmark, Northern Norway, during the 17th-century: Evidence for Ergotism as a Contributing Factor", *Economic Botany*, v. 57, no. 3 (2003), p. 403.
89. Rowlands, *Witchcraft Narratives*, p. 7.
90. Malcolm Gaskill, "Witchcraft and Evidence in Early Modern England", *Past & Present*, v. 198, no. 1 (2008), p. 34.
91. Anna Garland, "The Great Witch Hunt: The Persecution of Witches in England, 1550–1660", *Auckland University Law Review*, v. 9, no. 4 (2003), p. 1152.

victims actively seeking out their supposed tormentors.[92] More generally, the French total was fairly modest outside Normandy and Lorraine.

England experienced one of the lowest levels of legal activism against witches in early-modern Europe, far behind Bamburg and Scotland, and roughly on a par with parts of Scandinavia, such as Denmark, albeit ahead of Italy and Portugal, and far ahead of Ireland.[93] During the 178 years in which witchcraft was proscribed and prosecuted as a felony, there were probably a maximum of 500 executions for the crime, from the trials of about 2,000 people, although some commentators have suggested the former figure may have been as low as 400.[94] This was in a country that had about four million people in 1600, a figure that was set to increase steadily during the remaining years of proscription.

The numbers are uncertain, due to gaps in the documentary record. For example, 12 of the 36 Elizabethan witchcraft pardons were from the Home Circuit (five of them from Essex). However, the Eastern (Norfolk) Circuit produced 16. Can it therefore be inferred that most sixteenth century witchcraft prosecutions came from these two circuits (it probably can), and that the latter may even have seen more than the former (less certain)? Judges on the Eastern Circuit may have been more sympathetic to local pressure for reprieves, with more gentry being willing to petition the Crown for mercy on behalf of convicted witches.[95]

Some other alleged witches would have died in custody while awaiting trial in the country's appalling gaols, as was the case with Margery Coombes, one of three women committed to gaol in Somerset pending trial for witchcraft in 1690. (The other two were acquitted).[96] Typhus and, to a lesser extent, bubonic plague were a constant threat in such squalid environments. Elizabeth Stile had been entirely healthy when arrested for witchcraft in 1579. She had to be carried to Assizes in a barrow because her toes had rotted off during her short period of incarceration.[97] Four

---

92. Lipscomb, *Voices of Nimes*, p. 131.
93. Christina Larner, "Witch Beliefs and Witch-hunting in England and Scotland", *History Today*, v. 31. No. 2 (1981), p. 33.
94. Monter, "Re-contextualizing", p. 108.
95. Krista Kesselring, *To Pardon and To Punish: Mercy and Authority in Tudor England*, Ph.D. thesis, Queen's University, Ontario, 2000, p. 105.
96. C. L'Estrange Ewen (ed.), *Witchcraft and Demonism* (London: Heath Cranton, 1933), p. 337.
97. Krista Kesselring, *To Pardon and To Punish: Mercy and Authority in Tudor England*, p. 53.

women accused of witchcraft died within two weeks in Colchester Gaol during the early-summer of 1645.[98]

The most reliable estimates suggest that, in Europe as a whole, and making allowances for failures in recording through lost documentation, the number of executions for witchcraft during the early-modern period, was between 40,000 and 50,000, and that 100,000 were formally accused.[99] Thus (a maximum of) 500 executed witches in England would constitute just over one per cent of the European total if the lower figure is employed, and exactly one per cent if 50,000 is preferred, for the years between 1400 and 1700, although England made up about five per cent of the population of Europe for much of this period.[100]

The moderately lower conviction rate in England, compared to the average on the Continent, means that the difference is slightly less marked if trials resulting in any verdict (including acquittals) are compared. Even so, it can be argued that, for most of early-modern England, for the majority of the time, malefic witchcraft was a fairly minor concern. Without Essex, Kent (especially the east of that county), Lancashire, and some parts of East Anglia, the numbers tried would have been tiny.[101]

Essex was especially singular. It produced a clear majority of all witchcraft indictments prosecuted on the entire five-county Home Circuit. At the very peak of prosecutions for the crime during the Elizabethan period, about 13 per cent of indictments at the Essex Assizes over a ten-year period were for witchcraft, making it second in frequency only to theft. Nevertheless, even in Tudor and Stuart Essex, persecution was often highly localised. Of the 426 villages in the county, just over half, some 227, are known to have been connected in any way with witchcraft prosecutions. Although Hatfield Peverel, with a total population of roughly

---

98. Malcolm Gaskill, *Witchfinders: A Seventeenth-century English Tragedy* (London: John Murray, 2008), p. 75.
99. Robin Briggs, *Witches and Neighbours* (London: HarperCollins, 1996), p. 260.
100. Andrew Sneddon, "Witchcraft belief and trials in early modern Ireland", *Irish Economic and Social History*, v. 39, issue 1 (2012), p. 1.
101. J. A. Sharpe, *Early Modern England: A Social History, 1550–1760* (London: Edward Arnold, 1987), p. 311.

500 people, harboured 15 suspected witches who fell into the legal system over a period of 25 years, hundreds of other villages saw none at all.[102]

England experienced only one persecution that can properly be described as a craze, Matthew Hopkins' East Anglian crusade of 1645–1647, which occurred in the wholly unusual circumstances of the English Civil War. On some counts, this short-lived campaign and its satellites occasioned almost half the total number of English executions for witchcraft between 1563 and 1736. Most observers would, more plausibly, attribute at least a quarter of such deaths to it (see *Chapter 6*).

Areas that experienced no largescale witch-hunts were the norm rather than the exception, and some parts of the realm saw very little anti-witch activity at all. For example, in Sussex, apart from its separate non-county jurisdictions such as the Cinque Port of Rye, there were only about a dozen trials for the crime between 1563 and 1736. Only one witch was (it seems) capitally convicted and executed there, and this was a serious and, apparently, well-evidenced case. Margaret Cooper of Kirdford, the wife of a surgeon, was tried at the Assizes in 1574 for making "children of wax" (image magic) to bewitch people, reportedly causing several deaths. A few more suspected witches were convicted of non-capital forms of the crime. In 1577, Alice Casselowe from Mayfield was found guilty of killing an ox and three pigs using witchcraft, and sentenced to imprisonment and the pillory. Many others were acquitted outright. Similarly, although Cheshire has good legal records for much of the early-modern period, it appears to have had relatively few witch prosecutions.[103] In Surrey there were a significant number of indictments for witchcraft during Queen Elizabeth's reign, but in that of James I they were notably absent, only one case being preserved.

Although Wales was subject to exactly the same law and legal system as England (albeit administered by the great sessions rather than Assizes), it appears to have witnessed just five executions for the crime. Witch prosecutions arrived late in Wales, and were few in number, while women who were capitally convicted were more likely than their English

---

102. Alan Macfarlane, "Witchcraft in Tudor and Stuart Essex". In *Witchcraft Confessions and Accusations*, Mary Douglas (ed.) (London: Tavistock, 1970), p. 83.
103. J. A. Sharpe, "Yorkshire", p. 2.

counterparts to escape the gallows, despite a widespread Welsh belief in magic and witches. One factor may have been the language barrier in many parts of the principality, which would have helped to prevent the transmission of chapbook-based notions of witchcraft emanating from London. It may also have reflected wider aspects of Welsh culture and legal tradition, including attitudes towards women, many stretching back before the Union.[104] For example, in Denbighshire, from 1660 to 1730, just one indictment was brought for felonious witchcraft, and that was thrown out by the grand jury.[105]

The low number of witch cases found in England and many other parts of Europe has often been ignored. This is, perhaps, partly because it is much less eye-catching and marketable than accounts of largescale persecutions, partly because feminist scholars of a radical bent, who have sometimes been prominent in the field, have little interest in any work which might appear to downplay the impact of witch-hunts on early-modern women, and partly because cases of witchcraft that did not end in executions, or spawn larger campaigns, are harder to extrapolate from early-modern legal records.[106] Nevertheless, many contemporary believers in the phenomenon, in both England and on the Continent, such as Henry Holland, were well aware of, and sometimes shocked by, the generally widespread lack of anti-witch activism.[107]

Everyday life in early-modern England was fraught with danger. The inability to diagnose many of the phenomena, such as disease, that must have lain behind domestic disasters meant that witchcraft provided a potentially very attractive explanation for misfortune. William Drage (1637–1669), a Hitchin apothecary who published a treatise on diseases occasioned by witchcraft in 1664, was convinced that "the Devil can cause all Diseases that are Natural, but Nature cannot cause all Diseases that are Diabolical". As a result, even "natural" illnesses could be attributed to witches. Clerics regularly deplored the lack of stoicism found amongst

---

104. Sally Parkin, "Witchcraft, Women's Honour and Customary Law in Early Modern Wales", *Social History*, v. 31, no. 3 (2006), p. 295.
105. Sharon Howard, *Law and Disorder in Early Modern Wales* (Cardiff: University of Wales Press, 2008), p. 261.
106. Rowlands, *Witchcraft Narratives*, p. 7.
107. Henry Holland, *A Treatise Against Witchcraft* (Cambridge: University of Cambridge, 1590), p. 23.

ordinary people, feeling that there was no need to have recourse to witchcraft to account for any evils "that are suffered to befall'em, and much less so, where these evils are such as may proceed from natural causes, and are common unto men".[108] Given such attitudes, it must be asked why there were not many more executions for witchcraft than actually occurred, especially in England.

Several possible reasons for this comparative moderation have been put forward, including the English emphasis on *maleficium* as opposed to diabolism, the country's accusatorial legal procedure, the illegality of torture in England, and the mitigating effect of centralised legal supervision. More specifically, numerous legal hurdles had to be surmounted before a witch hanging could take place. Any of them could prevent matters reaching such a conclusion.

First, there had to be a plausible suspect and a convincing incident of potential witchcraft that could be attributed to him or her. Then there had to be credible people who were willing to make or support a formal complaint to a JP. In turn, this magistrate had to be willing to entertain such an allegation, or at least afraid to dismiss it. Next, a moderately sympathetic, or at least not hostile, grand jury had to be prepared to find a "true bill" for it to go to trial. At this stage it was still necessary to find a petty jury willing to convict and a trial judge who was not hostile to such actions and capable of leading the jurors away from such a course of action, and who was also unwilling or unable to effect a post-conviction reprieve.

The Wider British Isles

Scotland

In Scotland, with its separate, largely Roman-law, legal system, the level of anti-witch activity between the passing of the Witchcraft Act of 1563 (not to be confused with its less draconian English counterpart of the same year) and repeal of all such statutes, throughout the island, by the British Parliament's Act of 1736 (see *Chapter 5*), took place on a far

---

108. Tract 1736 p. 23.

greater scale than occurred south of the border. Scotland saw the most severe anti-witch campaign of any Protestant state in Europe. On one analysis, 3,887 people, largely drawn from the Lowlands, were tried for witchcraft, of whom two-thirds were found guilty and executed (a very high proportion); as Scotland had approximately a quarter of England's population, this gave it an execution rate for the crime that was 12 times as intense as that of its southern neighbour.[109] (Other Scottish estimates are slightly more modest).

Although witch-hunting got off to a relatively slow start after criminalisation in 1563, there were largescale trials in Scotland in 1590, 1597, 1628–1631, 1649–1650, and 1661–1662. The last of these was an exceptionally intense witch-hunt, despite its very late date. It started in the Lothians before spreading more widely. The Scottish Privy Council issued commissions to local authorities throughout the country to try suspected witches. Over a period of 16 months almost 700 people were accused. It seems that well over 100 were executed.

Witchcraft also lasted much longer as an actively prosecuted crime in Scotland than it did in England. For example, in one of the last largescale executions for witchcraft in Western Europe, five men and women were hanged and then burned in Paisley in 1697 for bewitching eleven-year-old Christine Shaw. Two others died in prison or committed suicide while awaiting trial. The prosecution of witches continued in Dumfries and Galloway in the southwest on a regular basis until well into the eighteenth century. From 1670 to about 1740, the very decades that were giving birth to the Scottish Enlightenment, learned interest in the supernatural was actually on the increase, and the topic received an unprecedented level of scrutiny. Ministers of religion appear to have actively contributed to the survival of belief in witches.[110]

Appropriately, the final witch to be executed in Britain was the elderly Janet Horne, at Dornoch in Sutherland, in June 1727. Janet and her daughter appear to have been arrested and imprisoned on the accusations of their neighbours. She was showing signs of senility or dementia, and

---

109. Sneddon, "Witchcraft belief", p. 1.
110. Lizanne Henderson, "The Survival of Witchcraft Prosecutions and Witch Belief in South-West Scotland", *The Scottish Historical Review*, v. 85, no. 219, part 1 (2006), p. 52.

Crimen Exceptum

her daughter had a withered hand and leg. A neighbour accused Horne of transforming her daughter into a pony and said she had "ridden her until lame". They were speedily convicted in front of the local sheriff, but the daughter appears to have escaped. Unfortunately, Horne was burned to death in a tar barrel.[111]

Ireland

Ireland largely avoided witch-hunting, despite criminalisation in 1586 (the relevant statute being almost identical to the English Act of 1563); there were only a handful of trials in the later seventeenth and early-eighteenth centuries. On one recent estimate, there may have been as few as four full trials and just one execution for the crime. Even at the time, observers appreciated that the island was unusual in this regard. An early-eighteenth century Anglican Archbishop of Dublin, William King (1650–1729), expressly noted that witch-hunting had never taken off there. Even when some Irish JPs were issued a handbook on how to identify witches, in the 1630s, the practice did not seem to grow.[112]

The lack of witch prosecutions in Ireland can be attributed to several factors. Belief in malefic, demonic witchcraft (as opposed to other forms of the craft) did not fully penetrate the culture of the Irish-speaking, Catholic majority of the population. They were also reluctant to use Anglophone Protestant-dominated legal institutions if under apparent witch-attack, preferring self-help. Furthermore, the Irish traditionally blamed fairies for various afflictions and illnesses that in other countries might have been attributed to malefic witches, while attacks on agricultural produce and livestock could be attributed to butter-stealing witches of a different type, who were never incorporated into the construct of black witchcraft prominent in Scotland and, to a lesser extent, England.[113]

The Islandmagee witch trial of March 1711 was the last (and easily the largest) of the very modest Irish total of such hearings, albeit not involving capital allegations. Eight women were put on trial at Carrickfergus, in largely Protestant County Antrim, and found guilty, after it

---

111. Brian Alexander Pavlac, *Witch Hunts in the Western World: Persecution and Punishment from the Inquisition through the Salem Trials* (Westport: Greenwood Press, 2009), p. 145.
112. Andrew Sneddon, "Witchcraft belief", pp. 145–146.
113. Andrew Sneddon, *Witchcraft and Magic in Ireland* (London: Palgrave Macmillan, 2015), p. 9.

was claimed that they had bewitched 18-year-old Mary Dunbar. Dunbar had exhibited classic signs of demonic possession such as shouting, swearing, blaspheming, throwing Bibles, having fits whenever a clergyman came near her, and vomiting nails, pins, buttons, glass, and wool. She had picked out the eight women, claiming that they had taken the form of spirits and attacked her. It is likely that Dunbar fabricated the whole business to become a local celebrity, drawing on Scottish accounts of the phenomenon that were prevalent in the area to form her narrative, and identifying eight women who were already socially marginalised because they were poor and uncouth. The women were jailed for a year and put in the pillory.[114] They received little sympathy and, when in the apparatus, were, apparently, severely pelted by the attendant crowd.

Isle of Man

As in Ireland, a rich and widespread belief in witches was firmly embedded in Manx culture. This had its own distinctive features, such as an emphasis on the significance of May Eve and May Day. For example, in a case from 1716, a woman complained to the ecclesiastical authorities about gossip that she and her husband had been out early on May morning, walking on the dew in their neighbours' fields, with the intention of harming their crops. However, charges of malefic witchcraft were rarely brought before the Court of General Gaol Delivery, the island's equivalent of the English Assizes. One woman was convicted of witchcraft before that court in 1569, but reprieved on grounds of pregnancy (as she would have been in England). In 1598 another woman accused of witchcraft escaped trial because of a mistake in legal procedure. As a result, it appears that only two people were executed for the crime in early-modern Man. Margaret Ine Quayne and her son John Cubon were burned at Castletown in 1617. It seems that the island's authorities, and in particular its ecclesiastical establishment, adopted an idiosyncratic attitude to witchcraft accusations. In general they maintained a fairly

---

114. Andrew Sneddon, *Possessed by the Devil: The Real History of the Islandmagee Witches and Ireland's only Mass Witchcraft Trial* (Dublin: The History Press Ireland, 2013), p. 9.

low-key approach, often treating them as signs of popular ignorance rather than as a satanic heresy that needed to be crushed.[115]

Meta-Narratives

The emergence of witch-hunting in early-modern Europe has prompted a plethora of explanations over the past century. Many of these say almost as much about the preoccupations of the decades that produced them as they do about the era of proscription. By the beginning of the twentieth century, various occultists, theosophists and spiritualists had identified witches as being amongst their forebears. In the early-1920s Sir James Frazer and Margaret Murray suggested (with almost no foundation in reality) that magical beliefs belonged to an ancient cult that had once been the religion of ordinary people.[116] According to Murray (1863–1963), an Egyptologist by training, this pagan religious cult had originated in the Middle East and survived underground throughout European history before coming to prominence in the sixteenth century.[117] More significantly, in the modern era, a variety of sociologists, anthropologists, historians, meteorologists, and even toxicologists have considered the issue from numerous perspectives, influenced by beliefs ranging from Marxism to feminism. A small selection will be very briefly considered.

It has been argued that it is not a coincidence that the arrival of the Little Ice Age largely coincided with the onset of largescale witch persecution in the 1560s. Perhaps significantly, in some parts of Europe witches were blamed or scapegoated for apparently "unnatural" climatic phenomena.[118] The decrease in temperatures produced the harsh economic conditions, increasing crop failure, and food shortages that lie behind some social explanations for the phenomenon, such as that found in the work of

---

115. James Sharpe, "Witchcraft in the Early Modern Isle of Man", *Culltural and Social History*, v. 4, issue 1 (2007), p. 13 and p. 16.
116. Malcolm Gaskill, "The Pursuit of Reality: Recent Research into the History of Witchcraft", *The Historical Journal*, v. 51, no. 4 (2008), pp. 1069–1970.
117. Thomas A. Fudge, "Traditions and Trajectories in the Historiography of European Witch Hunting", *History Compass*, v. 4, issue 3 (2006), p. 493.
118. Wolfgang Behringer, "Climatic Change and Witch-hunting: The Impact of the Little Ice Age on Mentalities", *Climatic Change*, v. 43, no. 1 (1999), p. 355.

Alan Macfarlane (considered elsewhere).[119] Indeed, some research on early-modern England, Scotland, and Germany might indicate a degree of correlation between witch prosecutions and wheat prices. Other, more recent, work has suggested that the bottom of the agrarian business cycle may have coincided with a doubling of witch trials in England.[120]

As far back as the 1970s, it was mooted that ergotism might have been a major contributory factor to early-modern outbreaks of alleged witchcraft. This condition is caused by grain, especially rye, becoming infected by *Claviceps purpurea*, a fungus that contains a number of alkaloids, some of which are psychoactive. It has been argued that symptoms such as convulsions and hallucinations, produced by ergot-tainted rye, might have been the source of some accusations of witchcraft. For example, it has been suggested that more than half of the 83 trials in the late-seventeenth century outbreak of intense witch prosecution in Finnmark (northern Norway), a place that was heavily dependent on imported rye flour, provide potential evidence of ergotism. In 42 of the trials, witchcraft may have been "learned" after consuming rye, usually in the form of bread or other flour products (17 cases), in milk or beer (23 cases), or a combination of foodstuffs (two cases). In the cases involving milk, several "witches" allegedly testified that some kind of black, grain-like objects were found in the foodstuff they had consumed.[121]

Nevertheless, the theory has not gained traction. For example, attempts to apply it to Scotland and its major witch-hunts have produced largely negative results, both with regard to documentation and the prevailing diet.[122] Even so, rye was widely grown in England, and it is possible that the presence of ergotism may have influenced a few, individual accusations of witchcraft.

More recently, and perhaps more plausibly, it has been suggested that competition between faiths in confessionally contested parts of Europe

---

119. Emily F. Oster, "Witchcraft, Weather and Economic Growth in Renaissance Europe", *Journal of Economic Perspectives*, v. 18, no. 1 (2004), p. 217.
120. Chris Hudson, *Witch Trials: Discontent in Early Modern Europe*, working paper HEIDWP11–2016 (Geneva: Graduate Institute of International and Development Studies, 2016), p. 3 and p. 33.
121. Alm, "Witch Trials", pp. 403–416.
122. Kirsty Duncan, "Was ergotism responsible for the Scottish witch-hunts?", *Area*, v. 25, no. 1 (1993), pp. 30–36.

during the Protestant Reformation and the Catholic Counter-Reformation helps explain the timing and location of peaks in the phenomenon, and why it ravaged certain areas, spared many others, and was largely absent in the Middle Ages despite widespread popular belief in witches.

According to this analysis, officials focused witch trial activity in confessional battlegrounds. Witch prosecutors advertised their religion's power to protect believers from manifestations of diabolical evil, so attracting the loyalty of undecided Christians. This might explain why Germany, the heart of the Reformation, saw nearly 40 per cent of all witchcraft prosecutions in Europe. By contrast, Italy, Spain, Portugal, and Ireland, which remained Catholic strongholds, even after the Reformation, and saw little serious competition from Protestantism, accounted for just six per cent of Europeans tried for witchcraft; the contest for religious adherents in these countries was minimal. In Spain, the Inquisition was especially cautious about witch prosecutions, even when a few women made extensive admissions under torture. Although Galicia was noted as a land of witches, trials for such activity were not even an annual event there, and none resulted in executions.[123] According to the confessional-conflict theory, it is not a coincidence that, after the treaties that made up the Peace of Westphalia of 1648 brought a close to the Thirty Years' War, and ended decades of religious conflict in Europe, witch prosecutions declined rapidly.[124] Perhaps significantly, in this context, something of a propaganda war developed in early-seventeenth century England between evangelical Puritans and Catholics as to their powers of exorcising those who were subject to demonic possession.[125]

By contrast, the anthropologist Marvin Harris argued that the witch-hunts of early-modern Europe could be explained by class conflict and manipulation by the elite. Witches could be blamed for the misfortunes afflicting society, while the clergy and nobility became the "great protectors of mankind against an enemy who was omnipresent but difficult to detect. Here at last was a reason to pay tithes and obey the tax

---

123. Allyson M. Poska, *Women and Authority in Early Modern Spain: The Peasants of Galicia* (Oxford: OUP, 2005), pp. 221–223.
124. P. T. Leeson and J.W. Russ, "Witch Trials", *Economic Journal*, v. 28 (2018), pp. 2066–2105. *The Guardian*, 7 January 2018.
125. Gaskill, *Witchfinders*, p. 29.

collector".[126] Such an analysis does not fully account for the popular pressure to pursue witches, something that the religious and political establishments frequently attempted to damp down, rather than actively encourage.

The notion that the persecution of witches was actually a mechanism used for the persecution of women has surfaced regularly since the 1960s, although early feminist historians sometimes vastly exaggerated the numbers of women executed, and failed to discuss the unusually heavy female involvement in witch prosecutions (see below). It provided a potentially attractive narrative, in which oppressors and oppressed could be readily identified, even if much of the evidence on which it was based was slightly dubious.[127] Even so, some modern scholars, albeit usually less far-reaching in their claims, still suggest that witch-hunting was a way of sifting out subversive females.[128]

None of these perspectives has been entirely satisfactory as a single explanation. As a result, they have sometimes been combined, so that, for example, witch-hunting has been described as a "ruling class campaign of terror directed against the female peasant population".[129] Arguably, such combinations are still too narrow to explain the phenomenon in an entirely satisfactory manner. One reason is the localism of intense witch-hunting and its relative infrequency, if not rarity, over much of Europe. Whatever "function" witch trials may have been fulfilling, it was not essential or irreplaceable in wider early-modern society. As a result, many modern scholars have adopted a multi-causal approach to the subject. There is not space in this short book, which focuses on the legal aspects of the topic, to explore these in great depth, but the role of women in witch prosecutions was fairly singular, and so worthy of special consideration, as is the presence of witches in early-modern urban environments.

---

126. Marvin Harris, *Cows, Pigs, Wars, and Witches: The Riddles of Culture* (New York: Random House, 1974), p. 238.
127. Diane Purkiss, *The Witch in History: Early Modern and Twentieth-Century Representations* (London: Routledge, 1996), p. 8.
128. Louise Jackson, "Witches, Wives and Mothers: witchcraft persecution and women's confessions in seventeenth-century England", *Women's History Review*, v. 4, no. 1 (1995), p. 64.
129. James Sharpe, "Witchcraft and women in seventeenth-century England: Some Northern evidence" *Continuity and Change*, v. 6, issue 2 (1991), p. 179.

Crimen Exceptum

Female Involvement

Women initiated many witch prosecutions, and were heavily involved in investigating and giving evidence against suspected witches, unlike their role in most other felony prosecutions. For example, in 1616 Emma Branch, a married woman from Tottenham in Middlesex, was accused of bewitching Edward Wheeler, a local nine-month-old infant, so that he became lame and died, and another two women, who became ill. Her prosecutors were all female: Mary Aldridge, Katherine Barbor, and Alice Smythe.[130] On a more statistical basis, in seventeenth century Yorkshire, of 43 adults whose gender can be identified and who claimed that they, their children, goods or animals had been bewitched, 22 were men and 21 women. However, of those identified as giving evidence at trial, 19 were men and 27 (almost 60 per cent) women. Furthermore, some 18 women were used on the five occasions when a search was made for the witch's mark.[131] (Groups of three or four females appear to have been usual on these occasions).

In the south of England, in the 1590s, the clerks of assize for the Home Circuit started to endorse the indictments tried before the Assizes with the names of the witnesses in the case. In witchcraft trials held on the Home Circuit between 1600 and 1702, it seems that 576 (48 per cent per cent) of the 1,207 witnesses called were women. This can be contrasted with typical felony cases in Hertfordshire between 1610 and 1619, in which only one in twelve witnesses were female.[132] In seventeenth century Norfolk, in all but one witch prosecution for which records exist, women took the lead in making a complaint (it was often men who backed these up with older stories), while females also made up half of the surviving witness depositions in such cases.[133]

The percentage of women involved in witch prosecutions may even have risen over time. In the last six years of the Elizabethan period the

---

130. William Le Hardy (ed.), *County of Middlesex. Calendar To the Sessions Records: New Series, Volume 3, 1615–16* (London: Middlesex County Council, 1937), pp. 288–312.
131. Sharpe, "Witchcraft and women", p. 185.
132. J. Sharpe, "Women, Witchcraft and the Legal Process". In *Women, Crime and the Courts in Early Modern England*, Jennifer Kermode and Garthine Walker (eds.) (London: UCL Press, 1994), p. 132.
133. Keith Parry, *Witchcraft in seventeenth-century Norfolk*, https://keithparry.org 2011.

proportion of female witnesses in witch cases on the Home Circuit was just over 38 per cent, rising to 43 per cent in the Jacobean period and 53 per cent during the Restoration (by which time it was 56 per cent on the Northern Circuit).[134] As a result of such evidence, some scholars have suggested that the business of deciding whether a person should be formally accused of witchcraft was primarily in the female sphere. Although it has been argued that women played a more passive role in the legal process against witches than the headline figures might suggest, it is apparent that females had an unusual degree of agency in such cases.[135]

Urban Witches

Many paradigms explaining witchcraft draw extensively on the stresses, strains, general remoteness and isolation of much early-modern rural life to account for the phenomenon and its distribution within particular countries. Nevertheless, caution is necessary before accepting any notion that urban life at this time was inherently more "rational", and so more likely to eschew popular belief in witchcraft than its rural counterpart. Accusations of witchcraft were made on a fairly regular basis in urban and suburban environments. London and its environs saw many of them, despite being one of the largest cities in Europe. For example, in the late seventeenth century, John Aubrey observed that most houses in the West End of the city still had a horseshoe over the front door to ward off witchcraft, and a century later, in 1797, the antiquarian John Brand noted that such protection could still be found in many houses in Monmouth Street, in the same area. On one assessment, use of a horseshoe for this purpose (as opposed to securing luck) disappeared only in the 1820s and 1830s.[136]

During the era of proscription the Metropolitan area (the City of London and adjacent parts of Middlesex) produced several noted witches, such as: Anne Kirk, from Castle Alley in the Square Mile, in 1599; Elizabeth Sawyer from Edmonton in 1621; and Joan Peterson from Wapping

---

134. Clive Holmes, "Women: Witnesses and Witches", *Past & Present*, v. 140, no. 1 (1993), p. 47.
135. Sharpe, "Witchcraft and women", p. 192; Holmes, "Women", pp. 56–58.
136. Owen Davies, "Urbanization and the Decline of Witchcraft: An Examination of London", *Journal of Social History*, v. 30, no. 3 (1997), p. 611.

in 1652. All of them went to the gallows. There were many others, albeit that some of them, such as Helen Spokes from St Giles-in-the-Fields in 1597, and Rose Mersam from Whitecross Street in 1607, were acquitted, while others were merely convicted of non-capital forms of the crime.[137] It is also apparent that formal allegations of witchcraft were made in the Metropolitan area until well into the eighteenth century. Thus, in the early-1700s, the fruiterer Sarah Morduck was mobbed by people in Southwark who were convinced that she had bewitched the fraudster Richard Hathaway, a belief that was not altered by her acquittal of such a charge at the Surrey Assizes. Money was raised for Hathaway, and prayers said on his behalf in local churches. More prosaically, at the Surrey Quarter Sessions, from 1699 to 1700, William Langham from largely urban Bermondsey, accused a scrivener named Thomas Watts "for being a sorcerer and using sorceries and witchcrafte".[138]

Of course, the profound changes brought about by urbanisation did affect the nature of such claims. This can be seen by comparing indictments taken from largely urban Southwark in Surrey with those drawn from rural parts of the same county. The bewitchment of domestic animals featured heavily in the latter, but was almost absent from the former. Witchcraft allegations in urban environments were more likely to involve accusations of interference with businesses than with, for example, butter-making.[139]

---

137. Andrew Pickering and David Pickering, *Witch Hunt: The Persecution of Witches in England*. (Stroud: Amberley Publishing, 2013), pp. 122–124.
138. Davies, "Urbanization and the Decline of Witchcraft", p. 611.
139. *Ibid.*

CHAPTER 2

Candidates for Witch-hood

Introduction

Allegations of witchcraft were not made at random. Those accused tended to be disproportionately female, poor, mature or elderly, quarrelsome and locally unpopular, ugly or deformed, single, and socially marginalised. They were likely to have been the subject of suspicion and informal allegations for long periods of time, sometimes decades, prior to being accused before a JP. Lightning was also prone to striking twice; if a person had been prosecuted for witchcraft on an earlier occasion but escaped the gallows there was a good chance that this type of allegation would be renewed. A family connection with another witch also greatly increased the likelihood of being identified as such. At least some of the people accused of witchcraft had tacitly encouraged others to believe they were witches, and possessed of magical powers, whether for personal protection, status, or as a way of reinforcing requests for charity. A few seem to have genuinely believed that they were witches.[1]

None of these factors was remotely conclusive. Most elderly, poor, deformed, single and unpopular women in England were not suspected of witchcraft, and the vast majority of those suspected were never indicted. This can be seen from the speed with which large numbers of people could be brought into the net as witches on the few occasions when there was active encouragement from the authorities, as occurred in East Anglia and Newcastle during the 1640s.

---

1. Machielsen, "'Moved and Seduced", p. 5.

Conversely, there were numerous exceptions to the general profile. Some alleged witches were well-to-do individuals. Alice Nutter, one of the Pendle witches in 1612, was described by Thomas Potts as a "rich woman [who] had a great estate, and children of good hope". The octogenarian Reverend John Lowes, one of the victims of the Hopkins persecution in 1645, was a Cambridge-educated clergyman and had been vicar of Brandeston in Suffolk since 1595. He had become extremely unpopular amongst some of his more puritanical parishioners, over a period of many years, because of his churchmanship, reluctance to preach, vexatious litigation, and apparently overenthusiastic collection of tithes. A pamphlet published in 1642, long before his death, described him as a witch, a conjurer, and the associate of recusants.[2]

Similarly, on some accounts, Anne Bodenham, the Salisbury witch executed in 1652, was not a typical suspect. She wore spectacles, wrote letters, owned books, and taught children to read. She was sensitive about her social status, preferring to be called "Mistress Bodenham" rather than simple "goodwife."[3] On a slightly more statistical basis, at one time, in early-modern Boreham in Essex, of the ten people receiving aid from the local overseers of the poor, none was prosecuted as a witch, despite the presence of four other suspected witches in the village at about the same time. Indeed, one of the latter, Margaret Poole, was married to the village constable.[4]

Furthermore, it was recognised that witches might be outwardly godly people, while several suspected women, far from being given to cursing, appeared good natured. Alice Nutter was widely thought to be even-tempered and "free from envy or malice", unlike many witches. Others appeared to be pious. In Suffolk, in the same year that Lowes met his fate, it was noted that Mother Lakeland had been a "professour of Religion, a constant hearer of the Word for these many years, and yet a *Witch* (as she confessed) for the space of near twenty years".[5] According to John

---

2. E. J. Kent, "Masculinity and Male Witches in Old and New England, 1593–1680", *History Workshop Journal*, v. 60, no. 1 (2005), p. 74.
3. Malcolm Gaskill, "Witchcraft, Politics, and Memory in Seventeenth-Century England", *The Historical Journal*, v. 50., no. 2 (2007), p. 292.
4. Macfarlane, "Tudor and Stuart Essex", p. 85.
5. Tract 1645 (1) pp. 1–8.

Stearne, Goody Kendall from Cambridge, another alleged witch, carried herself as if she were a "saint on earth". On a more statistical basis, in Hatfield Peverel (Essex), none of the ten women presented between 1584 and 1600 for non-attendance at church was among those from the village accused of being witches.[6]

Physically attractive witches were rare. In Newcastle in 1649, one woman was so far from being ugly that she was reprieved after being positively identified as a witch by a witch "pricker" (see below). A Colonel Hobson observed that she was far too "personable and good-like [a] woman" to be a witch, and asked that the test be run again. On this occasion, when the needle was stuck into her thigh, she bled profusely, proving she was not a witch. Nevertheless, even here there were exceptions. At her execution at Tyburn in 1652, it was noted that Joan Peterson, the alleged Witch of Wapping, "seemed not to be much above 40 years of age, and was not in the least outwardly deformed, as those kind of creatures usually are".[7]

There were also some regional variations in typical witch profiles. Cynthia Herrup found that Sussex witches did not conform to the national stereotype. Although she came across only a few examples of the crime in the county, they stood out because of the prominence of male defendants and the frequent parity in economic and social status between accused and complainant. Accusations appear to have reflected competition between the two, rather than guilt produced by a failure to provide charity.

More generally, this profile can also be seen in many of the relatively small number of male witches indicted for the crime outside Sussex, especially those without a close connection to suspected female witches. For example, in 1607 Nicholas Stockdale, a Norfolk yeoman, brought an action in Star Chamber against some of the villagers of Brancaster, on the north coast of the county. He claimed that, with the complicity of their constable, they had engineered his arrest for assault and then, by manipulating local JPs, added three charges of murder by witchcraft (allegedly committed between 1595 and 1602) while he was in custody.

---

6. Macfarlane, "Tudor and Stuart Essex", p. 88.
7. *The Faithful Scout*, 9–16 April 1652.

The case against him was thrown out by the court in 1602, just as a previous allegation of bewitching sheep had been. Stockdale was intensely unpopular with several other male villagers, having appeared in the Brancaster Manorial Court accused of riot and abusing communal resources, as well as being involved in enclosure disturbances, behaviour that could explain the prosecution.[8]

When they were indicted, male witches were very much more likely to be accused by other men, rather than by women, unlike females accused of the same crime.[9] Furthermore, their social status, higher on average than that of female witches, helps to explain the tendency for men to be involved in a slightly more "bookish" form of witchcraft. Of course, some were charged with acts of *maleficium*. For example, in 1658, two men were accused of bewitching Sara Smith so that "her body was greately wasted, consumed, payned and lamed". One of them, William Bones, died while awaiting their hearing at the Essex Assizes in August 1659, while the other man (and a woman) were acquitted at trial.[10] Even so, male witches were often prosecuted for using evil spirits in order to find the whereabouts of hidden treasure or similar magical crimes.

Nevertheless, with all these caveats, the stereotype of the English witch did largely match the reality. As a newspaper correspondent noted in 1726, he knew of an "old woman noted for poverty, deformity, and consequently for witchcraft". Once these factors were present, people were quick to find a "few unhappy circumstances, whereby, of an unhappy wretch, they may make an infernal witch".[11] In a letter to Sir Leoline Jenkins, the Secretary of State, in August 1682, Sir Francis North noted that the three elderly Bideford women who had been convicted before Sir Thomas Raymond (his coadjutor at Assizes) looked like caricatures of witches: "A painter would have chosen them out of the whole country for figures of that kind to have drawn by". A selection of contemporary descriptions makes clear what this entailed.

In the 1580s Reginald Scot viewed the women accused of practising witchcraft as generally "old, lame, bleary-eyed, pale, foul, and full of

---

8. Kent, "Masculinity", p. 74.
9. *Ibid.*
10. ERO T/A 418/152/13; TNA ASS 35/100/2/13.
11. *Weekly Journal, or The British Gazetteer*, 18 June 1726.

wrinkles; poor, sullen, superstitious, and papists, or such as know no religion". According to Samuel Harsnett, the popular idea of a witch entailed an "old weather-beaten Croane, having her chinne and her knees meeting for age, walking like a bow leaning on a shaft, hollow-eyed, untoothed, furrowed on her face, having her lips trembling with the palsie, going mumbling in the streetes".[12] During Matthew Hopkins' campaign, the sceptic John Gaule complained that every old woman was labelled a witch if she had a "wrinkled face, a furr[owe]d brow, a hairy lip, a gobber tooth, a squint eye, a squeaking voice, or a scolding tongue, having a ragged coat on her back, a skull-cap on her head, a spindle in her hand, and a dog or cat by her side".[13]

This continued to be the profile for witches to the very end of proscription. In 1736 the Reverend Joseph Juxon, responding to a recent attempt to "swim" alleged witches in his own parish, observed that those typically identified were pathetic rather than terrifying, and "destitute of friends. Bow'd down with Years, laden with infirmities; so far from annoying others, as not to have it in their power to take care of themselves".[14] For a specific example can be considered Elizabeth Sawyer, the "Witch of Edmonton", in 1621, whose body was "crooked and deformed" and who was noted for cursing, swearing, and blaspheming.[15] Some commonly recurring features can be considered on a more specific basis.

Gender

Unlike other felonies (apart from infanticide) far more women than men were accused of witchcraft. At various times, males made up between five per cent and (much less commonly) 20 per cent of those accused of the crime in early-modern England; the national average was just over ten per cent. As Christina Larner observed, witch-hunts were not gender-specific but they were gender-related. However, this does not appear to have been a new phenomenon in England in the years after 1563, but

---

12. Wallace Notestein, *A History Of Witchcraft In England From 1558 To 1718* (Washington, D.C.: American Historical Association, 1911), p. 66.
13. John Gaule, *Select Cases of Conscience Touching Witches and Witchcrafts*, (London, 1646), p. 6.
14. Tract 1736 p. 24.
15. Tract 1621 (2) pp. 1–10.

rather a product of the late medieval era. Church court evidence from the Canterbury diocese, from a prosecution in 1396 to the advent of the Elizabethan Witchcraft Act of 1563, suggests that the notion that malefic witches would normally be female was established during the fifteenth century.[16] (This also undermines those hypotheses that have explained the gender imbalance by reference to social changes in the 1500s).[17]

For example, in seventeenth century Norfolk, some 59 (just over 85 per cent) of 69 people (known to have been) charged with such an offence were women. Additionally, all 14 of those convicted were female (though some verdicts are missing). Similarly, the 20 sets of depositions in seventeenth century witchcraft cases recovered from Yorkshire (two from boroughs within the county) identify 30 alleged witches, of whom 27 (or 90 per cent) were women.[18] (The proportion of females had been more modest in this northern county during the Elizabethan era). In Kent, 73 (91 per cent) of the 80 people accused as witches in the 150 years up to 1700 were women.[19]

Furthermore, some of the relatively few male witches appear to have been indicted as satellites to accusations made against related females. For example, the three Yorkshire men (see above) included two husbands and the son of a witch.[20] Of the seven men who were prosecuted in Kent, four were co-defendants with accused women, some of whom were their wives.[21] More specifically, at the Chelmsford Assizes in March 1573, William Skelton and his wife Margery were accused of bewitching an infant named Agnes Collen so that she languished for a long period.[22] Nevertheless, this should not be exaggerated: a significant number of men were prosecuted for witchcraft offences without being associated with any female relative who was similarly accused.

---

16. Sweetinburgh, *Later Medieval Kent*, p. 206.
17. Karen Jones and Michael Zell "'The divels speciall instruments': women and witchcraft before the 'great witch hunt'", *Social History*, v. 30, no. 1 (2005), pp. 45–63.
18. Sharpe, *Yorkshire*, p. 13.
19. Adrian Pollock, "Social and Economic Characteristics of Witchcraft Accusations in sixteenth and seventeenth-century Kent", 1979, p. 38.
20. J. A. Sharpe, "Witchcraft and women in seventeenth-century England: Some Northern evidence", 1991, p. 184.
21. Adrian Pollock, "Social and Economic Characteristics of Witchcraft Accusations in sixteenth- and seventeenth-century Kent", *Archaeologia Cantiana*, v. 95 (1979), p. 38.
22. ERO T/A 418/21/33.

In England the proportion of male witches was lower than the Continental average, where 20 per cent or so of witches were men (a figure that was found in Germany), and slightly less than that found in Scotland where it was just over 15 per cent.[23] However, the male percentage was even lower in the bishopric of Basel and, albeit only just, in Hungary. Only in a very few countries and regions, some (but not all) situated at the peripheries of Europe, were a majority of witches men. For example, just over 90 per cent of witches in Iceland were male, the most extreme example.[24] There were high proportions of male witches in Normandy (over 70 per cent), Estonia (60 per cent), Burgundy (52 per cent), and Finland (49 per cent).[25] Russia and Ukraine also returned high male totals.

Contemporary observers were well aware that women were much more likely to be indicted for witchcraft, and some attempted to account for this phenomenon. Most explanations were fairly standardised. Although the blatant misogyny of the *Malleus Maleficarum* of 1486, whose German Dominican authors were convinced that women were inherently both credulous and deceptive, was not typical, its analysis was widely accepted.[26] That women were the weaker gender, both physically and mentally, explained their disproportionate involvement in the dark arts. Like many others, Richard Bernard also thought that Satan had been heartened by his initial success with Eve, encouraging him to focus his efforts on females.

Nevertheless, and unusually, Alexander Roberts rejected the notion that the high number of female witches was the result of their "frailtie and imbecility". He thought that many had stronger wills than men. The true explanation for their heavy involvement in witchcraft lay in their insatiable desire to revenge perceived "wrongs offered unto them". If they lacked the power to do this using ordinary means, as was often the case with women, they might become vulnerable to the devil's blandishments,

---

23. Roper, *Witch Craze*, p. 6.
24. Chris Hudson, *Witch Trials: Discontent in Early Modern Europe*, p. 9. Larner, "Witch Beliefs", p. 33.
25. Jacqueline Simpson, "Witches and Witchbusters", *Folklore*, v. 107, issue 1–2 (1996), p. 7. Lara Apps and Andrew Gow, *Male Witches in Early Modern Europe* (Manchester: Manchester University Press, 2003), p. 45.
26. Jacob Sprenger and Heinrich Kramer, *Malleus Maleficarum*, 1487. Translated by Montague Summers (London: Bracken Books, 1996), pp. 43–44.

seeing witchcraft as a way to achieve their aims.[27] Such explanations continued to circulate to the end of the era of proscription.

Perhaps unsurprisingly, modern scholars have often preferred to concentrate on the manner in which many suspected female witches defied contemporary notions of domesticity and the role of good wife and mother, some of them living independent of patriarchal control. They argue that many witch persecutions were focussed on disapproved patterns of female behaviour. Older single women were also more likely to be on the economic margins of society. However, it has also been argued that females were more likely to be thought of as witches simply because they were more likely to act like witches. Women were more prone to certain forms of behaviour, such as the cursing that flowed from open displays of emotion, than were men, because they were at a disadvantage when it came to utilising other forms of power, such as physical violence or recourse to legal actions.[28]

Although most witches were women, their victims were almost equally likely to be male or female. Unsurprisingly, given the relatively high age of many witches, they also tended to be somewhat younger on average than their tormentors and, given the latter's frequent poverty, and the costs of prosecution, somewhat richer.

Familial Connections

It was widely believed that witchcraft could run in families, passing from generation to generation. For example, Ellen Smith of Maldon, executed for witchcraft at Chelmsford in 1579, was the daughter of a woman hanged some years earlier for the same crime. Similarly, in a late witch prosecution conducted at the Ipswich Assizes in 1694, it was noted that the aunt and grandmother of the accused woman, Margaret Elnore, had been executed for witchcraft (the grandmother was said to have kept eight imps).[29]

---

27. Roberts, *Treatise*, p. 31.
28. Edward Bever, "Witchcraft, Female Aggression, and Power in the Early Modern Community", *Journal of Social History*, v. 35, no. 4 (2002), p. 976.
29. Arthur George Harper Hollingsworth, *The History of Stowmarket: The Ancient County Town of Suffolk* (Ipswich: F. Pawsey, 1844), p. 172.

In 1566 Elizabeth Francis was indicted at the Essex Assizes for non-capital witchcraft, accused of bewitching the infant son of William Auger of Hatfield Peverel. She admitted the charge and was sentenced to the standard one-year imprisonment. Francis claimed that she had become a witch when she was just 12-years-old, under the influence of her grandmother, Mother Eve, who gave her a cat as a familiar. Francis eventually passed on this animal to her sister, Agnes Waterhouse, who became one of the first people to be hanged for capital witchcraft in England after the same Assizes. There were several cases of mothers and daughters being jointly tried as witches. Thus, in 1589 Joan Cunny's daughters, Avice and Margaret, were brought before the Summer Assizes in Chelmsford, along with their mother.

It has been argued that a new stereotype of witch families, distinct from that of the normally solitary witch, emerged in print culture in the late sixteenth century and intensified during the early-1600s. Some Jacobean pamphlets even portrayed witch parents who taught their children a "trade", passing on magical techniques and familiars in the same way other parents taught normal work skills to their offspring. The children dutifully, if perversely, followed their instructions.[30]

As a result of such cases, it was widely believed that witchcraft could spread through communities and across generations. Unsurprisingly, experts such as Richard Bernard also thought that having a blood relative who had been a witch was relevant to the issue of guilt. However, it was certainly not conclusive. As even Bernard noted, some of the children of executed witches became zealous Christians.[31]

Previous Allegations

It is clear that anyone fortunate enough to survive an indictment for witchcraft was "marked", and a prime candidate for fresh allegations in the future. Elizabeth Francis (see above), executed at Chelmsford in 1579, had been convicted and sentenced to a year's imprisonment and the

---

30. Deborah Willis, "The Witch-Family in Elizabethan and Jacobean Print Culture", *Journal for Early Modern Cultural Studies*, v. 13, no. 1 (2013), p. 4.
31. Richard Bernard, *Guide*, p. 207.

pillory for bewitching a child in 1566 and again in 1572. Jennet Preston was acquitted at the Lent Assizes held at York in 1611 for murdering a child by witchcraft. (The parish register of Bolton-by-Bowland records a Thomas Dodgson being baptised in September 1610 and buried in April 1611). However, she was tried again at the Summer Assizes for York the following year, charged with having murdered Thomas Lister of Westby Hall by witchcraft. This time, she was convicted and executed.[32] Three years later, Joan Hunt of Hampstead in Middlesex, who had also been acquitted of witchcraft on two earlier occasions, was sentenced to death at the Old Bailey for the same crime.[33] In 1656 Judith Sawkins from Aylesford in Kent was indicted and acquitted of witchcraft after allegedly using it to kill Frances Long. Less than a year later, she was prosecuted again for a similar crime, convicted, and hanged.[34] Maria Verey was more fortunate. She had been acquitted of capital witchcraft at the powerful Yarmouth Quarter Sessions in 1645, was indicted for a similar crime before the same forum some 18 months later, but again found not guilty.[35]

Temperance Lloyd, one of the last women to be executed for witchcraft in England, in 1682, had already been indicted for the same type of crime at the Exeter Assizes in 1671; she had been accused of killing William Herbert, but acquitted at trial. The dead man's son was to take an active role in the prosecution a decade later, as he sought to right what he perceived to have been a miscarriage of justice. Furthermore, in May 1679, Lloyd had been formally accused of practising witchcraft against Anne Fellow, the daughter of a minor Bideford gentleman, although this matter did not get to trial.

Age and Marital Status

It is difficult to get statistical information on the age of those accused of witchcraft. However, coroners' inquisitions on five imprisoned witches

---

32. Potts, *Wonderfull Discoverie*, p. 164.
33. John Cordy Jeaffreson (ed.), *Middlesex County Records: Volume 2, 1603–25* (London: Middlesex County Record Society, 1887), pp. 217–218.
34. Gilbert Geis and Ivan Bunn, *A Trial of Witches: A Seventeenth-Century Witchcraft Prosecution* (London: Routledge, 1997), pp. 40–50.
35. NRO Yarmouth Sessions Book Y/S 1/2.

in 1645 show that two were 70-years-old, one was 40, one "about 50", and one "about 84".[36] Thus three were very old for the time. Alice Fowler, the Witch of Wapping, was also an octogenarian, as were several others, and one or two were reputed to be nonagenarians. Most witches were over-40, and many, probably a majority, had reached their half-century, though there were a few youthful exceptions, especially when the children of established witches were accused of the crime. Given that witches had usually acquired a longstanding reputation as such before they were formally accused, this is not entirely surprising.

Female (i.e., most) witches were significantly more likely to be single than the average for women, but this was far from universal, and only a minority were spinsters. For example, when two of John Harvey's cows sickened in Buntingford he blamed Alice Sparke for bewitching them. In March 1576, she was tried and acquitted of the crime at the Hertfordshire Assizes, although described on her indictment as the wife ("uxor") of Stephen.[37]

Married women and spinsters frequently appeared in roughly equal numbers although, like Alice, the former were less likely to be convicted, while the largest single marital category was often made up of widows, as was the case in seventeenth century Yorkshire.[38] In a sample of three Essex villages, of 15 female witches whose marital status can be identified, only one had never married, and eight were widowed. The same county's assize records indicate that of 117 suspected witches whose marital status was given, 40 per cent were widows.[39] On a smaller scale, the three Bideford witches consisted of a spinster and two widows.[40] However, proportions varied with time and place; at the Kent Assizes, widows accounted for just 26 per cent of prosecuted witches between 1565 and 1635, and 37 per cent during the Interregnum.[41]

The preponderance of widows amongst the witches found in many areas was partly linked to their high average age (see above) and the

---

36. Macfarlane, "Tudor and Stuart Essex", p. 87.
37. TNA ASSI 35/18/5 m 18.
38. Sharpe, "Witchcraft and women", p. 185.
39. Macfarlane, "Tudor and Stuart Essex", p. 87.
40. Frank J. Gent, *The Trial Of The Bideford Witches*, Crediton, 2001, p. 12.
41. Malcolm Gaskill, *Crime and Mentalities in Early Modern England* (Cambridge: Cambridge University Press), 2003, p. 49.

tendency of women to live longer than men, as well as the increased likelihood that such women would fit the stereotype of a witch. In a male-dominated society, older women who were not subject to the control of a husband might occasion concern, while many women in this situation were also likely to be poor and needy, and so to satisfy other features of the typical witch stereotype.

Character and Social Status

Witches were often obstreperous, foul-mouthed, and uncouth, all of these characteristics that helped make them locally unpopular. The "presumptions" against witches included being given to "cursing, and bitter imprecations".[42] For example, Joan Flower's neighbours thought she was a "monstrous malicious woman", noted for swearing and generally irreligious behaviour.[43] Similarly, the elderly Alice Fowler, long reputed as a witch, had always been known as a "malicious ill-natured woman". She lived by selling biscuits to bawdy houses, where she regularly got drunk, being a "very debauched and leud woman". Furthermore, alleged witches were often needy and "continually in want", although rarely entirely destitute. It was noted that Fowler was: "always poor, as it is observable that those kind of people are".[44]

Many suspected witches lived outside the norms of respectable society. Some (though not a majority) were associated with other forms of (conventional) deviance, as was the case with most of the women tried for bewitching Edward Fairfax's two daughters in 1621. Among them, both Margaret Waite and her husband had an "evil report for witchcraft and theft". Indeed, Waite's husband was subsequently executed for property crimes. They also had an allegedly lewd and slatternly daughter who kept a house that was the resort of petty thieves.[45]

Similarly, in 1589 it was noted that Joan Cunny's two daughters, Avice and Margaret, who (like their mother) were brought before the Essex Assizes in Chelmsford charged with witchcraft, each had illegitimate

---

42. Tract 1645 (1) pp. 1–8.
43. Tract 1619 p. C2.
44. Tract 1685 pp. 1–4.
45. Tract 1621 p. 7.

children although, in this heavily Puritan county, little more than one per cent of the population was born out of wedlock at this time. Thomasine Short, who was tried for capital witchcraft at the County of Exeter Quarter Sessions in 1581, was probably already familiar to Exeter's magistrates, which cannot have helped her case. Less than two decades earlier she appears to have been ducked in the city's river for "scolding", while some years later she may have been bailed for an unspecified felony.[46]

Much more seriously, as a result of John Stearne's campaign, John Bonham and his wife Bridget were tried for witchcraft at Ely in 1647; both were acquitted. A decade earlier, John Bonham had been prosecuted for the murder of his eleven-year-old son, who appears to have disappeared in 1627; a pot of bones of juvenile size was subsequently found buried near his house. The grand jury at Assizes seems to have thrown this case out, as the couple were prosecuted again (and found not guilty) for the murder in 1662 (grand-jury discharge not constituting an acquittal). It is safe to assume that his neighbours were convinced that John was a killer and a man whose presence they could do without.[47]

---

46. Stoyle, "'Olde Wytche Gonne'", p. 138.
47. Gaskill, *Witchfinders*, pp. 272–273.

Crimen Exceptum

CHAPTER 3

A Witch's Career

Introduction

Most English witches were gradually identified in their neighbourhoods, with likely candidates being marked out by a combination of their social profiles, age and general behaviour, and then becoming associated with specific acts of *maleficium*. The types of misfortune attributed to them included sudden illness and death, accidents, lingering diseases for which no explanation could readily be given (as frequently happened in a period of limited medical knowledge), the effects of stroke or epilepsy, the drying-up of cows and failure of crops (especially where neighbours did not suffer the same misfortune), strange behaviour in animals, and, for fishing villages, disasters at sea.[1]

However, witches had to "acquire" their powers from somewhere, at a distinct time and in a specific place; they were not born with them, even if there was sometimes a familial link to other witches (see *Chapter 2*). Furthermore, such powers had to be granted for a purpose. If pressed, most contemporary observers would have subscribed to the belief that witches entered into some kind of formal pact with the devil, what William Perkins termed a "league or covenant", in which they bound themselves to each other.[2] Under this agreement, the witch received assistance from the devil in exchange for surrendering her immortal soul to him, and swore allegiance to a cult that was aimed at subverting Christian

---
1. Larner, "Witch Beliefs", 1981, p. 34.
2. William Perkins, *A Discourse of the Damned Art of Witchcraft*, 1608. In *The Work of William Perkins*, I. Breward (ed.) (Abingdon: Sutton Courtenay, 1970), p. 593.

society.³ To an extent, the pact could be seen as a sinister inversion of the covenant between God and his chosen people that was at the heart of Calvinist theology.⁴ Thus, after the supposed witches Margaret and Phillip Flower became embittered with their lives, the devil, ever alert to such an opening, was presumed to have offered them his services. They agreed to "give away their soules for the service of such spirits, as he had promised them; which filthy conditions were ratified with abhominable kisses, and an odious sacrifice of blood".⁵

If suitably cajoled and encouraged when examined, many suspected witches obliged by describing, or assenting to the questioner's description of, a covenant with Satan. For example, Mother Lakeland confessed "the Devil came to her first between sleeping and waking, and spake to her in a hollow voyce, that if she would serve him she should want for nothing. After often sollicitation she consented to him." The devil then gave her three familiars in the form of two little dogs and a mole.⁶

Sometimes the devil appeared directly to the future witch, often as a dark man; at other times he appeared in the shape of a familiar. The latter was said to be the case in 1646, when the devil supposedly appeared to Ellen Shepherd (who was profoundly unhappy with her life) in the form of a rat. He promised her "all happiness" (a promise that, of course, he did not keep), in exchange for giving him her soul and letting him (the rat) suck her blood.⁷

However, in many English cases, the existence of this formal agreement was tacitly assumed and little explored. Instead, the legal emphasis was on identifying and punishing specific acts of *maleficium*. Just as it was sometimes thought to be inappropriate for the ecclesiastical courts to be dealing with serious damage to life and property, so consorting with the devil and invoking demons was not necessarily viewed as a matter for secular forums.⁸ Indeed, most forms of diabolism were not, per se,

---

3. Edward Bever, "Witchcraft Prosecutions", p. 263.
4. Andrew Cambers, "Demonic Possession, Literacy and 'Superstition' in Early Modern England", *Past & Present*, v. 202, no. 1 (2009), p. 21.
5. Tract 1619 p. 12.
6. Tract 1645 (1) p. 5.
7. Charlotte-Rose Millar, *Witchcraft, the Devil, and Emotions in Early Modern England* (London: Routledge, 2018), p. 3.
8. Gaskill, *Witchfinders*, p. 28.

a crime under the 1563 Act, and they constituted only a relatively small part of the 1604 statute. The typical English witch was not prosecuted for being a witch but for the physical harm she had caused to others by practising her malign craft.

Furthermore, the average person had little incentive to pursue acts of diabolism through the courts, even when it was a crime. Unsurprisingly, the primary concern for ordinary people was harmful witchcraft that directly affected their lives. The country's lay-dominated common-law accusatory and adversarial system was largely premised on a victim-complainant — rather than a state prosecutor — who would make a formal allegation before a JP and then pursue a matter all the way to trial. Private individuals who had suffered personal injury might (sometimes) be willing to carry-out this onerous burden with regard to their own assailants, whether witches or robbers. They would not do so for crimes that did not concern them directly, any more than they would for high treason. Unsurprisingly in these circumstances, many examining JPs did not bother to explore the witch's pact or meeting in any great depth.

By contrast, investigating magistrates in Scotland and on the Continent stressed witches' pacts, Sabbaths, and meetings, the latter two often involving banquets, dancing, obscene rites, sexual activity, and even a personal appearance by the devil. Thus, the formal counts (or "articles") against Scottish witches were often general allegations of diabolism and consorting with Satan. Specific instances of *maleficium* were used to back up these claims, rather than constituting the count itself, even if they were what had initially brought the matter to light. For example, during the 1590s, the North Berwick trials in Scotland frequently had the witches' Sabbath at their core. At one meeting, it was claimed that the devil was present, with the witches kissing his buttocks to seal an agreement to kill the king.

Similarly, in 1617, on Guernsey, one of the Channel Islands just off the French coast with a Norman-French legal system, Collette Du Mont confessed in court that the Devil had regularly arranged for her to attend a witches' Sabbath. He had given her a black ointment which, when administered to her skin, allowed her to fly through the air to the place where the meetings were being held. On arrival at the Sabbaths she met up to 16 other wizards and witches, who were disfigured, blackened, and accompanied by their own devils who were present in the form of cats, dogs and hares.⁹

At times the apparent neglect of diabolism has led observers to suggest that a popular belief in witches' pacts and Sabbaths was largely absent in England, which was, it has even been claimed, a country of fairly unsociable, solitary, witches who only rarely met, unlike their continental counterparts, who associated in covens, at witches' Sabbaths (Sabbats), or to celebrate black masses, sometimes with the devil being present, and even flying to their communal events. Certainly there is very little evidence of any belief in witches holding a black mass in England. It would not have been expected in an essentially Protestant country, as it would have been the inversion of a foreign religious rite.¹⁰

Nevertheless, educated Englishmen who took an interest in such matters necessarily had to have recourse to diabolism to produce an intellectually coherent and structured explanation for the phenomenon; *maleficium* flowed from diabolism, while the central role of the familiar in English witch trials also promoted such notions.¹¹ For example, in Thomas Middleton's play *The Witch* (1613 and 1616), many of his characters' activities, such as flying through the air and meeting at nocturnal Sabbaths, are similar to (and probably based on) continental demonology.¹² Similarly, the Pendle witch-trials of 1612 reveal well-developed notions of diabolism, complete with large-scale witches' meetings, and probably reflect, in part, an awareness of demonological theory by at least one of the examining magistrates. In like manner, Matthew Hopkins and John Stearne, the East Anglian witchfinders of the 1640s, appear to have been well-versed in continental theories, as seen in their questioning of suspects; the admissions they extracted often make reference to sexual intercourse between the witch and the devil (only rarely noted prior to this time). Thus Elizabeth Clarke confessed to having had "carnal copulation with the Devil" for up to seven years. Apparently, he would

---
9. Gragg, "Witchcraft", p. 137.
10. Larner, "Witch Beliefs", 1981, p. 33.
11. Sheilagh Ilona O'Brien, "The discovery of witches: Matthew Hopkins's Defense of his Witch-Hunting Methods", 2016, p. 32.
12. Levack, *Witchcraft Sourcebook*, p. 329.

appear at her bedside as a handsome, dark man and say, "Bessie, I must lie with you", before vigorously making love to her for half the night.

However, and more significantly, recent research also suggests that many ordinary people also subscribed to such beliefs, even if they had little cause or opportunity to publicly enunciate them in a recordable fashion. For example, in a series of depositions made to JPs in 1673, Anne Armstrong, a young servant from Birchen Nook in Northumberland, testified that the previous August she had met an old man who warned her that she was going to be bridled like a horse and ridden to a meeting where she should on no account eat any of the food offered to her. She described what appears to have been a witches' Sabbath, with feasting and dancing, the presence of the devil in a gold chair, the reporting to him by those in attendance of various acts of *maleficium*, and the saying of the Lord's Prayer backwards, albeit that there was an absence of sexual promiscuity (often found elsewhere in Europe).[13]

Familiars

Witches' familiars were a particularly, though not quite uniquely, English phenomenon. They were often called "imps", and were supernatural creatures that acted as both demonic spirits and domestic pets. They were usually, but not invariably, granted to witches after they had entered the service of Satan, sometimes after a meeting with the latter entity. However, familiars frequently acted on the devil's behalf, as his representatives, or were even seen as an incarnation of the devil when entering into a pact. Some were inherited from other witches; others approached the witch of their own accord. Even though the familiar might have an independent life, it remained closely linked to the witch, unless and until permanently abandoning her.

Of course, in some cases familiars were simply domestic pets, the attribution being given to a real animal. The witchcraft sceptic Thomas Ady spoke of a woman being executed for witchcraft in 1645 for "keeping a tame frog in a box". He may have been referring to a case from the

---

13. James Sharpe, "In Search of the English Sabbat: Popular Conceptions of Witches' Meetings in Early Modern England", *Journal of Early Modern Studies*, no. 2 (2013), p. 161 and p. 166.

previous decade. According to tradition, the eminent physician William Harvey, aware that a reputed witch had a toad familiar, tricked his way into her home and took the animal away to kill and dissect; he found that it was exactly like any other toad, and nothing more than a cherished milk-fed pet.[14]

Familiars might provide their (often needy) mistresses with money, food, or possessions, or give them practical advice. In 1579 Elizabeth Stile admitted that she had gone to Windsor hoping to beg some milk; she could not obtain it, as the maid was out milking, "but her Ratte had prouided for her bothe Milke and Creame, againste her commyng home".[15] Another familiar would present the occasional shilling to his witch.

As these cases suggest, such gifts were usually modest, and if more substantial would often prove to be illusory and swiftly disappear. This was necessary, as it was patently obvious that most witches were far too poor to be receiving large amounts of supernatural aid; at times, in the early eighteenth century, the impoverished Jane Wenham, the last convicted witch in England, had even been reduced to stealing turnips out of hunger. As Thomas Ady observed, given their supposed access to diabolical help, it was strange to see the number of "poor lean starved people" executed as witches.[16]

The much more important—and plausible—function of familiars was to carry out specific acts of *maleficia*, usually to effect revenge, for their witches, something that was viewed as being close to the latters' wicked hearts. According to Elizabeth Stile, in 1579, if anyone had annoyed a witch, they would "go to their Spirites and saie, suche a one hath angred me, goe dooe them this mischief, and for their hire, would giue them a droppe of their owne blood, and presently the partie was plagued by some lamentable casualtie".[17]

---

14. Cathy Gere, "William Harvey's Weak Experiment: The Archaeology of an Anecdote", *History Workshop Journal*, v. 51, no. 1 (2001), p. 27.
15. Tract 1579 (2) pp. 1–10.
16. Thomas Ady, *A Candle in the Dark* (London: 1656), p. 141.
17. Marion Gibson, *Early Modern Witches: Witchcraft Cases in Contemporary Writing* (London: Routledge, 2000), p. 38.

The Essex JP Brian Darcy claimed that Ursula Kemp had admitted to having four familiars, two male spirits that killed people and two female spirits that brought sickness and destroyed domestic animals. Kemp went on to confess to sending her familiars to make Grace Thurlow lame and to kill Joan Thurlow.[18] A century later, in 1678, when Mary Neale of Wissenset in Norfolk admitted that she and two other women had used witchcraft to kill several local people, she claimed that she had sent a mouse to Alice Atkins which "did soone dispatch her in five dayes". She also alleged that one of her accomplices "did send a Duck" to John Willis, with the same result.[19]

As this suggests, familiars took on many animal guises, including squirrels, polecats, farm animals, and even fish or insects. According to Reginald Scot, during Queen Mary's reign (when witchcraft was not a secular crime), a Kentish JP had put a man in the stocks for cheating in an archery competition by using a "divell or familiar" in the form of a fly.[20] Nevertheless, as the canine familiar in *The Witch of Edmonton* (1621) noted, they tended to manifest themselves as "coarse creatures", such as dogs, cats, hares, ferrets, frogs and toads. The last was especially popular amongst malefic witches in the West Country, something that was discussed by a cunning man from Dorset in 1566, who noted that "mens goods & Cattels be hurt by the Todes".[21] The collective memory of familiars survives as the witches' black cats of nineteenth century fiction.

Much more rarely, a familiar might appear as a homunculus or child, as can be seen from a late near panic that appears to have taken place in Kent, in 1692. A county JP there examined three women accused of witchcraft in June that year. The results were later published. One of the women apparently confessed, in the presence of numerous witnesses, to having signed in blood (taken from her nose) a covenant with the devil, and to having four familiars, three the size of mice, the fourth a little black man, with whom she had had "carnal copulation" on two occasions. They assisted her in working *maleficium* against man and beast.

---

18. Tract 1579 (2) pp. 1–10.
19. TNA ASSI 16/32/3.
20. Reginald Scot, *The Discoverie of Witchcraft*, 1584. (Facsimile reprint, Wakefield: E. P. Publishing, 1973), p. 65.
21. Tract 1566 (2) pp. 1–6.

(This alleged witch was later found dead by her bed in an unusual posture, about five days before she was due to stand trial, so the matter could not be examined further).[22]

Some witches had only one familiar, while others possessed several. They were nearly always given personal names, like any other type of pet. When Alice Samuel, about to be executed in 1592, was asked about her familiars, which had appeared as dun-coloured chickens, and what the "names of those Spirites (wherewith shee bewitched) were called, shee said, they were called Plucke, Catch, and White".[23] These were sometimes conferred in a parody of baptism.[24] However, other familiars were said to have volunteered their own names.

In return for their assistance, witches would care for their familiars, usually providing them with sustenance in the form of their own blood. One of the first witches to be executed, Agnes Waterhouse in 1566, rewarded her familiar by allowing him to drink her blood at various ad hoc places. She would cut her hand or face and put the wound to his mouth, which he then sucked leaving visible spots on her skin.[25] This swiftly gave way to the notion of a permanent specialist nipple, often in the genital area. In 1621, Elizabeth Sawyer gave some indication as to how this was formed, when she admitted that the devil came to her in the form of a dog, putting his head under her coat and sucking her blood for 15 minutes at a specific spot in her nether regions; there, as a result of his "continual drawing, there is a thing in the forme of a Teate". The process was painless.[26]

In 1653, the elderly Anne Bodenham was found to have a teat on her shoulder and another near her genitals. They were about the length and "bignesse of the Nipple of a womans breast, and hollow and soft as a Nipple, with a hole on the top of it". After Alice Fowler, who had long been reputed to be a witch, died from natural causes in Shadwell in the early 1680s, several of her neighbours decided to search her body and all of them subsequently affirmed that they found in the "private parts of

---

22. *Athenian Gazette*, 28 February 1693.
23. Tract 1593 p. 112.
24. Bernard, *Guide*, p. 109.
25. Tract 1566 (1) pp. 1–8.
26. Tract 1621 (2) pp. 1–10.

the Corps five Teats; to wit, four small ones and one very big, and that they were all of them as black as a Coal".[27] Some witches had a teat for each familiar that they possessed.

Familiars quickly came to be regarded as classic indicators of an English witch and an important part of popular lore on the topic. Even so, witches sometimes had recourse to other methods of enchantment, rather than relying solely on their "imps".

Alternative Forms of Enchantment

Many observers accused witches of using sympathetic or "image" magic to effect *maleficium*, something that had been expressly noted in (and well before) the 1542 Act, and which had been discussed by Reginald Scot in the 1580s, and James VI in the 1590s. In these situations, the devil would teach his acolytes to make pictures of wax or clay, "[t]hat by the rotting thereof, the persones that they beare the name of may be continuallie melted or dryed awaie by continuall sicknesse".[28] In 1612 the octogenarian witch Elizabeth Sowtherns claimed that the quickest way to kill a man by witchcraft was to make a clay picture of him and then: " … take a Thorne or Pinne, and pricke it in that part of the picture you would so have to be ill".[29]

The construction of such images might be accompanied by special spells and incantations. Abraham Chad, when giving evidence against Susan Cock and Rose Hallbread at the Worcester Assizes in 1647, observed that the women had lit a fire, crafted the shapes of their victims in wax, and then put them on a spit. As one of them turned the spit, the other stuck pins and needles in the figurines, while both "muttered to themselves strange kind of words".[30]

One of the last women to be executed for witchcraft, Temperance Lloyd in 1682, was pressed on the issue of image magic, and was asked whether she had any wax or clay pictures that she pricked to torment

---

27. Tract 1685 pp. 1–4.
28. James VI &1, *Daemonologie In Forme of a Dialogue*, p. 44.
29. Tract 1613(1) p. B3.
30. Tract 1670 p. 6.

Grace Thomas. She denied having images made of such materials, but admitted having a piece of leather that she had pricked nine times. [31]

Aside from images, some witches were believed to use potions or formal spells, as the actions of the trio portrayed by Shakespeare in *Macbeth* suggest. Margaret Flower confessed that she had often heard her mother curse the Earl of Rutland and his lady, and "thereupon would boyle feathers and blood together, using many Devilish speeches and strange gestures".

However, in other cases, the witch does not appear to have used familiars, material aids, or even complex formal words in her attempt to effect *maleficium*, but simply cursed her victim. Keith Parry has noted that in seventeenth century Norfolk, *maleficium* was far more commonly effected by simple words, in the form of threats, than by familiars.[32] Other cases were said to have been brought about by physical contact, or simply by an invisible power givenced out by the witch's eyes, so that the victim was said to be "overlooked" or "fascinated".[33] In practice, once there was a will to attribute malign witchcraft to a suspect, finding an appropriate method by which it had occurred posed few problems.

---

31. Gent, *Bideford Witches*, pp. 7–8.
32. Parry, *Norfolk*.
33. Keith Thomas, *Religion and the Decline of Magic* (London: Weidenfeld & Nicolson, 1971), p. 519.

CHAPTER 4

Living With the Witch

Introduction

Witches were usually well-known to their victims, their *maleficium* normally thought to be conducted for personal reasons. In Essex, witch and victim came from the same village in 410 out of 460 recorded cases.[1] Similarly, of 130 indictments for witchcraft made at Assizes in Kent, only eleven involved accusations in which the suspected witch and her victim did not live in the same community. Even in these cases, the distance between the two averaged just two-and-a-half miles (in a straight line) and was never more than six.[2]

It is apparent that communities lived with suspected witches for years, often decades, without taking formal action against them, and that the majority of suspected witches died natural deaths without coming before a court, especially a secular forum, even though they might be "vehemently suspected for witchcraft as the common fame goeth".[3]

For example, in 1603 Mary Panell, who was eventually executed for witchcraft at Ledston in Yorkshire, had a reputation as a witch that stretched back at least a decade, but probably far longer; she had been accused of killing a man with witchcraft in 1593. In 1617, in the same county, Thomas Brooke claimed that a woman whom he had accused of bewitching his goods had been a witch for 14 years. In 1652 it was alleged that Hester France of Huddersfield had practised as a witch

---
1. Tracy Borman, *Witches: A Tale of Sorcery, Scandal and Seduction* (London: Jonathan Cape, 2013), p. 133.
2. Pollock, "Social and economic", p. 42.
3. Hussey, "Visitations", p. 46.

for 20 years.⁴ At the very end of the witch-trial era, the Hertfordshire farmer John Chapman had thought for many years that Jane Wenham was behind the strange deaths of local cattle and horses before eventually taking action in 1712.

Once the reputation of being a witch was acquired, it was very difficult to dispel. Gossip and informal accusation were constrained only by fear of an action for defamation in a church court or, less commonly, a secular forum.⁵ Nevertheless, a few rumoured witches did pursue this route. For example, in 1606 Thomas Herold of Pulborough sued Elizabeth Hitchcock for defamation in a Sussex ecclesiastical court, claiming that she had accused him to a third party of bewitching her husband's cattle and their children. The case made little progress for the initial six months, a delay the plaintiff later alleged was due to hopes of reaching an agreement and settlement. However, it continued without resolution, and at one point the defendant was excommunicated for contumacy and then absolved. The plaintiff eventually won, and was awarded his costs, while the defendant was sentenced to do public penance in Pulborough church in May 1608, on pain of further excommunication if she failed to carry it out.⁶

Changing forum, in 1578 William Netlingham sued Ralph Ode in the Court of King's Bench for making a similar allegation of witchcraft. He received more than £11 in damages. More than a century later, in October 1696, John Vick, an Epping locksmith, entered into a recognisance to answer an allegation of having defamed the married Ann Bartmaker by falsely reporting that she was a witch.⁷

Other secular avenues were also used for dealing with such abuse. In the 1680s a youth who used to shout "Witch!" at an elderly woman, who was resident in an almshouse, so enraged her that "she threatened him with a *Warrant;* and accordingly did fetch one from a Neighbouring *Justice of the Peace;* at which he was so frightened, that he humbled

---

4. Sharpe, *Yorkshire,* p. 10.
5. Peter Rushton, "Women, Witchcraft, and Slander in Early Modern England: Cases from the Church Courts of Durham, 1560–1675", *Northern History,* v. 18, issue 1 (1982), p. 116.
6. Peter M. Wilkinson (ed.), *Chichester Archdeaconry Depositions 1603–1608* (Lewes: Sussex Record Society, 2017), p. 230.
7. ERO Q/SR 491/4.

himself to her, and promised never to call her so again".⁸ The Star Chamber provided another (if rarely used) legal forum in which people who felt they had been the victims of malicious or unfounded allegations of witchcraft could take proceedings against their attackers.

However, suits for defamation were unlikely to be possible for the poor. Furthermore, such actions, whether in the ecclesiastical or secular courts, were not without their own risks. The precipitating event in the Wenham case in 1712 occurred after an angry local farmer, John Chapman, called Wenham a "Witch and Bitch". Shortly afterwards she went to the local JP, Sir Henry Chauncy, asking for a warrant for slander, with a view to obtaining some sort of financial compensation from Chapman and also, bearing in mind her longstanding reputation as a witch, hoping "to deter other People from calling her so any more". However, the elderly magistrate made enquiries about her character (very poor), which did not help her case. He referred the matter to the local minister, the Reverend Gardiner, for what amounted to low-level arbitration, so beginning the chain of events that would result in her prosecution and conviction for witchcraft.⁹

The Dangers of Prosecution

There were several reasons for the general reluctance to prosecute suspected witches. The main ones were fear of revenge (supernatural or not), the cost and risks of prosecution (especially its low prospects of success), and an unwillingness to disturb local harmony by endangering the life of a neighbour. For example, Dorothy Durrant, whose evidence was to play a large part in the case against Amy Duny in 1662, had asked her to look after her baby some five years earlier, even though she knew of Duny's reputation as a witch.¹⁰

As to potential expense, in 1654, the Norfolk Quarter Sessions order book describes Mary Childerhouse, who engaged in numerous disputes with her neighbours, and made periodic allegations of witchcraft against

---

8. Tract 1689 p. 1.
9. O. Davies, *Witchcraft, Magic*, p. 84.
10. Geis and Bunn, *A Trial of Witches*, pp. 40–41.

them, as being elderly and "impoverished" and so "unable to prosecute law".[11] Similarly, when Elizabeth Field was asked at the trial of Jane Wenham why she had not prosecuted nine years earlier, when she first believed that the defendant had bewitched her daughter, she stressed that she had "no friends able to bear the cost of prosecution".

Very occasionally, there were also direct legal risks in making formal allegations. At the Chelmsford Assizes in July 1621, Anne Godfrey, a married woman from West Ham, was indicted for attempting to procure the death of Elizabeth Edlyn. She had told two JPs in Barking that Edlyn had bewitched her. Godfrey was convicted and sentenced to be placed in the stocks for two hours during market day in Chelmsford and Barking, and then to be committed to the House of Correction until the following Assizes.[12] There was also the possibility of a costly civil action for malicious prosecution.

Instead of formal action, many people who lived near suspected witches preferred appeasement, informal methods of protection, counter-magic, and direct action against the source of their trouble if they thought they were bewitched.[13] As has frequently been noted, private suspicions of witchcraft did not easily become public accusations.

Appeasing the Witch

One obvious way to protect against witches was to avoid being victimised in the first place. The simplest way to do this was to keep them "on side". This could often be done by the sensible use of charity. In the 1580s Reginald Scot observed that witches were so feared that few people dared offend them, or deny them when they begged: "These go from house to house, and from door to door for a pot full of milk, yeast, drink, pottage, or some such relief; without the which they could hardly live". Such charity was not confined to simple people. Edward Fairfax noted that one of the alleged witches who afflicted his daughters had "so powerful a hand over the wealthiest neighbours about her, that none of

---

11. Parry, *Norfolk*.
12. J.S. Cockburn (ed.), *Calendar of Assize Records: Essex Indictments, James I*, (London: HMSO, 1982) p. 251.
13. Gaskill, "Witchcraft Trials", p. 284.

them refused to do anything she required".[14] Just as a village scold could get her way on various local issues by wearing people down, a suspected witch could gain considerable benefits by scaring her neighbours, helping to explain why some would publicly adopt such a persona.[15] The Reverend Francis Trigge, a Lincolnshire cleric who died in 1606, shared some of Reginald Scot's belief in a link between a rise in witch-hunting and a decline in charity in the country. He thought the latter was the best remedy against witchcraft.[16]

Even after victimisation, those who had been on the receiving end of a witch's attentions might be able to pacify her. For example, in Yorkshire one of Mary Midgley's suspected victims, a married woman whose cattle had sickened, went to the supposed witch, admitted offending her, and asked to remedy her error if possible. After some hesitation, Midgley accepted sixpence from the woman and informed her "the kyne should mend".[17]

Passive Defence

It was possible to defend against some witch-attacks using various forms of counter-magic. For example, charms and so-called witch bottles or jars could be employed to provide protection against spells by neutralising them or even deflecting them back at the witches involved. Such charms and bottles were used from at least the sixteenth to the nineteenth centuries, and were often prepared by a cunning man or woman. Some of the earliest documented witch bottles were Bartmann jugs (salt-glazed stoneware with the image of a bearded man). Traditionally a witch bottle contained the (potential) victim's urine, hair, or nail clippings. Joseph Glanvill described the preparation of such a bottle in 1681: "Take your Wive's Urine as before, and Cork it in a Bottle with Nails, Pins and Needles, and bury it in the Earth". A sealed witch bottle was discovered five

---

14. Tract 1621 (1) p. 7.
15. Edward Bever, "Witchcraft, Female Aggression, and Power in the Early Modern Community", *Journal of Social History*, v. 35, no. 4 (2002), p. 976.
16. Peter Elmer, *Witchcraft, Witch-Hunting, and Politics in Early Modern England* (Oxford: Oxford University Press, 2016), p. 32.
17. Sharpe, *Yorkshire*, p. 16.

feet below ground in Greenwich, London, in 2004. It contained bent pins and nails, a nail-pierced leather heart, fingernail clippings, and hair in a solution of urine. [18]

Other witch bottles and jars were concealed in buildings and underneath fireplaces. Excavations of old buildings at Charing in Kent revealed several anti-witch charms, including witch bottles and jars, from about the seventeenth century, although there were no witch prosecutions recorded in this village. In several cases bottles were hidden in chimneys. As elsewhere, some contained pins that had been bent double, along with hair and iron nails (witches disliked ferrous metal).[19] Such vessels were believed to remain active for as long as they were hidden and unbroken.

It was often believed that, after being buried, the bottle captured evil, which was impaled on its pins and needles. Others thought that its presence meant that a witch who had placed a spell would be unable to pass water until her curse had been removed. In 1670, Margaret Kemp of Great Yarmouth remembered that when she had been ill, 14 years earlier, her friends suspected one Margaret Ward of bewitching her. Their response was to cut a piece of red cloth into a heart shape and to put it into a bottle together with some nails and pins. This was then put on the fire for two hours. Within a fortnight she was well again.[20]

At a more basic level, apotropaic symbols or "witch's marks" were often scratched or carved into the beams of houses, barns, and even churches to protect them from witches and evil spirits; these were much simpler to produce than "witch bottles", and correspondingly widespread. They often appear as, *inter alia*, flower-like patterns made with compasses and dividers, designs based on the intertwined letters V and M (for the Virgin Mary), tangled skeins of lines, thought to confuse spirits who attempted to follow them, and tadpole-shaped scorch marks made with a candle flame.[21]

---

18. *New Scientist*, 4 June 2009.
19. Patricia Winzar, "Witchcraft Counter-Spells in Charing", *Archaeologia Cantiana*, v. 115 (1995), pp. 24–28.
20. Parry, *Norfolk*.
21. *The Guardian*, 31 October 2016.

Active Defence

Sometimes a more aggressive approach was necessary to deal with a troublesome witch. Occasionally a good thrashing was enough to make the witch change her mind, and withdraw her spell, although this must have taken a degree of nerve on the part of the victim. Nevertheless, in 1648 Nicholas Baldwin of Reedness in Yorkshire beat Elizabeth Lambe with a cane after three of his foals died in mysterious circumstances. One witness claimed that, after doing this, Baldwin had "never since been disturbed by her". Several other people who thought Lambe had bewitched their cattle were emboldened by this, followed suit, and also thrashed her, with equally positive results.[22] Much more commonly, those who were subject to bewitchment would seek to draw the witch's blood by scratching her.

Scratching

A longstanding belief in England was that the victim of bewitchment could break a spell, at least in the short term, and gain relief from its symptoms, by scratching the witch with fingernails, a frond of holly or similar barbed foliage, a needle, awl, or other pointed implement. As was noted in 1691, "there's a custom that the bewitched party, is to pinch, bite, scratch, or prick the witch till she draw's blood, and then she's well".[23] In giving relief, it also, of course, provided a means of identifying the witch behind the spell.

Some believers in witchcraft did not favour such stratagems, feeling that, as they were not founded in scripture or medicine, they were useless or would make those using them guilty of using magic themselves. Nevertheless, the practice was very widespread throughout the country, during the entire era of proscription, and for long afterwards, being referred to in numerous sources.

For example, in 1604 Joan Guppy complained to the Star Chamber that one Margaret Abington had defamed her as a witch. It seems that

---

22. Sharpe, *Yorkshire*, 1992, p. 2.
23. *Athenian Gazette*, 27 September 1691.

Abington, her husband, Andrew, and several other people, lay in wait for Guppy as she rode to market in Crewkerne, Somerset, then ambushed her and scratched her face with overgrown brambles and pins, saying that she "was a witch and they came for the blood". It was a vicious attack, which left her seriously wounded.[24] In 1618, when Mary Dalton was on her deathbed in Yorkshire, she became convinced that Isabel Morris was the cause of her affliction and attempted to scratch her when she came into the house selling bread.[25] In 1712 Jane Wenham, the last woman convicted of witchcraft in England, was also subjected to such treatment. One of her alleged victims "flew upon her to scratch her, saying, I must have your blood, or I shall never be well".

Officials sometimes sanctioned such a procedure, even at the start of the eighteenth century. In 1702 Alderman Sir Thomas Lane, an *ex officio* JP in the City of London, ordered Richard Hathaway to scratch Sarah Morduck in his presence and that of other several aldermen. These magistrates manifested some nervousness about allowing such a procedure, but eventually concurred with Sir Thomas's decision. (He also ordered that Morduck be stripped and searched for marks by some women in his house).[26] It seems that such scratching would not be conducted in court, but its outcome might be reported at trial.

However, as the aldermen's nervousness in Morduck's case suggests, the legal status of scratching was always dubious. Strictly speaking, it might constitute an assault. In 1600 the elderly Margaret Francis was sent to Norwich gaol to await trial on suspicion of bewitching Joan Harvey, a Hockham maid who had started barking, having fits, and experiencing muteness, blindness, and lameness. However, Augustine Steward visited the alleged victim, and came to the conclusion that she was suffering from a form of hysteria. He wrote to Sir Bassingbourne Gawdy, the JP who had committed Francis to prison, asking that she be freed. The magistrate appears to have issued an order for her release, but before it was enforced Harvey was allowed to visit her alleged tormentor "who having been blooded in the usual manner by scratching, shortly after she died".

---

24. Ross, Richard S., *Before Salem: Witch Hunting in the Connecticut River Valley, 1647–1663* (Jefferson, N.C.: McFarland, 2017), p. 296.
25. Sharpe, *Yorkshire*, 1992, p. 15.
26. Tract 1702 (2).

It seems that it was subsequently alleged that the two events were linked, with a criminal prosecution mooted, and potential witnesses prepared to give evidence against the maid, whether for manslaughter or assault. Fortunately for her, it was also noted that "all the[se] witnesses are very poor". This made a successful prosecution of the maid unlikely.[27]

In 1674, when Joseph Weeden, a grazier who thought that he was bewitched, identified Ann Foster as the source of his woes, he decided to have recourse to "fetching the blood" of the suspect. As a result, he cut her above the hand. An infection formed within the cut, and Ann threated to have him arrested. Weeden was sufficiently worried by this possibility to initially offer to pay for Ann to go to a healer.[28] (Had she accepted, she would never have been prosecuted).

As attitudes changed, the courts became more robust about punishing such self-help measures. In early 1720 there were reports that the landlord of an alehouse and his wife had attacked an elderly woman and suspected witch in Cripplegate, "cutting and slashing her arm to fetch blood of her", so that she was seriously injured. The landlord was bound over by JPs to attend Quarter Sessions.[29] Even so, the scratching of suspected witches continued on a popular basis until well into the nineteenth century.

Use of Ecclesiastical Courts

Even when it was felt that some form of legal action against a witch was required, it did not necessarily have to be conducted in a secular forum. The advent of the 1563 Act did not bring an end to the involvement of the much more lenient ecclesiastical courts in dealing with witchcraft. Such forums could not prescribe the shedding of blood, and often merely imposed penances. For example, in 1566, three years after the new statute, John Walsh appeared before an ecclesiastical court in Devon accused of witchcraft. He was a physician but appears to have doubled as a cunning man. Although he seemed rather ignorant of the legitimate uses of

---

27. Ewen, *Demonism*, pp. 190–191.
28. Tract 1674 p. 2.
29. *Original Weekly Journal*, 9 April 1720.

herbs, he stressed that he did not use magic or any "secret meanes" for his cures, but did admit to familiarity with various types of fairy. He also utterly denied that he had a familiar when questioned, but eventually confessed that he had had one for four years in the past, given to him by the master who had trained him, and who had appeared as either a dog or a small man with cloven feet. This imp might guide him to the whereabouts of stolen property. (It was very uncommon for cunning folk to have familiars). He had also had a "booke of Circles" or charms, but this had been taken away from him by the constable of Crowkhorne the previous year.[30]

Essex may have been the epicentre of secular witch prosecutions in England, but in the years from 1560 to 1680 at least 230 cases (and probably many more) involving witchcraft or sorcery of all types were presented at the various ecclesiastical courts in the county. There were several of these, reflecting overlapping jurisdictions, including those of the Bishop of London and the Archdeacons of Colchester and Essex.[31] Similarly, in the sixteenth century, the Canterbury Archdeacon's Court met fortnightly, and went on circuit regularly in the western part of the diocese. It heard occasional witchcraft cases, amongst numerous others, and continued to do so after 1563, although the number of such offences that might, alternatively, have been indicted in the secular courts under the 1563 Act declined during the 1570s.[32]

Even so, in 1582 the Archdeacon of Canterbury cited one "Goodwife Swane" because she was "vehemently suspected" of being a witch. Some of her actions were standard cunning-folk activity: it was reported that Swane claimed that she could make powerful love potions that worked on young men. However, it was also said that she had "threatened one of her neighbours and upon words fell out with her, and told her that she would make her repent her falling out with her. And it is come to pass this same woman her neighbour hath never been well since".[33] This was quintessentially malefic witchcraft that could easily have been

---

30. Tract 1566 (2) pp. 1–6.
31. Alan Macfarlane, *Witchcraft in Tudor and Stuart England: A Regional and Comparative Study* (New York: Harper & Row, 1970), p. 66.
32. Sweetinburgh, *Later Medieval Kent*, p. 201; Gaskill, *Introduction*, p. 63.
33. Hussey, "Visitations", p. 19 and p. 31.

(non-capitally) indicted under the 1563 statute but was dealt with in a much milder fashion.

Such actions were found elsewhere in England. For example, in the period between 1567 and 1640, there were 117 presentments for witchcraft in the church courts at York alone. Of these 62 alleged "charming" — that is, some form of cunning-folk activity. However, more than two-thirds of the remaining 55 cases involved damage to the health of either men or animals (malefic witchcraft).[34]

Being presented for witchcraft before an ecclesiastical court did not preclude a similar case being brought at Assizes, although this was unusual. Nevertheless, in the transitional period before and after the passage of the 1563 Act, Elizabeth Lowys was cited before the Archdeacon's Court in Essex (the result is unknown) and, a month later, for an overlapping set of offences (one had been heard by the ecclesiastical court, two were new) at the Essex Assizes in July 1564 (the first to be prosecuted in the county). She was found guilty on all three counts but (initially) successfully pleaded pregnancy.[35]

The ecclesiastical courts ceased operating during the Civil War and Interregnum. Although restored after 1660, they did not fully regain their pre-war vigour.

Vagabond Actions

Furthermore, lesser allegations of witchcraft that might, potentially, have come under the 1563 or 1604 statutes (see *Chapter 5*) were occasionally dealt with using alternative criminal provisions in the secular courts. For example, in June 1573 Robert Wallys was indicted at the Essex Assizes for cozening after telling people he could conjure spirits to detect gold, in exchange for payment. He was ultimately convicted of being a vagabond and bound in service to a Mr Mede.[36] This might be done for

---

34. Philip Tyler, "The Church Courts at York and Witchcraft prosecutions, 1567–1640", *Northern History*, v. 4, issue 1, pp. 84–110.
35. Alan R. Young, "Elizabeth Lowys: Witch and Social Victim, 1564", *History Today*, v. 22, issue 12 (1972), p. 879.
36. J.S. Cockburn (ed.), *Calendar of Assizes Records: Essex Indictments, Elizabeth I* (London: HMSO, 1980), p. 114.

administrative or evidential convenience—for example, in the absence of a willing prosecutor or where a case appeared otherwise weak.[37]

---

37. *Ibid.*

CHAPTER 5

The Witchcraft Statutes

Introduction

Throughout Europe, the crime of witchcraft was defined on a national basis, so that although the offences produced had many similarities, there were also variations from country to country. In England witchcraft was prohibited by a series of parliamentary statutes that listed outlawed behaviours. As already noted, these acts focussed mainly on witchcraft as hostility towards a particular individual or for a specific malign purpose (*maleficium*), rather than as a pact or other form of covenant or association with the devil (diabolism). This would become a general characteristic of English witchcraft prosecutions, and one way in which they often differed from those on the Continent and in Scotland.

Criminalisation did not merely give a legal avenue of expression to an already strongly held popular belief, channelling a force that would otherwise have found an informal outlet in extra-legal activities. It actively encouraged such a belief by giving it an official sanction. As Christina Larner observed, the "labelled" witch, in a community where the control of witchcraft is not backed up by the state, is usually a less frightening character, often requiring only social marginalisation rather than elimination. By making witches guilty of a serious secular crime, the state also made them more potent in popular perception.

The Witchcraft Acts were statutes like any others; they were not general licences to punish any activity which might be associated with or deemed to be witchcraft. Indeed, they were passed in an era that was increasingly concerned about the rules and canons of statutory intepretation, as can be seen, for example, in the discussion of the "mischief rule" in the Exchequer Court in *Heydon's Case* in 1584.[1] The statutes were complicated, and there was considerable debate and dispute as to what their provisions meant. Treatises on the 1604 Act have been found with handwritten annotation from informed readers challenging the author's interpretation as to whether certain forms of contact with the devil were necessarily criminal. However, although witches, like all felony defendants, could technically have legal representation on points of pure law in court, most were far too poor to avail themselves of it, reducing the practical significance of the statute's subtleties.

The 1542 Act

The first English Witchcraft Act (33 Henry VIII. c. 8) came into force in 1542 (a similar statute had been drafted in 1533 but not pursued).[2] It is not known precisely what prompted Henry VIII and Parliament to such action, although concerns about treasonous prophecies made with regard to the king's reign may have been a factor. It may also have been influenced by equivalent provisions on the Continent, such as the article against witchcraft contained in the Carolina Code of 1532.

More generally, it seems that malefic witchcraft was occasioning increased concern amongst the secular authorities around this time. For example, in January 1538 Thomas Wriothesley, the Earl of Southampton and variously Secretary of State and Lord Chancellor, along with Paul Withipol and Dr Starky, examined a man named Fulk Vaughan about an alarming discovery. A few days earlier, Vaughan had seen a number of people clustered around something in the churchyard next to his master's house in London. Initially they appeared to think that it was the illicit burial of a small child. However, when the church clerk removed a piece of cloth shaped like a winding sheet from the ground, and ripped it open, he discovered a wax model in the form of a young child with two pins thrust into it. Vaughan took the sheet to a scrivener

---

1. *Heydon's Case* [1584] EWHC Exch J36 76 ER 637.
2. Gaskill, "Evidence", p. 39.

The Witchcraft Statutes

named Pole in Crooked Lane who told him "it was made to waste one. But, quoth he, he that made it was not his craft's master, for he should have put it either in horse dung or in a dunghill". He also told him that such sympathetic magic could kill a man. Pole seems to have acquired his knowledge from personal experience (he appears to have been some sort of cunning man), and Vaughan was examined about whether he had heard Pole speak of conjuring matters before.[3]

The 1542 Act expressly noted that people had been conjuring spirits and pretending by such means to find buried gold and silver, and had used sorcery and witchcraft to destroy their neighbours and their property. It also discussed how images had sometimes been used for this purpose (as seen in the Vaughan case). This claim is well supported by other contemporary sources.

Under the 1542 Act it was an unclergyable felony (one for which the death penalty was mandatory) to use the conjuration of spirits, witchcraft, or sorcery to destroy another person's body or goods; to find money or treasure; to find lost or stolen property; to promote unlawful love; or for any other illegal purpose. Consequently, it can be said that the far-reaching statute was aimed both at fraudsters who made money by claiming magical powers that allowed them to know where treasure was buried and at those who genuinely used witchcraft, whether for such purposes or for the "destruction of their neighbours' persons and goods".

Although it covered a huge range of behaviours of very varying degrees of gravity, from murder by witchcraft to finding stolen items using magic, the felony created was undifferentiated as to its consequences. Because it was unclergyable, and no lesser punishment was specified, all such activities (real or feigned) were necessarily capital on conviction, even for a first offence, unless reprieved by the Crown or deferred because of pregnancy. (Pleading benefit of clergy allowed literate criminals to be transferred to an ecclesiastical court for sentence; these forums could not authorise the shedding of blood). Like most other felonies, conviction also led to attainder and the complete forfeiture of the "lands, tenants, goods and chattels" of the convicted person (normally to the Crown).

---

3. James Gairdner (ed.), *Letters and Papers Foreign and Domestic: Henry VIII, Volume 13, Part 1, January–July 1538* (London: HMSO, 1892), pp. 1–20.

Crimen Exceptum

The 1542 Act was the strictest witchcraft statute ever passed in England, not just for the witch, but also for any "counsellors, abettors, and procurers" of the offences as well. It struck at cunning folk and tricksters, as well as malefic witches, and punished them equally. If the statute had been systematically enforced, its consequences would have been very severe. However, in practice, it does not seem to have resulted in a surge in prosecutions in the secular courts during the five years that it was in force. Indeed, it appears that there were almost no prosecutions at all. There is one very belated reference to witches being executed in Devon during this period. In his book *Psonthonpanchia*, first published in 1664, John Heydon claimed that two witches were hanged near Exeter in the reign of Henry VIII. However, this account appears fairly unreliable.[4]

Nevertheless, in October 1542 John Morris of Brampston in Leicestershire received a pardon for all felonies involving witchcraft committed since 1 May that year (when the statute came into force), suggesting that he had been convicted, or at least threatened with prosecution, for such an offence.[5] In 1546 Henry Neville, the dim, gullible, and debt-pressed heir of the Earl of Westmoreland, appears to have been arrested and questioned under the 1542 Act after he was accused of counselling or procuring a fraudulent magician to murder his wife and father using the dark arts (a capital offence given that spells had been cast). In an eight-page confession, made in his cell, Neville also admitted that he had paid cash to the same man for: making a magic ring that guaranteed success at gambling; promising to discover a cache of gold allegedly hidden under a cross in Yorkshire using magic (expressly forbidden under the statute); and creating a spell to make him (Neville) play the lute in an accomplished fashion. However, in 1547 Neville was pardoned, and, by the end of the year, Henry VIII was dead, and the 1542 Act, along with other recent Henrician legislation, had been repealed.[6]

---

4. Stoyle, "'Olde Wytche Gonne'", p. 138.
5. James Gairdner and R. H. Brodie (eds.), *Letters and Papers, Foreign and Domestic: Henry VIII, Volume 17, 1542* (London: HMSO, 1900), pp. 550–569.
6. Alec Ryrie, *The Sorcerer's Tale: Faith and Fraud in Tudor England* (Oxford: Oxford University Press, 2008), p. 27.

The young Edward VI did not enact any witchcraft statute of his own, and Mary I (1553–1558) felt no need to restore such legislation, so England was without an equivalent provision for more than a decade.

The 1563 Act

Following the accession of Queen Elizabeth I in 1558, there was almost immediate concern at the lack of secular powers available to combat witches. This was partly linked to concern that Catholics might employ sorcery against the new queen, but was also strongly influenced by the swift return of numerous influential Protestant divines from abroad; as Bishop White of Winchester had warned at Queen Mary's funeral: "The wolves be coming out of Geneva, and other places of Germany". Among them was Edmund Grindal (1519–1583), who had been an exile during the reign of Mary, living in Strasbourg and Frankfurt, and who appears to have absorbed continental notions about witchcraft. On his return to England, he became Bishop of London and later Archbishop of Canterbury. John Jewel (1522–1571), made Bishop of Salisbury in 1559, had also been an exile in Germany, and held equally strong views on the subject. (It should be stressed that in England Calvinism did not *necessarily* produce a propensity to prosecute witches. Several Puritans deplored the fact that witches were blamed for natural misfortune and the working out of the divine will).

Many observers felt that the Henrician witch statute had been repealed through inadvertence, the Act being lumped in with other legislation. As a result, another witchcraft Bill was introduced to Parliament in 1559. This appears to have failed for procedural reasons.[7] It passed through the House of Commons but, after an initial reading in the House of Lords, Parliament was dissolved in May 1559, before it could be enacted.[8]

However, the matter did not rest there; high-level clerics continued to press for change. Jewel appears to have warned Queen Elizabeth about the threat of witchcraft in a letter written at some point in the winter of

---

7. G. R. Elton, *The Parliament of England, 1559–1581* (Cambridge: Cambridge University Press, 1986), p. 110.
8. R. Trevor Davies, *Four Centuries of Witch Beliefs* (London: Methuen, 1947), p. 15.

1559–1560. In April 1561 Grindal wrote to the queen's secretary, Sir William Cecil, urging reform of the law and action against a priest named John Coxe who was, allegedly, guilty not only of popery but also of "magic and Conjuration". (The conflation of Catholicism and witchcraft was to become a fairly common trope amongst Protestants, especially Puritans, in post-Reformation England). In the letter Grindal lamented the secular law's lack of jurisdiction to deal with such matters: "My Lord Chief Justice sayeth the temporal law will not meddle with them. [while] Our ecclesiastical punishment is too slender for so grievous offences".[9]

It is tempting to think that the stress on Bible reading in newly Protestant England also made a contribution, encouraging readers to dwell on the maxim in *Exodus* that "Thou shalt not suffer a witch to live". However, there was to be a long-lasting debate as to the meaning of biblical mentions of witches and the quality of their translation into the various vernacular versions of the Bible (up to and including the King James Bible of 1611). For example, one cleric claimed that the phrase "familiar spirit" in a translation of *Isaiah* "by no means expresses the sense of the original language".[10]

As Grindal's comment suggests, and as already noted, the church courts had continued to exercise their historic, if relatively mild, jurisdiction over witchcraft by hearing cases between 1547 and 1563. Thus in 1560, during one of his visitations in Kent, with a view to presenting ecclesiastical cases, the Archdeacon of Canterbury noted that one Mother Bush was "suspected to be a witch".[11] In December that year, one of John Jewel's first tasks as the newly appointed Bishop of Salisbury was to discipline the Reverend Leonard Bilson, the prebendary of Teynton Regis, who was accused of being involved in witchcraft. He was found guilty in an ecclesiastical court and punished. Henry Machyn recorded in his diary entry for 23 June 1561 that "one priest Master Bellston of Winchester was set on the pillory for conjuring". The following year, the same cleric was also deprived of all his positions in the church.[12]

---

9. *Ibid.*, p. 18.
10. Tract 1736 p. 10.
11. Hussey, "Visitations", p. 21.
12. Clifford Dobson, *The Jewel of Salisbury* (Much Wenlock: RJK Smith, 1996), p. 12.

It has been argued that there was even a minor surge of presentments for magic and witchcraft before the ecclesiastical courts during the late 1550s, in Kent and some other counties — most of these cases being brought by laymen (rather than the clergy) — and that their main concern was the physical harm caused by the accused witch, just as it would be in secular forums during ensuing years.[13] This might suggest a degree of localised pressure from below, as well as from above, to introduce a new witchcraft Act.[14]

Furthermore, although it was not a specific secular offence between 1547 and 1563, allegations of witchcraft did, very occasionally, come before the criminal courts in these years. For example, two cases involving witchcraft went before the Chelmsford Assizes in July 1560. Joan Haddon, a spinster from Witham in Essex, was indicted for "cozening money" and bewitching people early in the same year as a common witch (*communis facinatrix et incantatrix*). Conveniently, she was acquitted of witchcraft (not then a secular crime) but found guilty of the conventional offence of fraudulently receiving money; she should have been pilloried for this (it was a misdemeanour rather than a felony), but may have been pardoned.[15]

Rather more problematically, John Samond, a Danbury "berebruer", who appeared at the same Assizes, was accused of fatally bewitching John Grant and Bridget Peacock the previous year in his capacity as a "common wizard".[16] It appears that the jury initially found him guilty. However, he seems to have challenged the basis of his conviction. At the next Assizes, conducted at Chelmsford in March 1561, the court received a writ directed to the Assize judges for Essex from the Court of Queen's Bench. Samond was then, it seems, acquitted of the crime for which he had, apparently, been convicted six months earlier.[17] It is possible that the Queen's Bench had quashed the finding of the jury the previous year as being without proper legal foundation.[18] (Samond appears to have been

---

13. Jones and Zell, "'The divels speciall instruments'", pp. 45–63.
14. Gaskill, "Witchcraft and Evidence", p. 39.
15. ERO T/A 418/4/7.
16. ERO T/A 418/4/8.
17. J. S. Cockburn (ed.), *Calendar of Assize Records: Essex Indictments, Elizabeth I* (London: HMSO, 1978), p. 16.
18. J. S. Cockburn (ed.), *Crime in England 1550–1800* (London: Methuen, 1977), p. 27.

an incorrigible wizard; he was to reappear before the courts on several occasions, for both witchcraft and conventional felonies, until finally executed for capital witchcraft in 1587).[19]

Pressure for a fresh witchcraft statute came to fruition with a new Parliament in 1563. An Act that year (5 Elizabeth I c. 16) suggested, with an apparent lack of historical awareness given that it was hardly ever invoked, that repeal of the 1542 Act had resulted in "many fantastical and devilish" persons destroying their neighbours' bodies and goods. The new statute was much more merciful than that of 1542. It introduced a bifurcated penal regime in which only very grave witchcraft offences were capital while others, deemed to be less serious, were subject to a year's imprisonment and quarterly pillorying, for six hours at a time, in different market towns during business hours.

Execution was mandated only where witchcraft had supposedly been used to inflict harm on another person that had resulted in their death; effectively, this was "murder by witchcraft". However, where it had been used to cause a non-fatal human injury, to injure or kill domestic animals, or to damage property, it would merely be subject to the lesser regime for a first offence. (A second such conviction would be a capital felony). Thus when Mary Burgess was acquitted of murder by witchcraft at the Hertfordshire Assizes in July 1590, and merely convicted of two lesser counts of using witchcraft to kill a horse and to temporarily paralyse a man's arm, she was sentenced "according to statute" — that is, to imprisonment and the pillory. Catherine Dewsbury received the same sentence six years later, at the same forum, for a similar crime.[20]

Furthermore, those who provided what might be termed typical cunning-folk services, such as locating buried treasure, also fell within the scope of the 1563 statute, in certain circumstances, and would also be subject to a year's imprisonment and the pillory for a first offence. In practice, such forms of witchcraft only rarely came to court. Nevertheless, and for example, at the Lent Assizes held at Chelmsford in 1598, Robert Browning, a labourer from Aldham, was indicted for attempting

---

19. Apps and Gow, *Male Witches*, p. 50.
20. J. S. Cockburn, *Calendar of Assize Records: Hertfordshire Indictments: Elizabeth I*, (London: HMSO, 1975), p. 75 and p. 118.

to acquire great sums of money by the conjuration of evil spirits. He was convicted, largely on the evidence of a single witness, and sentenced to the pillory.[21]

Although a second conviction for lesser forms of witchcraft was supposed to be capital, this was predicated on the court's being aware of an earlier finding of guilt. This was not always the case, as access to records was often poor, and an earlier conviction might be missed or (it seems) deliberately overlooked to avoid a draconian disposal. For example, in 1566 Elizabeth Francis of Hatfield in Essex pleaded guilty ("confesses") to the non-fatal bewitching of a small child named John Auger, and was sentenced according to the statute to a year in prison. In 1572 Francis was again before the court, and on this occasion convicted of making a woman ill by witchcraft; she was pilloried and imprisoned, although, under the 1563 Act, she should have been executed. (She was hanged a few years later for capital witchcraft).

There are occasional indications that, in the early years of the new statutory regime, some Assize judges had reservations about its novel, and sometimes very harsh, nature, remanding capital cases so that a pardon might be considered more frequently than they would in ensuing decades. For example, in February 1568 Margaret Robinson from St. Olave's parish in Southwark was capitally convicted at the Surrey Assizes for bewitching two people to death. Even so, she was remanded without sentence. She seems to have ultimately received mercy, as she appears to have been the same person as a widow by that name who was capitally convicted and executed for infanticide at the Surrey Assizes in July 1584.[22]

Similarly, in the immediate aftermath of the advent of the 1563 Act, the Exeter magistrates, who had power of gaol delivery, were still prepared to punish those who had been accused of witchcraft in the traditional manner, merely banishing them from the city bounds. However, attitudes gradually changed, and by 1581, at the very latest, the execution of a convicted witch took place at the city gallows, albeit only after a temporary reprieve had been granted to consider a pardon. (It is possible that Maud Park and Alice Mead, convicted at the Borough Sessions at

---

21. ERO T/A 418/65/53.
22. Cockburn, *Surrey Indictments*, pp. 64–65 and p. 259.

Exeter Guildhall in 1566, were amongst the very first people in England to be hanged for witchcraft, but this cannot be confirmed).[23]

After a slightly slow start, prosecutions in England quickly increased, to reach their peak in the 1580s and 1590s, apart from the Civil War years during the following century. For example, in Kent there were 23 prosecutions in the final two decades of the sixteenth century. This had fallen to 13 in the first 20 years of the seventeenth century, and just eight between 1620 and 1639 (many were brought under the 1604, rather than the 1563, Act).[24]

Elizabethan Prosecutions: A County Profile

Most of the Hertfordshire Assizes records survive for the Elizabethan period, from 1572 onwards (a few cases during these years have been lost). Some 22 women and men were indicted for offences under the 1563 Act, some for capital forms of malefic witchcraft, others for non-capital types, and a few, such as Mary Taylor in 1598—who was said to have used magic to kill both man and pigs—for both. Twelve were acquitted outright. However, the conviction rate varied significantly with the type of witchcraft alleged.

Of the 14 people who faced capital charges, only three (just over a fifth) were found guilty for murder by witchcraft, one of whom, Agnes Morris of Stevenage, was temporarily reprieved from execution. There is a good chance that this was made permanent by the Queen/Privy Council. Four defendants accused of both capital and non-capital counts of witchcraft were merely convicted of the latter. Thus in 1593 Joan Garret, acquitted of four cases of murder by witchcraft, but found guilty on a fifth count of bewitching a horse to death, was sentenced to a year's imprisonment. This suggests that the early-modern jury's well-noted desire to punish without killing, where possible, remained intact, even when it came to witchcraft. In another case, from 1601, Sarah Asser was indicted for murdering a woman by witchcraft and for petty larceny in her village, Little Munden. She was acquitted of the serious charge but convicted

---

23. Mark Stoyle, *Witchcraft in Exeter: 1580–1660* (Exeter: The Mint Press, 2017) p. 17.
24. Pollock, "Social and Economic", pp. 37–48, p. 38.

of stealing an ash cloth valued at just two pence. She would have been flogged and discharged for this offence.[25]

Seven people — more than half of the 12 indicted for non-capital forms of witchcraft (including those who were indicted for both capital and non-capital crimes) — were convicted; this was usually after bewitching humans, so that they sickened and languished (but did not die) or animals (whether they died or not). They received the punishment set out under the 1563 Act, but there may have been some court-imposed variation. For example, in 1579, in a very minor case, Alice Cowle, who had been found guilty of bewitching a brewing vat from which two cows were drinking water, was sentenced to be pilloried four times, for six hours, but there was no mention of imprisonment.[26]

Interestingly, the first case of witchcraft of any type to produce a (preserved) conviction in Hertfordshire, that of Thomas Heather in 1573, involved an allegation of conjuring spirits in a wood at Hoddesdon to help find large sums of money. Perhaps significantly, he was subsequently pardoned. This was the only instance of this form of witchcraft to come before the Hertfordshire Assizes during the Elizabethan period, although such activity was regularly associated with cunning folk and must have been fairly widespread.[27]

The 1604 Statute

There has been considerable debate as to why Parliament thought it necessary to pass a new statute against witchcraft in 1604, and even whether it was more draconian than the 1563 Act that it replaced, although the statute itself expressly declared that it was aimed at the "more severe punishing" of witches. In some respects, its advent is a little surprising, as there had not been a plethora of witch trials immediately before it became law. Indeed, a case from December 1602, in which the elderly Elizabeth Jackson had been tried at the Old Bailey for bewitching 14-year-old Mary Glover, the daughter of a prosperous London shopkeeper and

---
25. Cockburn, *Hertfordshire Indictments*, p. 166.
26. *Ibid.*, p. 28.
27. Cockburn, *Hertfordshire Indictments*, p. 2.

noted Puritan, might have been expected to engender caution. Jackson and Glover had had a bitter quarrel and, a few days later, the latter fell ill, allegedly suffering sudden bouts of muteness, blindness, and swelling in her throat. The case attracted much attention from the London medical, religious, and legal establishments, including members of the London College of Physicians and Richard Bancroft, the Bishop of London, who thought her illness was either the result of natural causes or entirely fraudulent.

Unfortunately for Jackson, the presiding judge at her trial was Lord Chief Justice Sir Edmund Anderson, a judicial scourge of witches, who successfully dissuaded the jury from believing a medical explanation of Glover's illness. Jackson was found guilty and, under the Witchcraft Act of 1563, sentenced to a year in prison. (She had not killed anyone). It appears that she was released shortly afterwards, possibly due to Bancroft's intervention.[28] Had Jackson been convicted under the 1604 statute for the same conduct, she would have been executed.

The timing of the 1604 Act must have been linked to the then recent accession of James I to the English throne. Certainly, casual observers assumed that this was the case. Edward Fairfax, in the preface to his *Demonologia: A Discourse on Witchcraft* (1621), thought that the King had found a defect in the statute "by which none died for witchcraft but they only who by that means killed, so that such were executed rather as murderers than as witches". In reality there is little reason to suppose that it must have been James I himself who drew attention to any "defect" in the existing Act. Fairfax's observation seems to have been an attempt to flatter the King.[29]

Nevertheless, even if indirectly, the arrival of the new monarch explains these developments. During the first year of James's residence in London, from May 1603, there was a flurry of interest in witchcraft. The accession of a monarch with a known interest in the subject, one who claimed to have been personally attacked by storm-raising witches from

---

28. Michael MacDonald (ed.), *Witchcraft and Hysteria in Elizabethan London: Edward Jorden and the Mary Glover Case* (London: Routledge, 1991), p. xviii.
29. P.G. Maxwell-Stuart, "The New King and the Crucible of the Act: King James's Experience of Witches and the 1604 English Witchcraft Act". In *Witchcraft and the Act of 1604*, John Newton and Jo Bath (eds.) (Leiden: Brill, 2008), p. 45.

The Witchcraft Statutes

North Berwick when returning by sea to Scotland in 1590 with his new wife, Princess Anne of Denmark, was likely to have prompted fresh interest in the phenomenon. Perhaps indicative of this, the King's book on witchcraft, *Daemonologie,* was republished in London in April 1603. It is possible that the 1604 Witchcraft Act was simply an attempt to curry favour with the new monarch by refreshing legislation along lines that, it was thought, would please him.

However, the King may well have taken an interest in the law once an initial proposal for a new statute had been made, and it is apparent that the monarch took an active interest in the initial prosecutions under the 1604 Act, and also that he was still fairly committed to stamping out witchcraft in his new realm at this point.[30] At the start of 1605, the Reverend James Montagu and Sir Thomas Lake wrote to Viscount Cranborne noting that James had become personally involved in persuading a male witch named Butler to stand by his confession and wanted to discover whatever he knew about witchcraft. The King apparently thought that Butler was within the compass of the 1604 statute, and so would become the first person to be tried under its provisions if indicted. Nevertheless, he referred the matter to the Lord Chief Justice for further consideration.[31]

The 1604 "Act Against Conjuration, Witchcraft and dealing with evil and wicked spirits" was drafted by a committee of the House of Lords, which included amongst its members the Earls of Northumberland, Northampton, and Derby, along with the Bishop of Lincoln, Sir Edward Coke (the Attorney General), Sir John Tindal (an ecclesiastical lawyer), and four senior judges from the Westminster courts.[32] Foremost amongst the judiciary was Sir Edmund Anderson, Chief Justice of the Court of Common Pleas, an able if bad-tempered lawyer, hostile to both Catholics and Puritans, but — as the Glover case suggests — also a man who had an inveterate fear of witches. When presiding over that case, he had even informed the jury that he was an expert on the subject, that the country was "full of witches", that he had hanged at least 26 of them, and that they would overrun the kingdom if not subject to draconian

---

30. *Ibid.*, p. 38.
31. M. S. Giuseppi (ed.), *Calendar of the Cecil Papers in Hatfield House: Volume 17, 1605* (London: HMSO, 1938), pp. 15–43.
32. R. T. Davies, *Four Centuries*, p. 22.

punishment.³³ Doubtless Anderson played a very active role in drafting the new Act.

The 1604 statute made several important changes to the 1563 Act, which it "utterlie repealed". Witchcraft that produced human injury but not death—that is, where the victim merely "wasted consumed pined or lamed in his or her bodie"—had been non-capital for a first offence under the 1563 statute; it became capital under the 1604 Act. Two of the three Bideford witches executed in 1682 (almost the last in England), Mary Trembles and Susannah Edwards, were hanged for this lesser offence, unlike their co-defendant, who had (allegedly) killed using witchcraft.

Another major, and very noteworthy, distinction between the 1563 and the 1604 statutes, was that the latter no longer confined the capital crime purely to physical harm produced by witchcraft (*maleficium*). It introduced notions of diabolism as an offence in itself, something that was often more of an elite rather than popular concern. To a modest degree, these brought English law slightly closer to that found in Scotland, where, under the terse but draconian Scottish Witchcraft Act of 1563, any form of "Witchcraftis, Sorsareis or Necromancie" was a capital offence, and on the Continent. As a result, people could be punished simply for being witches (in certain circumstances), even if no harm could be laid at their door. Interestingly, the Renaissance magus John Dee, famous for consulting angels using a crystal ball, apparently believed that the 1604 Act had been passed specifically to target him.³⁴

The new Act extended the death penalty to anyone who simply conjured or entertained evil spirits for any purpose. Thus, at the December 1607 borough sessions for Rye, in Kent, indictments were preferred against two women for conversing with and feeding wicked spirits in order to obtain treasure; their prosecution was based on a provision in the 1604 statute which made it a felony, inter alia, to "feede or rewarde any evill and wicked Spirit to or for any intent or purpose". One was found guilty and sentenced to be hanged (albeit later reprieved), which was then almost unprecedented in a case that did not involve any damage

---

33. Maxwell-Stuart, "The New King", p. 43.
34. Machielsen, "'Moved and Seduced'", p. 5.

to persons or goods.³⁵ Similarly, at the Lent Assizes for Essex in 1616, three women, a widow and two spinsters, were prosecuted for feeding evil spirits who were capable of harming the King's subjects. All were acquitted, although 17 witnesses' (12 of them female) were called for the prosecution.³⁶ At the following Summer Assizes, held in July 1616, a married woman, Margaret Lambe from South Ockendon, was indicted for entertaining spirits with the intention of exercising witchcraft, and also found not guilty. However, Richard John was less fortunate at the same forum in March 1612. He was convicted of feeding three evil spirits, apparently named "Jockey", "Jacke" and "Will", with the intention of using them to destroy his neighbours' livestock, and sentenced to death.³⁷ As late as 1712 Jane Wenham was capitally convicted for conversing with the devil, who had allegedly appeared in the shape of a cat, albeit swiftly reprieved.³⁸

The 1604 Act also extended capital punishment to anyone who took a corpse, or any part of it, including human skin, from a grave with a view to using it for witchcraft. However, this provision, not found in either the 1542 or 1563 acts, was rarely indicted. On one of the few such occasions, one of the allegations against Susan Barker, tried at the Essex Assizes in July 1616, was that she had removed a skull from a grave in Upminster churchyard with a view to utilising it to bewitch one Mary Stevens. (She was acquitted on this count).³⁹

Nevertheless, the 1604 Act preserved the bifurcation of witchcraft into capital and non-capital crimes. Thus, and as with the 1563 statute, harm of any degree inflicted on animals and goods (rather than humans) remained a non-capital offence for a first conviction, for which a year's imprisonment and quarterly pillorying might be imposed. (Subsequent convictions of the same type became capital).

For example, in August 1612, Margaret Pearson, one of the Pendle witches, was tried on three counts: murder by witchcraft (capital);

---

35. Annabel Gregory, "Witchcraft, Politics, and 'Good Neighbourhood' in Early Seventeenth-Century Rye", *Past & Present*, v. 133, issue 1 (1991), p. 37.
36. ERO T/A 418/88/44.
37. Cockburn, *Essex Indictments, James I*, p. 114.
38. Charles Jones, "A Hertfordshire Trial for Witchcraft" (*St. Albans & Hertfordshire Architectural & Archaeological Society*, Transactions, 1929), pp. 279–286.
39. Cockburn, *Essex Indictments*, p. 171.

bewitching a neighbour and damaging their health (capital); and bewitching a horse (non-capital). She was acquitted of the first two counts and (alone among the accused) convicted only of the third, after a witness testified that Margaret had a "spirit in the likeness of man with cloven hoofs, that she and the Spirit had entered Dodgeon's stable through a loophole and had sat on the mare, which later died". She was sentenced to a year's imprisonment and four successive market days in the pillory in Clitheroe, Padiham, Colne and Lancaster, with a printed-paper upon her head, stating her offence.[40]

As late as 1704, after Hannah Baker of Elham pleaded guilty to "witchcraft and *inchanting cattell*" at the Kent Quarter Sessions, she was sent to prison for a year. She was also made to stand in the pillory on the day after Lady Day (25 March), St John's Day (24 June), Michaelmas (29 September) and Christmas for six hours, as required by the 1604 statute, becoming one of the last people to be convicted under the Act.[41] By then it would have been debatable whether she would have been found guilty had she challenged the indictment.

Furthermore, and as with its predecessor statute, typical cunning-folk magic, such as using sorcery to identify buried gold and treasure and lost or stolen goods, or to prompt others to fall in "unlawfull love", received the same non-capital punishment, although (as with its predecessor) not frequently prosecuted. Nevertheless, in 1651 John Lock, a Colchester weaver and, it seems, local cunning man, was sentenced to gaol and the pillory for using witchcraft to inform another weaver where he would find some stolen yarn.[42]

A novel provision of the new statute was the criminalising of a completely unsuccessful attempt to use witchcraft to hurt or destroy any person in their body ("although the same be not effected and done"). This was a non-capital offence for which punishment was also limited to the standard year's imprisonment and quarterly pillorying. Thus, at the Chelmsford Assizes in March 1613, Robert Parker was convicted of unsuccessfully taking "upon him charms and sorceries to hurt and

---

40. Potts, *Wonderfull Discoverie*, p. V4.
41. Gaskill, *Crime and Mentalities*, p. 92.
42. Pickering, *Witch Hunt*, p. 80.

destroy" Thomas Brown, and sentenced according to the statute.[43] Inchoate offences, such as attempt and conspiracy, were very little developed at common law at this time, helping to explain the need for such a provision.

Non-malefic forms of witchcraft were not indicted very frequently after 1604, and often failed to produce convictions when they were. However, there were some localised exceptions to this general pattern. On one analysis, entertaining the devil and consulting with spirits (taken together), account for more than 36 per cent of witchcraft cases in seventeenth-century Norfolk. Significantly, all these charges were brought in trials that involved Matthew Hopkins and his associates, who showed an awareness of, and interest in, continental demonology.[44]

Even so, it has been estimated that, taking the era of proscription as a whole, some 95 per cent of English witchcraft prosecutions were for *maleficia*. Indeed, even after the advent of the Jacobean statute, most hanged witches had been indicted for using witchcraft to kill people rather than for inflicting lesser forms of harm (such as injuring human victims) that would not have been capital under the Elizabethan statute, but were under the 1604 Act. Unsurprisingly, after the 1604 Act made these less serious crimes punishable by death, a higher proportion of people indicted for such crimes were acquitted than had been the case with its predecessor.

The advent of the 1604 statute appears to have given a limited, short-term impetus in some (but not all) places to witchcraft investigations. In January 1605 the Earl of Mar wrote to Viscount Cranborne, noting how he was then engaged: "We are here continually busied either at hunting or examining of witches, and although I like the first better than the last, yet I must confess both uncertain sports".[45] Nevertheless, this enthusiasm quickly levelled off, especially as cases of fraud under the new statute swiftly emerged.

---

43. Cockburn, *Essex Indictments*, p. 131.
44. Parry, *Norfolk*.
45. Giuseppi, *Cecil Papers*, pp. 15–43.

Jacobean Prosecutions: A County Profile

Essex was the heartland of English witch-hunting, and it would be mistaken to view it as in any way typical. Four people, three women and a man, were prosecuted in Essex under the 1563 Act during the early months of James I's reign. Slightly unusually, both prosecutions involving capital forms of the crime produced convictions, while both non-capital indictments resulted in acquittals. A hiatus then appears to have ensued before the first (preserved) prosecution under the 1604 statute, which took place in 1607.

A total of 28 people were indicted in Jacobean Essex under the 1604 Act. Four of them were prosecuted, in three trials, for the new and potentially capital offence of entertaining spirits; all but one of these defendants was acquitted. This crime did not require any type of injury to man, beast, or object. One woman was indicted for using body parts for magic, as well as for other counts of witchcraft; she was acquitted (see above). Nobody was indicted, let alone convicted, for using magic to find gold or stolen goods or to make someone fall in love. Cunning folk were not, it seems, actively persecuted under the statute in the county.

This leaves 24 people accused of malefic witchcraft, six of whom stood trial in pairs, on three occasions, as co-defendants. One of the 24 died in prison, prior to their hearing. As a result, 23 people were indicted under the 1604 Act. Of the 13 who were tried in cases in which someone had allegedly been killed by the witchcraft, five were convicted and sentenced to death (as they would have been under the 1563 Act), and eight acquitted. Another ten were prosecuted for non-lethal forms of malefic witchcraft. These forms of the crime would not have produced a death sentence for a first conviction under the 1563 Act, but some of them were capital under the 1604 statute, as they included harmful (but not fatal) witchcraft exercised against humans. Of these, just one produced guilty verdicts, and nine resulted in acquittals. Given the higher conviction rates under the previous statute, it seems likely that, as with conventional felonies, the likelihood of a death sentence had a significant effect on the willingness of trial juries to convict.

Significantly, the sole exception, that of Mary Wade, a married woman who was convicted of bewitching three women who merely "pyned and lamed" in the summer of 1609, did not produce an (immediate) execution. She was found to be pregnant, and punishment was deferred.[46] Perhaps the trial judge was uncomfortable with execution in this case.

Although the capital witchcraft offences were unclergyable (something that affected only male defendants prior to the seventeenth century), they were still open to other forms of mitigation, most pertinently pregnancy (discussed elsewhere) and pardon. Thus in March 1618 Mary Holt from Leighs was capitally convicted of murder by witchcraft and sentenced to death, but remanded after sentence, presumably to allow a pardon to be considered. A possible reason for this might be the date of the allegation. Margaret Ellis, the woman she was alleged to have killed, had died some seven years earlier.[47]

---

46. Cockburn, *Essex Indictments*, p. 62.
47. *Ibid.*, p. 202.

Crimen Exceptum

CHAPTER 6

Entering the Criminal Justice System

Introduction

England had an accusatory criminal justice system. Complainants initiated cases by making allegations and then pursuing them to trial and conviction. The court might lend its procedures to the complainant/prosecutor, but it did not normally take a particularly active role in proceedings by, for example, seeking out suspects or gathering evidence, unlike some Continental forums. However, as will be seen, motivated JPs could have an impact in this regard.

The English common law criminal justice system differs from those in the "inquisitorial" Roman-law countries of continental Europe and (to some extent) Scotland. These systems, of course, also required someone to make a complaint; however, once this was done, the judicial officers took a much more active role in conducting further investigations, shaping charges, and bringing matters to court.

The worst witch-hunts in Europe involved states with an inquisitorial or quasi-inquisitorial system, whether Protestant Scotland or some of the Catholic prince-bishoprics in the Holy Roman Empire. Of course, given that most Europeans lived under such systems, apart from those in England, Wales, parts of Ireland, and (eventually) the English colonies in the Americas, this is perhaps unsurprising. However, it does appear that a "mutated" inquisitorial system that had lost its inherent safeguards, as was sometimes the case with witchcraft trials (because it was *crimen exceptum*) could, in exceptional circumstances, produce large numbers of convictions very quickly. Nevertheless, this was certainly not a frequent occurrence. More typically, the transcripts of witchcraft trials conducted before the court of the Roman Inquisition in Venice reveal a forum that struggled to overcome the numerous hurdles present in convicting those accused of performing *maleficia*.[1]

Triggering Event

Formal witch prosecutions would usually start with a triggering event; frequently this was a suspected act of *maleficium* that the "victim" took to law. This might have been done because the act was especially vicious, local patience with the suspected witch was exhausted, or the victim was unusually thin-skinned and/or affluent and influential. In practice, some or even all of these factors might be present concurrently.

Sometimes, a suspected witch's own misguided behaviour, at a time when local suspicion was already on the verge of giving way to formal action, helped prompt a complaint to a JP. In 1712, had Jane Wenham accepted a clergyman's suggestion that a farmer pay her a shilling (admittedly, a very modest sum) as compensation for calling her a witch and alleging that she had cast a spell on one of his workers, rather than flouncing-off muttering threats of some description, she would probably not have been prosecuted for the crime.[2]

Although the *casus belli* that prompted a formal allegation varied enormously, the most common scenario involved a suspected witch forming a grievance against an individual for a specific reason and resorting to "threatnings to be revenged, and their imprecations, or some other mischief presently followeth".[3] This scenario lasted until the end of proscription; as a physician noted in the early-eighteenth century: "If any Mischief befals a Person, or his Family, after the passionate, but impotent threats of an Old Woman, it's a sure Argument of her being a Witch".[4]

Statistically, it was almost inevitable that such assumptions would be made. As Reginald Scot observed, over time a suspected witch's

---

1. Jonathan Seitz, *Witchcraft and Inquisition in Early Modern Venice* (Cambridge: Cambridge University Press, 2011), p. 102.
2. Davies, *Witchcraft, Magic*, p. 84.
3. Tract 1645 (1) pp. 1–8.
4. Tract 1712 (2) pp. 1–10.

neighbours would all have displeased and been cursed by her. Eventually, some of them (or their domestic animals) would become ill or die, or their children would be visited with diseases that would "vex them strangely"; ignorant people then attributed these misfortunes to the "vengeance of witches".

In 1616, after Mary Smith was hanged at King's Lynn for malefic witchcraft, the Reverend Alexander Roberts described the incidents that prompted her attacks on local people. John Orkton, a sailor, had hit her son (not very hard) after the boy misbehaved.[5] Elizabeth Hancocke, a local woman, was mistakenly accused of stealing Smith's prized hen.[6]

The most common ground for suspecting witchcraft was a misfortune suffered by a person who had refused charity to a poor woman who was already widely suspected of being a witch. For example, in the late 1670s, when John Castleton, who was in charge of distributing an annual charitable grant amongst the poor of his Norfolk parish, gave Anne Diver a lesser amount than she had become accustomed to, she warned him that he should "take heed lest some mischeife came to him or his". He duly experienced misfortune.[7] In the case of Joan Robinson in Essex, it was claimed that her various acts of witchcraft were precipitated by, *inter alia*, the refusal of payment for goods "at her own reckoning".[8]

However, most such cases involved a simple refusal of alms, and were especially likely if the beggar had been heard to curse the person who had denied them. For example, in 1646 in Yorkshire, Mary Midgley became annoyed when she was given alms of milk rather than wool, as she had hoped, and "departed very angry". She was subsequently blamed when an infant died.[9] In 1682 Mary Trembles had gone around Bideford in Devon begging unsuccessfully for bread. She then accompanied Susanna Edwards to the house of John Barnes in the hope of being given some food. Unfortunately, he was away, and his wife, Grace, and her servant would not give them anything (1682 was an economically very straitened year). The two women then tried to beg a farthing's worth of tobacco,

---

5. Roberts, *Treatise*, p. 48.
6. *Ibid.*, p. 51.
7. Parry, *Norfolk*.
8. Macfarlane, "Tudor and Stuart Essex", p. 92.
9. Sharpe, "Witchcraft and Women", p. 187.

which tiny request was also refused, so that they were annoyed when they went away. Grace Barnes was taken ill that night and accused them of bewitching her.[10]

As the Barnes' case suggests, frequently, the alleged victim of witchcraft immediately made the association between their refusal of charity to the suspected witch and their ensuing misfortune, rather than it being proposed by a third party, suggesting that it was a widely known scenario.

This pattern continued after the end of proscription in 1736. The series of events that culminated in the murder of the elderly Ruth Osborn in Hertfordshire in 1751 began when she approached a local farmer, and asked him for some buttermilk. This was met by a very blunt refusal, which angered the elderly woman, who went away muttering that he would be paid out for it. When he subsequently, if rather belatedly, experienced misfortune in his health and business, it merely required a cunning woman from Northamptonshire to join the dots and identify the source of his troubles, who already laboured under a reputation for being a wicked old woman who had done "much damage by her witchcraft".[11]

Such a background to allegations was also found in other parts of the British Isles. For example, in December 1661 the elderly Florence Newton begged for a piece of bread or meat at the home of John Pyne in County Cork in Ireland. Pyne's housemaid, Mary Longdon, refused and sent Newton away. Shortly afterwards, Newton ran into and violently kissed Longdon, exclaiming, "Mary, I pray thee, let thee and I be friends." Subsequently, Longdon began to experience violent fits and trances, which she attributed to bewitchment. Newton was tried at the Cork Assizes in September 1661, although her fate is not known.[12]

So common was this scenario that Alan Macfarlane used it as the basis of a wider paradigm in which the acute economic pressures found during much of the witch-hunting era (the result of a combination of population increase, climate change and inflation) led to a lessening emphasis on traditional bonds of neighbourliness. This prompted better-off villagers to withhold alms that they had previously given to their local poor.

---

10. Gent, *Bideford Witches*, p. 9.
11. *London Evening Post*, August 24 1751–August 27 1751.
12. Sneddon, "Witchcraft Belief", pp. 1–25.

In turn, this engendered both guilt on the part of the rejecter and fear that the rejected supplicant would retaliate. This then led to accusations of witchcraft after the party withholding charity suffered some form of misfortune. As with many such paradigms, what is sometimes referred to as the "charity-refused model" provides a valuable perspective rather than a universal explanation for witchcraft allegations.

Supporting Allegations

Frequently, a victim's willingness to make a formal allegation to a JP would prompt other local people to come forward in support, adding their own accounts of other malefic acts by the suspect. As the Reverend Joseph Juxon observed, "[W]henever the alarm is given, there is always a party formed, a very secure one too, against these poor ignorant and helpless creatures". [13]

Sometimes these allegations would themselves become the subject of formal prosecution, eventually featuring as counts in an indictment. More often they would simply be adduced as supporting material, helping to persuade the examining JP that the case should be committed for trial, and being advanced at trial as incriminating evidence, but not constituting formal allegations. In an extreme example, in the final case to produce a conviction for witchcraft in England, the prosecutors originally wished to charge Jane Wenham with bewitching a woman named Anne Thorn but ultimately indicted her only for "conversing" with the devil in the form of a cat. However, at trial, the prosecution called evidence from a dozen witnesses, who spoke of more serious allegations to support this count, including the testimony of several neighbours who blamed Wenham for the deaths of a woman, an infant, and several sheep.[14]

The case of Thomas Cutting, from Runhall in Norfolk, provides another classic example of the accumulation of complaints after a triggering allegation. In 1679 Cutting alleged that a local woman, Anne Diver, had made his cow sick and bewitched his family after he had refused to

---

13. Tract 1736 p. 24.
14. Phyllis J. Guskin, "The Context of Witchcraft: The Case of Jane Wenham (1712)", *Eighteenth-Century Studies,* v. 15, no. 1 (1981), p. 51 and p. 63.

give her some herbs from his garden; as a result, he claimed, he broke his leg, and his wife and daughter fell ill. Other witnesses then came forward with supporting allegations. For example, John Calfe claimed that, when he had fallen sick a year or so earlier, a cunning man had shown him Diver's face in a glass. Elizabeth Pitts alleged that, six years before that, she had purchased a goose from Diver and was ill for four months after eating it. Even further back, Frances Beales noted that a decade earlier she had refused to give Diver some beer one summer's day, but when she then drank some of the beverage herself she had fallen sick for three weeks. Most extreme of all, and indicative of the long memories found in such cases, Susan Major alleged that, some 20 years before, Diver had gone to her master's house to beg some meat for her father, but left before receiving any, saying that she was too proud to accept it. A week later Susan fell ill, losing her speech and sight, and suffering strange fits.[15]

Taking Action

Once a complainant decided to take action, he or she would have to bring the suspected witch before a JP. To do this, the supposed victim might obtain an arrest warrant (and any ancillary search warrants) from a magistrate, and then enforce it, usually with the aid of a parish constable. For example, in 1652, when three men had Joan Peterson arrested for witchcraft, they first obtained a warrant from a Mr Waterton, a JP resident near Wapping (where Peterson lived), to "apprehend the said *Petersons* person, and to search her house for Images of Clay, Hair, & Nails, which accordingly they did; but upon strict search and diligent inquiry could find no such thing; whereupon the said confederates carried her before the said Justice, to have her examined".[16] Although obtaining such warrants was not particularly difficult, they were occasionally refused. For example, in 1682 the Mayor of Bideford, Devon, refused to issue a warrant for Mary Beare's arrest for suspected witchcraft.[17] Alternatively, presumed victims could effect what in the modern era would

---

15. Parry, *Norfolk*.
16. Tract 1652 pp. 1–11.
17. Gent, *Bideford Witches*, p. 17.

be termed a citizen's arrest and, effectively, frog-march the suspect before a magistrate.

The JP's role was vital, and could not be circumvented. The experiences of Richard Galis in 1566 are indicative of its significance. The allegedly "slack" magistrates of Windsor had thwarted Galis's efforts to initiate criminal proceedings against a group of witches who were, he claimed, tormenting him (the Elizabethan Witchcraft Act was still only three years old). He eventually seized their supposed ringleader by the arm and marched the woman to the town prison, where he asked the jailer to detain her. Quite properly, the jailer refused to do this without a JP's warrant or *mittimus*. Galis then took the woman before Richard Readforth, the Mayor of Windsor and an *ex officio* magistrate for the town (an incorporated borough). Readforth was not impressed with his allegations and ordered her immediate release.[18] By contrast, more than a decade later, Elizabeth Stile (or Rockingham), a 65-year-old widow from Windsor, was less fortunate after she was apprehended and brought before Sir Henry Neville, a Berkshire JP, for examination on suspicion of witchcraft. Satisfied that there was a case to answer, after hearing evidence from her neighbours, he committed Stile to the common gaol at Reading, to await trial at the next Assizes.[19]

The suspected witch might have to be held temporarily if arrested when a magistrate was not immediately available. For example, on a Saturday at the start of July 1682, Thomas Eastchurch, a Bideford shopkeeper, complained to the town's constables that Temperance Lloyd had committed acts of malefic witchcraft against Grace Thomas and had had familiarity with the devil in the form of a black (dark) man. They arrested her and locked her in an old chapel, where she remained until produced before the town's appointed justices on the Monday morning. These men, the mayor, Thomas Gist, and one of the borough's aldermen, John Davie, conducted her initial examination and that of potential prosecution witnesses. The town clerk, John Hill, acted as a justice's clerk and recorded their statements.[20]

---

18. Tract 1579 (1) pp. 1–32.
19. Tract 1579 (2) pp. 1–5.
20. Gent, *Bideford Witches*, p. 7.

Crimen Exceptum

Pre-Examination Questioning

An unusual feature of witchcraft cases was the significant involvement of members of the public other than JPs in examining witches using specialist investigative techniques. Sometimes this might be done in the presence of such magistrates; for example, clerics might bring their specialist knowledge of demonology to an examination. Thus in 1712 Jane Wenham was examined in front of three clergymen as well as a justice of the peace.

Occasionally the supposed witch might be examined *before* being handed over to the magistrates, with the results being reported to the JPs; the procedure formed the backdrop to the latter's own (better-regulated) formal investigation, while providing a powerful motive to repeat earlier admissions to the magistrate. At times this seems to have occurred extra-legally, the suspected women's gender, single-state, isolation, and low social status allowing a violation of their rights, and an improper limitation on their liberty, to pass without comment. At others it had some form of authorisation. This was the case when Hopkins and Stearne, for instance, questioned Elizabeth Clarke for several days before extracting appropriate admissions and, allegedly, witnessing her familiars. They then gave the Essex JPs, Sir Harbottle Grimston and Sir Thomas Bowes, a full account of what had transpired and asked that she be formally examined. The magistrates did, at least, insist that she first be allowed to rest from her ordeal so that she would have a clear head when questioned. Clarke was then woken and taken before them, when she made a full confession.[21]

Justices of the Peace and the Witch-Hunting Process

JPs were unpaid, untrained, part-time magistrates normally drawn from the ranks of the major gentry. They were vital to the witch prosecution process (as they were for all crimes). As already noted, they would receive the initial allegation(s), issue arrest warrants, examine suspects

---

21. Gaskill, *Witchfinders*, pp. 51–53.

and potential witnesses, and decide whether a witch should be indicted, as well as committing her to gaol (or less commonly bail) pending trial. However, some went further, and actively and enthusiastically investigated cases of witchcraft, seeking out evidence and potential witnesses. Such men, who included Brian Darcy in 1580s Essex, and Roger Nowel in early-seventeenth century Lancashire, could play an important role in initiating or pursuing major prosecutions.

In the increasingly sceptical post-1660 period, fewer magistrates shared this enthusiasm, and more were actively opposed to such prosecutions. After about 1670, most cases of witchcraft that came for trial involved the influence of one or more continuing "believers" in the local Commission of the Peace. One example is the final prosecution to produce a conviction, that of Jane Wenham in 1712. The role of the 80-year-old Sir Henry Chauncy, Squire of Ardeley and local JP, was central to this case. At 15-years-of-age, Chauncy had matriculated at Caius College, Cambridge; he entered Middle Temple at 17, and was called to the Bar in 1656, at the age of 24. Subsequently he became a JP for Hertfordshire, a magistrate for the borough, and its first Recorder in 1680, when Hertford obtained its charter. He was knighted in 1681. An intelligent, well-educated man, an important historian of his county, and a moderately successful lawyer, if rooted in the mores of an earlier era due to his advanced age, he does not seem to have pre-judged the matter, but eventually became firmly persuaded of Wenham's guilt. In part this may have been because he had "enquired after her Character, and heard a very ill one of her". He examined Jane, as well as the other witnesses, at his home and in a local village.[22]

Conversely, sceptical J.P.s would have a restraining influence on witch prosecutions, especially after the Restoration. For example, in 1664 (or 1665), Robert Hunt (1609–1680), an experienced and diligent Somerset JP and qualified barrister, who had been actively engaged in witch-hunting (as well as searching out other types of felon) for several years, believed that he had discovered a "hellish knot of witches" in two covens in Stoke Trister and Brewham in the east of the county. He examined

---

22. Guskin, "The Context of Witchcraft", pp. 48–71.

numerous suspects. However, with the exception of Elizabeth Style (who died in prison after conviction) he was unable to see them successfully prosecuted because of the allegedly negative attitude of his fellow magistrates. Joseph Glanvill subsequently deprecated the way in which Hunt's endeavours met with "great opposition and discouragements from some then in authority". Francis Hutchinson agreed with his analysis, albeit not his regret, approvingly noting how "poor people were saved" because of this official stance.[23]

In January 1672 (sometimes mistakenly given as 1686), a 12-year-old boy named Thomas Webb fell ill in Malmesbury and started having regular fits, during which he would "curse and swear" and name several women as bewitching him, sometimes speaking to them as if they were present. One of them, Anne Tilling, a local woman, was questioned by the boy's mother, and apparently confessed to bewitching him, saying that several other women (whom she named) had assisted her. An alderman magistrate from the town and three JPs from the county (specially called in) eventually questioned eleven women and three men as suspected witches, putting their examinations in writing, as required by a 1556 statute (see below). Satisfied that all of them had a case to answer, the justices' clerk was in the process of drawing up the appropriate *mittimus* to commit them to the county gaol, when a fourth county magistrate arrived, a man who was not, it seems, enormously popular with his fellows, but also "not perhaps very credulous in matters of witchcraft". This justice did not deny the existence of witchcraft, but thought its extent was greatly exaggerated, especially in Malmesbury.

The late arrival asked that the examination room be cleared of casual observers so that he could speak to his colleagues in private, although local gentlemen were allowed to remain, and several others were sent for. The sceptic then addressed the assembled magistrates at length. He mooted that the boy might be an "impostor", warned them about the precipitate nature of the proceedings and the "very light evidence" against eleven of the suspects. He also expressed a fear that they would be "severely censured" by the Assize judges and others in authority for

---

23. Geis and Bunn, *A Trial of Witches*, p. 6. Barry, *Witchcraft and Demonology in South-West England*, pp. 14–15 and p. 35.

sending so many people, on such an unusual charge, on the 40-mile journey to Salisbury to await trial. As a result, he persuaded the other magistrates to moderate their decision, and they agreed to restrict themselves to committing three of the accused to gaol, with a strong warning that they should not be subject to the traditional tests for witchcraft (swimming, etc.) while held in custody. The rest were released.[24]

It seems that the same sceptical JP also suggested that Anne Tilling's apparently voluntary confession, which had been the source of the proceedings, might be the result of "madness, deep melancholy, or hatred of life".[25] Even so, Tilling, Elizabeth Mills, Elizabeth Peacock, and (the appropriately named) Judith Witchell appear to have been tried at the Lent Assizes in Salisbury in 1672 before Sir Nicholas Rainsford. Tilling and Witchell were convicted, while Mills and Peacock were found 'not guilty'.[26] It seems that the two guilty witches were subsequently hanged at Malmesbury, making this a very late double-execution for the crime.

The JPs' Examination

As the Malmesbury case suggests, before deciding whether to allow an allegation of witchcraft to go for trial and (usually) remanding a witch in custody prior to their hearing, JPs would conduct an examination of the accused person(s), as they would with any other felony suspects. They would also question potential prosecution witnesses. Throughout the period of effective proscription (i.e. the years after 1563), a Marian statute from 1556 (1 & 2 Philip & Mary c. 13) regulated this procedure. A JP (sometimes more than one) would conduct such examinations in their own home, a tavern, or some other convenient place. They were often open to members of the public, but the defendant would not normally be legally represented when questioned. In 1652 the examination of Joan Peterson was unusual, but still telling in its irregularity. Her accusers brought a solicitor and several other observers, one of whom "sate at the table as the Justices Clerks to take her examination, where

---

24. Reproduced in *The Gentleman's Magazine*, v. 102, 1832, pp. 489–491.
25. Gere, "William Harvey", p. 23.
26. Pickering, *Witch Hunt*, p. 195.

the said Justice examined the said *Peterson* upon oath (contrary to law) concerning her using of witchcraft and sorcery to take away the life of the Lady *Powel* of *Chelsey*".[27]

As this suggests, the justice or his clerk (not usually a casual or partisan observer as in Peterson's case) would record the statements made by suspects and potential prosecution witnesses (the latter under oath), which might then be read back to them, and which they would usually be invited to sign or mark (if illiterate). This was not normally a verbatim record but a mediated summary of the magistrate's questions and answers, albeit that there might be direct quotation of key phrases, especially if they were incriminating. In theory, the JP had two days to produce this record, but the best magistrates would ensure that it was prepared fairly swiftly, and organize the depositions into a coherent narrative.[28]

The Role of Confessions

The nature of witchcraft crimes, particularly their inherent lack of tangible evidence, meant that securing an out-of-court confession during the examination was of enormous significance when it came to founding a prosecution and obtaining a conviction, more so than with most other offences. This became especially marked as evidential requirements in witch cases tightened after the early-seventeenth century. In many respects, it was the surest way to prove guilt, something that was expressly recognised by Michael Dalton in his legal handbook of 1618, *The Country Justice*. Many other observers thought that, when it came to witches, their "own voluntary confession ... exceeds all other evidences".[29] Similarly, at the trial of the Pendle witches at the Lancaster Assizes in 1612, Sir Edward Bromley stressed that nearly all of them had been convicted on their "owne voluntarie confessions and examinations".[30]

Such admissions could be formally presented in court by being read out to the jury. An account of the major witch trial held at the Huntingdon

---

27. Tract 1652 pp. 1–11.
28. Holger Schott Syme, *Theatre and Testimony in Shakespeare's England: A Culture of Mediation* (Cambridge: Cambridge University Press, 2012), p. 37.
29. Tract 1645 (1) pp. 1–8.
30. Potts, *Wonderful Discoverie*, p. V3.

Assizes in 1593 noted that the confession elicited during Alice Samuel's pre-trial examination was presented as evidence of her guilt: "So also was read the confession of the saide mother Samuell made at Burkden afore saide the 29 day of December 1592 before the saide reuerent father in God. William Bishop of Lincolne, Fraunces Cromwel, & Richard Tryce Esquires, Justices of her Maiesties peace within the countie of Huntington".[31]

A significant number of suspected witches made confessions. To modern observers this is surprising, because they were confessing to something that was untrue, and putting their lives in peril. By the end of the seventeenth century, this also troubled some contemporary observers. When, in 1692, a Kent JP questioned a witch who claimed to have turned herself into a cat to effect *maleficium*, she was openly ridiculed by a gentlewoman who was watching the examination, who told her, "[Y]ou do confess impossible things".[32]

However, the proportion of suspected witches making formal confessions should not be exaggerated. Many made no admissions when questioned by a JP. They simply denied everything, and were not prejudiced in any way by their examining magistrates for doing so. Many JPs were simply fulfilling the duties of their office rather than acting as enthusiastic witch-hunters, and questioned them as they would any other suspected felon, without recourse to subterfuge or oppressive investigative techniques. This might reflect an innate sense of fairness on the part of the magistrate involved, scepticism about witchcraft in general or in the instant case, or both. Such cases have necessarily left very few records, as the absence of a confession made it much less likely that a matter would proceed to trial. However, they are sometimes hinted at. For example, it was noted that Elizabeth Sawyer, the Witch of Edmonton, had been "laboriously and carefully examined" by a Middlesex JP on several occasions over a period of years, with no formal action being taken, before she was eventually charged.[33]

---

31. Tract 1593 p. 110.
32. *Athenian Gazette*, 28 February 1693.
33. Tract 1621 (2) p. 1 & p. 6.

Cases in which there was no confession were also much less likely to produce a conviction, even if they did get to trial. For example, in September 1653 Edward Hodge of Benenden in Kent formally accused Elizabeth Wood, from the same village, of bewitching his six-year-old son, who had been pining for several months and allegedly suffered from fits in which he shouted, "Here comes Bes Wood". Wood was already "reputed to be a witch" in the area and, it was claimed, had fallen out with Hodge's wife shortly before the boy started to "languish". Three county JPs duly examined her. However, the questioning appears to have been conducted in an orderly manner. Wood vigorously denied that she had bewitched Hodge's son or fallen out with his wife, or that she had "any skill or knowledge at all in any kind of witchcraft whatsoever". An indictment was brought against her at (unusually) the Michaelmas Quarter Sessions in West Kent, but was thrown out by the grand jury there.[34]

Nevertheless, a significant number of witchcraft cases, especially those that produced convictions, rested, at least in part, on out-of-court confessions. In a handful of them it is possible that these confessions were invented by examining JPs. Even so, there is nothing to suggest this was widespread, so that it remains the case that a significant number of suspected witches "confessed" to their crimes. For example, in 1678 Mary Neale of Wissenset in Norfolk admitted that she had killed local people, and signed a confession, allegedly crying out, "O wicked wretch that I am, I have destroyed two poore soules". She also implicated two other women in the crimes. (Both of them denied the charge).[35]

Even at the time, some observers knew that many of the admissions of witchcraft were groundless. In 1693 Widow Chambers, a poor woman from Upaston in Suffolk, was committed to Beccles gaol after being accused of witchcraft. She died in prison before coming to trial. However, she was "walked" while in custody (see below), after which she confessed to killing her husband and Lady Blois, although the latter's close relations were satisfied that she had died a natural death. Most pertinently, and anticipating modern practice when dealing with potentially false

---

34. Elizabeth Melling (ed.), *Crime and Punishment, Kentish Sources VI* (Maidstone: Kent County Council, 1969), p. 61.
35. TNA ASSI 16/32/3.

admissions, "some for Experiment sake ask'd her, if she had not killed such and such; and she confessed she had, though the Persons were then living".[36]

Contemporary observers were not oblivious of the dangers of admissions, whether made in front of a JP or to third parties, and what might have prompted them. In 1646 Mary Midgley confessed that "she could witche a little" when questioned by an alleged victim (not a JP) in Yorkshire, who also conceded that he had first struck her; a bystander witness stressed (perhaps a little unconvincingly) that he was "verily persuaded that the confession was not made from fear but according to truth".[37]

Nevertheless, such awareness was by no means universal or even typical. In his journal, the prolific diarist Nehemiah Wallington, a middle-aged Puritan wood turner, originally from the City of London, and a contemporary commentator on the witch trials promoted by Matthew Hopkins in 1645, noted that many suspected witches in East Anglia "voluntarily and without any forcing or compulsion freely declare that they have made a covenant with the Devill, to forsake God and Christ and to take him to be their Master and Like wise do acknowledge that divers Cattell and som Christians have been killed by their meanes".[38]

Had England sanctioned torture such cases would be readily explicable. It was a highly effective way of inducing admissions from innocent people. As a result of his experiences as a witch confessor during the intense persecution at Wurzburg, Friedrich Spee (1591–1635) became convinced that almost all confessions to witchcraft were worthless, a belief that he set out in his *Cautio Criminalis* of 1631. Spee was convinced that torture did not elucidate the truth as suspects could end their suffering equally well by telling lies.

However, in England, torture was forbidden at common law. Quite exceptionally, prior to 1640, an order from the Privy Council could derogate from this rule, and a warrant authorising its use in a specific case might be issued, but only one or two such cases seem to have had overtones of sorcery, all involving men. A former schoolmaster named

---
36. Hutchinson, *Historical Essay*, pp. 130–150.
37. Eileen Rennison, *Yorkshire Witches* (Stroud: Amberley, 2009), p. 50.
38. *Yorkshire Post*, 4 July 2011.

Samuel Peacock was incarcerated in the Tower of London in 1620 for plotting to influence James I by witchcraft, and appears to have been racked during questioning.[39]

It seems that English witches confessed for a variety of reasons, among them blatant physical coercion just short of torture, more subtle intimidation, trickery, suggestibility, the effects of depression ("melancholy") and cognitive impairment. Sometimes several of these factors were present. It must be remembered that many of those examined were fragile individuals: relatively elderly people, physically and sometimes even mentally weak, poorly educated, and probably thoroughly disoriented by something so outside their experience as being arrested and then questioned by a JP.

Deep Interrogation

In the modern era, the use of various forms of "deep interrogation" involving sleep deprivation, stress positions, and the subjecting of suspects to continual noise has been used and outlawed in various environments. Some of those who investigated English witchcraft, especially the East Anglian witch finders, appear to have stumbled on them. Matthew Hopkins and his associates perfected the art of examining witches without shedding blood and so (arguably) without violating the ban on torture in English common law. Their techniques involved "watching" and "walking" the witch. The former was described by John Gaule in *Select Cases of Conscience Touching on Witches and Witchcrafts*. He noted that the suspected witch was "placed in the middle of a room upon a stool, or Table, crosse legg'd, or in some other uneasie posture, to which if she submits not, she is then bound with cords, there is she watcht & kept without meat or sleep for the space of 24 hours". In cases involving "walking" the prisoner was kept awake by being walked up and down her cell until a confession was secured. It was also hoped that, by keeping the witch under continuous observation, her familiars would be forced to break cover in their search for nourishment from their mistress.

---

39. John Langbein, *Torture and the Law of Proof* (Chicago: University of Chicago Press, 1976), p. 77 and p. 135; James Sharpe, *Instruments of Darkness* (London: Penguin, 1997), p. 49.

Such techniques were highly productive. At the start of his East Anglian campaign, in 1645, Matthew Hopkins was allowed to hold and question the elderly Elizabeth Clark. She was "watched" for three consecutive nights, with almost no sleep. Initially, she revealed nothing. However, having been constantly prompted by Hopkins, she eventually broke, and confessed on the fourth night to being a witch. She claimed that she kept and nourished five familiars — a white kitten, a fat spaniel, a black rabbit, a polecat, and the most singular, "Vinegar Tom", a greyhound with a head like an ox. Even more significantly, according to Hopkins no fewer than eight people swore that they had seen these creatures in the room. (Clarke also implicated other witches during the course of her interrogation).[40] Exactly what happened in that darkened chamber is impossible to establish; there were several people present, and blatant falsehood appears unlikely, although not impossible. Perhaps it was a form of mass hysteria, brought about by the darkness or by fatigue after many hours of watching.

Similarly, in Brandeston, Suffolk, in 1645 the elderly Reverend John Lowes firmly denied his guilt when first questioned. However, after being kept awake for three days and nights by Hopkins, and forced to walk without rest until his feet were blistered, the clergyman became "scarce sensible of what he said or did". According to the parish register, he became "delirious", duly confessed to witchcraft and familiarity with the devil, and showed marks on his head and tongue where he had fed his imps. These admissions had great weight with his trial jury, although the cleric retracted his confession on the scaffold.[41]

Such techniques were certainly not confined to England. They were found on the Continent and widely used in Scotland, even though that country also had the possibility of recourse to unabashed torture. During the 1640s, the process was also referred to in Fife's church court and burgh records as "watching" (as well as "warding") the witch. In Scotland a period of at least 24-hours' watching prior to examination was suggested.[42]

---

40. Garland, "Witch Hunt", 2003, pp. 1152–1180.
41. Gaskill, *Witchfinders*, p. 143.
42. MacDonald, "Torture", pp. 102–103.

The interrogations conducted by Matthew Hopkins and his associates were at the extreme end of a continuum of abusive questioning, and condemned, even at the time, by members of the judiciary. They were not typical of most such cases (and not normally carried out by JPs). Nevertheless, slightly less extreme methods of investigation cropped up periodically during the era of proscription.

More commonly, suspected witches might be subject to robust or even aggressive questioning. For example, the Essex JP Brian Darcy, enthusiastically engaged in investigating the alleged St Osyth witches in 1582, used threats with Ales (Alice) Newman when she was reluctant to make admissions: "The said Brian Darcey finding this examinat to bee obstinate, and that shee coulde be brought to confesse nothing, said to this Examinat, that hee woulde sever and part her and her spirites a sunder".[43]

Even so, it is also apparent that some accused witches incriminated themselves by making admissions without being subjected to blatant mistreatment. As Richard Bernard noted, "If any thinke that it is almost impossible to make Witches confesse thus much [to familiars and pacts], they are deceived; for I find by Histories exceeding many to have confessed".[44] This does not mean that they were questioned in an entirely proper manner by modern standards. Trickery was sometimes employed.

For example, Brian Darcy had no hesitation about giving a false assurance to Ursula Kemp so as to obtain admissions, even though these ultimately helped lead to her conviction and execution. This does not appear to have occasioned concern at the time, although it would become a ground for excluding confessions in the eighteenth century: "The saide Brian Darcey then promising to the saide Ursley, that if shee would deale plainely and confesse the trueth, that shee should have favour: & so by giving her faire speeches shee confessed as followeth".[45]

However, even ignoring such cases, it is still apparent that some people confessed to witchcraft without being subjected to trickery, let alone coercion. For example, in early-1666 Sir Roger Bradshaigh, a Lancashire JP, noted in a letter that he had recently examined four reputed witches;

---

43. Tract 1582 pp. 1–5.
44. Bernard, *Guide*, p. 100.
45. Tract 1582 pp. 1–5.

one had confessed that she, her father, and her mother, had each ridden a black cat nine miles to Warrington, and that the cats had sucked blood from her mother. Bradshaigh expressly noted that he had little faith in this account, although it was given on oath, but felt it necessary to send two of the four to gaol as a result.[46] Clearly, he was not actively looking for admissions.

Even more dramatically, in a letter sent by Lord Keeper North to Sir Leoline Jenkins, the Secretary of State, in August 1682, the former considered the implication of pardoning the three elderly Bideford witches who had been convicted before Sir Thomas Raymond a short while earlier. Very problematically, although the apparent evidence against them was very full, their "own confessions exceeded it. They appeared not only weary of their lives, but to have a great deal of skill to convict themselves. Their description of the sucking devills with sawcer-eyes was as natural that the jury could not chuse but beleeve them".[47]

A century before the Bideford case, the phenomenon of apparently voluntary confessions to witchcraft had troubled Reginald Scot who, like Jenkins, concluded that the women concerned must be suffering from some form of mental disturbance. He suggested that their vivid imaginations were brought on by melancholy or depression, so that if their wits were not "confounded with this humor, they would not so voluntarilie and readilie confess that which calleth their life in question".[48] The physician John Webster (1610–1682) shared Scot's belief that out-of court confessions in witch cases were often made by "deluded, melancholy, and mad persons, and so their confessions [are] of no credit, truth, or validity".[49]

Modern psychology has concluded that apparently unforced confessions are sometimes made by those who score high on tests for eagerness to conform in social situations, especially (but not solely) if they are suffering from mental illness or are of limited intellectual capability. Even at the time, observers appreciated that simple and ageing women, perhaps

---

46. Mary Anne Everett Green (ed.), *Calendar of State Papers Domestic: Charles II, 1665–6* (London: HMSO, 1864), pp. 215–227.
47. Gent, *Bideford Witches*, p. 18.
48. Jackson, "Witches, Wives", p. 67; Reginald Scot, *Discoverie*, pp. 56–57.
49. Darr, *Marks*, p. 253.

no longer in full possession of all their mental faculties, who had long been labelled as witches in their communities, might adopt and internalise the identity ascribed to them. Such people could also be highly suggestive when questioned by examining JPs, so that a witch suspect might admit to being "what they had stigmatiz'd her for, without either knowing the Hazard of Confession, or the Properties of a witch".[50]

However, it seems clear that even in cases where coercion was applied, the beliefs of both the accused and their accusers, rather than solely those of the latter, had a significant impact on the narrative the suspects provided.[51] They were drawn from shared traditions, cultural tropes, and a wider mythology, and normally came together in a mutually agreed story, one that had apparently persuasive details, such as their familiars' names. They were not simply put into the mouths of suspects.

Growing Caution About Confessions

By the final years of proscription, an increased degree of caution can sometimes be seen towards witch confessions, especially if they were unsupported. This can be identified in a late near-panic that appears to have taken place in Kent in 1692. A county JP examined three women accused of witchcraft in June that year. The third suspect admitted that she had been a witch for 50 years, but claimed she had committed only one act of harm, against a child. At their trials, the two surviving women denied their earlier admissions and "there being no other material evidence against them but their own confessions were acquitted".[52] A century earlier this would not necessarily have been the case, convictions being secured on such evidence.

---

50. Tract 1712 (2) p. 23.
51. Sheilagh Ilona O'Brien, "The discovery of witches: Matthew Hopkins's Defense of his Witch-Hunting Methods", *Preternature: Critical and Historical Studies on the Preternatural*, v. 5, no. 1 (2016), p. 30.
52. *Athenian Gazette*, 28 February 1693.

The Decision to Prosecute

At the conclusion of the questioning process, the examining JP(s) would have to decide whether to dismiss a matter or refer it to trial. In theory the latter required only belief that a crime had been committed and that there was some evidence to connect the suspect to it. In practice JPs were often slightly more robust about rejecting witch cases, as Elizabeth Sawyer's earlier experiences with the law suggest; she had been questioned and released on several occasions before her final, fatal encounter with the criminal-justice system.

Bail

JPs were encouraged to be cautious about granting bail in all felony cases (not just witchcraft), and could not usually do so on their own; a second JP had to be present, and at least one of them had to be of the quorum (a group of senior justices). If examining magistrates did not grant bail, an application could be renewed before petty or Quarter Sessions. Thus, in 1615 Alice Stevens was committed to the common gaol in Buckinghamshire, but a few days later arranged bail at the Quarter Sessions for the county, being released on recognisance to appear at the following Assizes.[53]

Although bail was rare in capital cases, it was granted to a handful of witches accused of the gravest crimes, especially if the evidence against them appeared weak and they could produce substantial recognisances, guaranteeing their appearance at trial (on pain of forfeiture of the value of the recognisance for non-attendance). For example, in 1673 Charles Pitfield, a Middlesex JP, granted bail to Elizabeth Row, a married woman from Hackney, after she secured recognisances of £40 each from John Thinn, a gardener, and Henry Cratch, a weaver. She was ordered to appear at the next Sessions of the Peace for Middlesex to answer all matters objected against her by John Tinson, who had accused her of having

---

53. C. L'Estrange Ewen, *Witchcraft in the Star Chamber* (privately printed, 1938), p. 43.

an "evill tongue, and is by him vehemently suspected to have feloniously bewitched his cow and other cattel to death".[54]

More seriously, at the Hertford Assizes in July 1618, two women appeared for trial, each accused of murder by witchcraft, after securing substantial recognisances from fellow villagers. Both were acquitted, as was fairly normal with accused witches who had secured their liberty before trial.[55] Similarly, in 1616 Emma Branch, a woman married to a labourer, was accused of capital witchcraft and bailed at Middlesex Quarter Sessions at Hicks Hall. Her trial was delayed because the evidence was not considered complete, and she, too, was eventually acquitted.[56] In 1682 the mayor and a fellow JP from Bideford bailed Elizabeth Caddy, unlike three other women from the town who were also accused of witchcraft. Her prosecution did not even get to trial, being rejected by the Assize grand jury.[57]

Occasionally, conditions apart from recognisance and appearance at trial were added to the grant of bail. In 1578, when Thomas Barker, a surgeon from Gestingthorpe in Essex, was bailed to appear for a minor allegation of witchcraft, a condition stipulated that in the meantime he was "in no way to conjure or invoke spirits, contrary to the statute".[58]

Ancillary Orders

The examining JP(s) would also deal with any ancillary orders necessary for a prosecution. Most important, they would bind over prosecutors and (sometimes) prosecution witnesses to attend trial. In July 1616, for example, Andrew Cansfield, a London fruiterer, entered into a recognisance for £40 before Thomas Sanderson, a Middlesex JP, to appear at the next session of the peace, to "give evidence against Margaret Wellam accused vpon suspition to be a witch".[59] Wellam was eventually delivered by

---

54. John Cordy Jeaffreson (ed), *Middlesex County Records: Volume 4, 1667–88*, (London: Middlesex County Record Society, 1892), pp. 42–43.
55. Cockburn, *Hertfordshire Indictments*, p. 204.
56. William Le Hardy (ed.), *County of Middlesex. Calendar To the Sessions Records: New Series, Volume 3, 1615–16*, 1937, p. 306.
57. Frank J. Gent, *The Trial Of The Bideford Witches* (Crediton: 2001), p. 17.
58. ERO Q/SR 65/6.
59. John Cordy Jeaffreson (ed.), *Middlesex County Records: Volume 2, 1603–25*, 1887, pp. 119–126.

proclamation; apparently the complainant/witness had failed to appear, though it meant forfeiting his recogisance.[60]

Choice of Forum

In theory, cases of witchcraft could be tried at both the main jury courts — that is, the Quarter Sessions, which were conducted four times a year by county JPs — and the Assizes, presided over twice a year by visiting judges from the three Westminster courts. In chartered towns (those with royally granted laws and privileges) the equivalent of the former were termed borough sessions, and presided over by local officials (*ex officio* magistrates for the relevant town). In London and Middlesex the Old Bailey took the place of Assizes, with trials being heard before the Recorder of London and members of the Westminster judiciary sitting collegially.

Nevertheless, although Quarter Sessions had the power to try all felonies, including witchcraft, by the Elizabethan period they were increasingly reluctant to deal with serious crimes, especially unclergyable ones, particularly after 1590. As a result, in 1614, when Alice Battle, a widow from Toppesfield, was indicted at the Essex Quarter Sessions for using witchcraft to kill a local infant, the lower jury forum transmitted her case to the Assizes for trial (where she was acquitted).[61] In like manner, in 1653 the case of Elizabeth Beeman, accused of bewitching Margery Bowman at the Wiltshire Quarter Sessions, was sent to the higher jury court.[62]

Even so, very occasionally a (potentially) capital witchcraft case did go to the lower jury forum, particularly in certain counties. For example, in the late sixteenth century a woman was accused at the West Riding Quarter Sessions of bewitching a man to death.[63] In the West Country, Thomasine Short was tried for capital witchcraft under the 1563 Act at the County of Exeter Quarter Sessions in 1581, albeit that this was an unusual forum. (During the 1530s, Henry VIII had granted its mayor

---

60. Le Hardy, *County of Middlesex*, pp. 264–287.
61. ERO Q/SR 206/19.
62. Ewen, *Demonism*, p. 440.
63. Sharpe, "Yorkshire", p. 2.

Crimen Exceptum

and aldermen the right to sit as justices of the peace with power of gaol delivery).[64]

A similar process, whereby serious cases were transmitted to the Assizes, can be seen in many, but not all, of the country's boroughs. For example, two serious, potentially capital, witchcraft proceedings were commenced at the Maldon Borough Sessions during the 1570s, but the town magistrates were reluctant to handle them. One involved Alice Chaundler, who was accused of bewitching eight-year-old Mary Cowper and three other people (two of them children) to death. All were found to be true bills at the Maldon Sessions, but appear to have been referred to the Assizes at Chelmsford for trial (along with two new matters), where Chaundler was found guilty and hanged.[65]

Nevertheless, a few boroughs, such as Great Yarmouth and Bishop's (now King's) Lynn, jealously guarded their privileges and continued to hear capital cases, including witchcraft, throughout the period of proscription (and beyond). Indeed, the first preserved references to witches being condemned to death in Norfolk come from these two towns. In 1583, one "Mother Gabley" was probably hanged at King's Lynn, and the following year Elizabeth Butcher and Joan Lingwood were condemned to death at Great Yarmouth.[66]

Even so, the vast majority of allegations of capital witchcraft were tried at the Assizes or the Old Bailey. For example, all 35 people indicted for witchcraft in late-seventeenth century Yorkshire were tried at Assizes rather than Quarter Sessions.[67] However, non-capital witchcraft offences might still go to the lower forum (although many also went to the Assizes).

For example, Christopher Hall appeared before the Norfolk Quarter Sessions when accused of practising as a cunning man and giving a charm to Goodwife Smithbourne.[68] In 1617, when David Farman accused three of his neighbours in East Sussex (a married couple and another man) of

---

64. Stoyle, "'Olde Wytche Gonne'", p. 133.
65. Scott McGinnis, "'Subtiltie' Exposed: Pastoral Perspectives on Witch Belief in the Thought of George Gifford", *The Sixteenth Century Journal*, v. 33, no. 3 (2002), p. 669.
66. Parry, *Norfolk*.
67. Sarah Anne Barbour-Mercer, *Prosecution and Process: Crime and the Criminal Law in Late Seventeenth-Century Yorkshire*, Ph.D. thesis, University of York, 1988, p. 135.
68. NRO C/S 3/box 41a.

using witchcraft to harm his animals, the matter was also dealt with at the county Quarter Sessions.[69] (Ironically, one of the men accused, John Rolfe, had himself made an allegation of witchcraft against another neighbour at the Sussex Assizes, some 15 years earlier).[70] Similarly, in October 1623 Elizabeth Creary from Northalteron in Yorkshire was presented at Quarter Sessions in Pickering Lythe for bewitching and injuring a black cow worth 50 shillings. She was convicted and sentenced to the statutory year's imprisonment.[71] In 1704, in one of the last convictions secured for the crime, Hannah Baker of Elham pleaded guilty to "witchcraft and inchanting cattell" at the Kent Quarter Sessions, and she, too, was sent to prison for a year.[72]

Pre-Trial Detention

The Assizes were held twice a year, during Lent and the summer, although Old Bailey sessions occurred more frequently, usually at least six times a year. Nevertheless, many accused witches would have spent months in custody before coming for trial. For example, Elizabeth Pratt was accused of witchcraft and examined before Bedfordshire JPs in April 1666, when she made some admissions to the offence. She was also examined for the devil's mark by a group of women who found a "piece of flesh which grow upon her privities". For some reason, Pratt missed the Summer Assizes in 1666, and was not listed for a hearing until the Lent Sessions in 1667, by which time she would have been in custody for almost a year. By then, and like many others in her situation, she had succumbed to the harsh prison regime, and died.[73]

Given that witches were supposedly possessed of supernatural powers, it might be asked why contemporary observers thought they could not use these to escape. One reason was that "it was a received Opinion, That Witches had no Power over a Person after being in the Hands

---

69. Cynthia B. Herrup, *The Common Peace* (Cambridge: Cambridge University Press, 1987), p. 33.
70. Brian P. Levack, *New Perspectives on Witchcraft, Magic and Demonology, Volume 4, Gender and Witchcraft* (London: Routledge, 2001), p. 162.
71. Ewen, *Witchcraft and Demonism*, p. 394.
72. Gaskill, *Crime and Mentalities*, p. 92.
73. Eric Stockdale, *A Study of Bedford Prison, 1660–1877* (Luton: Bedfordshire Historical Record Society, 1977), p. 16.

Crimen Exceptum

of Justice".⁷⁴ Throughout the era of proscription it was widely thought that, once in custody, a witch was shorn of her powers, although there were reported instances of bewitchment from behind bars. In a refinement of this theory, in the 1650s, a passenger on the *Mayflower*, riding at anchor off Bermuda, remembered a conversation in England some four years earlier in which she had heard Elizabeth Page, a suspected witch, say that she had made the doors of Maidstone Gaol "stand open, so that others might or did goe forth, but she [Page] had no power to goe forth herselfe".⁷⁵

---

74. Tract 1712 (2) pp. 1–10.
75. Bernhard, "Religion, Politics", p. 704.

CHAPTER 7

Specialist Tests for Witchcraft

Introduction

A range of specialist tests developed to establish that a suspect truly was a witch. These included "swimming", "pricking" a special bodily mark, identifying a witch's teat, requiring her to recite the Lord's Prayer or other well-known passage of scripture without making a mistake, and any positive results obtained from the various techniques, such as scratching a suspect or boiling a victim's urine that were used to break a spell or to identify who had cast it.

The status of these tests within the criminal process varied greatly with time, location, and the inclinations of those in authority. They could be carried out by members of the public, to confirm widely held suspicions, prior to taking a suspect before a JP, although the Reverend Juxon was to warn that when private individuals "without any authority, and by vain and deceitful tests, take upon 'em to determine the Guilt or Innocence of persons unjustly suspected, it is high time to put a stop to such proceedings".[1] Alternatively, the JP himself might order the test to justify committing a woman for trial. If the first and/or second options took place, the results might (or might not) then be reported at trial, so becoming evidence in the case, material that could be used by the petty jury to determine guilt. Finally, the court itself could order the test to be conducted at trial, the results of which would, of course, then become evidence for all purposes.

---

1. Tract 1736 p. 26.

The first scenario occurred on numerous occasions, and in very different circumstances. These ranged from extremely informal actions, sometimes conducted by a small mob on the spur of the moment, to carefully organized tests carried out by local notables, even by members of the gentry, sometimes in a quasi-scientific manner, before involving the authorities. The second was also fairly common, the third much less so. The various tests and when they were employed will be dealt with *seriatim*.

Reciting Scripture

A long-standing belief, one that was present in the sixteenth century and which lasted until well into the 1700s, was that witches would find it almost impossible to repeat the Lord's Prayer or (more rarely) some other well-known passage from scripture, without making mistakes or important omissions. It was thought that reciting them accurately would be offensive to the devil. Although widely used, the test was not definitive or conclusive anywhere in the British Isles, especially when it produced a negative result. For example, most of the seven women accused in the Islandmagee witch case in Ireland in 1711 had no trouble reciting the Lord's Prayer, yet a jury found all of them guilty. Nevertheless, a failure was viewed as indicating that the speaker was a witch.

This test was used both at the magistrates' examination and in court at trial. Thus, in 1712 the Reverend Strutt, the vicar of Ardley, asked Jane Wenham, when she was examined by a local JP, to recite the Lord's Prayer. She started well but was unable to correctly say "Lead us not into temptation; but deliver us from evil". She tried doing so six or seven times, her versions including the unfortunate "Lead us into temptation and evil." In response, she claimed that she was "disturb'd in her Head" and needed to rest. As a result, further tests were carried out the following day at the house of the village constable, who was holding her in custody, but Wenham was still unable to recite the words accurately. This failure appears to have prompted her to confess to witchcraft.[2]

---

2. Jones, "Hertfordshire Trial", p. 283.

However, the recitation of scripture was also used in a forensic environment. In December 1602, at the elderly Louise Jackson's trial at the Old Bailey, the presiding judge, Lord Chief Justice Anderson, insisted that she recite the Lord's Prayer and the Creed, which she mangled at several points.[3] Since many accused witches were both elderly and largely uneducated, it is likely that some of them did not know or could not remember the correct form of the prayer. Florence Newton, tried in Ireland in 1661, and subjected to the same technique, said that she could not fully recall it because of her poor memory and advanced age. Others undoubtedly erred through being terrified.

Scratching

The positive results of "scratching" (discussed in *Chapter 4*) could be given in court to identify a witch, like other successful results from anti-witch stratagems (many of them suggested by cunning folk). At the trial of Elizabeth Stile in 1579, an ostler from Windsor was called to give evidence "viva voce" against her. He claimed that she had bewitched him after he had refused her what she thought were reasonable alms, and said that he had consulted a "wiseman" named Father Rosimonde about the source of his malady. This individual told him that he was bewitched, and asked him about likely suspects. When the ostler identified Stile, Rosimonde advised him to scratch her, so that he drew blood, and said that he would recover. At trial, the ostler testified that he subsequently did this, scratching her "by the face, that he made the blood come after, & presently his paine went awaie, so that he hath bin no more greved".[4] This confirmed Stile as a witch.

The Witch's Teat

The concept of the witch's teat had gradually been identified and developed during the Elizabethan period (see *Chapter 3*). The earliest record

---

3. Michael MacDonald (ed.), *Witchcraft and Hysteria in Elizabethan London: Edward Jorden and the Mary Glover Case* (London: Routledge, 1991), p. xvii.
4. Tract 1579 (2) pp. 1–10.

of a forensic out-of-court search for such a teat or mark (it is not clear which) relates to a case from 1579, in which a Southampton Leet court jury urged that the forum find five or six honest matrons to strip and search the elderly Widow Walker, to see if a witch's mark could be found. If the result were negative it would quieten gossip about the woman; if positive, the court could proceed further. In the mid-1590s a list of "presumptions against witches" drawn up for Yorkshire JPs suggested that they were "seldom without some strange mark on their bodies".[5] Again, it is not clear if this refers to a teat or another type of witch's mark (see below).

Nevertheless, in the late sixteenth century, the search for such a teat was not necessarily conducted as part of a forensic investigation, as can be seen from the lengthy (and very influential) chapbook on the three Warboys witches published in 1593. That year, *after* the trio had been convicted and hanged, their gaoler, who had the responsibility for seeing them buried, stripped off their clothes and found on the body of the elderly Alice Samuel a little lump of flesh "sticking out, as if it had beene a teate, to the length of halfe an inch". At first the gaoler and his wife were reluctant to disclose this information publicly because it was adjoining her genitals, and so "not decent to be seene". However, they eventually decided that it should be witnessed and, having covered Samuel's private parts as best they could, showed it to up to 40 people. The gaoler's wife then took the teat in her hand and squeezed it, initially producing what appeared to be a mixture of yellow milk and water. When she squeezed it a second time, clear milk came forth, and the third time blood.[6]

It is apparent that a thorough body search for a teat, for forensic purposes, was not normally used until the early-1600s. Over ensuing decades it gradually became a set part of witch investigations and prosecutions, often being carried out by groups of three or four matrons. By the 1630s, the formal search for teats had become quite routine and continued to be so to the end of proscription. For example, in Bermuda, in the 1650s, a panel of women was appointed to search two females suspected of

---

5. Darren Oldridge, *The Supernatural in Tudor and Stuart England*, (Abingdon: Routledge, 2016), p. 141.
6. Tract 1593 p. 114.

being witches. After a diligent examination, they reported, "[We] cannot find any outwards or innwards mark soe far as wee can p.ceave whereby wee can in conscience find them or either of them guilty of witchcraft". How these women knew what to look for is uncertain. None is known to have been present at a witch trial, but most likely they had heard talk or read of such matters.[7]

By 1652 the process was so mainstream that there were complaints, after Joan Peterson had been physically examined in London, with negative results, that she was illegally searched a second time: "Then they caused her (contrary to Law) to be searched againe in a most unnaturall & Barbarous manner, by fower women whom they themselves for that purpose had brought along with them, one of which women told the Justice that there was a Teat… whereupon the said Justice committed her first to New-prison and from thence to Newgate".[8] Such examinations were still being carried out in 1712, when four women searched Jane Wenham, the last witch convicted in England, for teats and marks (none was found), and beyond.

The absence of teats was never conclusive of innocence: it was thought that the devil could conceal them, and that some witches might deliberately cut them out. In 1726, a newspaper correspondent could note that, after an old woman in Kent who was reputed to be a witch, was accused of bewitching a young lady, the "matrons of the neighbourhood resolved to search this unhappy wretch that had caused these calamities, in hopes to find her unnatural teats; and search her they did, but finding none, they gravely concluded, that the Devil for the present had rendered them invisible".[9]

Even male witches might have teats, which would be searched for by other men. When in June 1647 Adam Sabie was accused of being a witch by a Haddenham man named John Kirby, John Stearne claimed to have conducted an intimate search of Sabie, and to have found near his fundament "one Teate of the greatest length that ever he sawe upon the body of any man". (He also claimed that Sabie had subsequently

---

7. Bernhard, "Religion, Politics", p. 691.
8. Tract 1652 p. 6.
9. *Weekly Journal, or The British Gazetteer*, 18 June 1726.

confessed to him that a spirit in the shape of a young child had first appeared to him 12 years earlier "when he was in trouble"). Similarly, in 1653, in Wiltshire, unusual spots were found on William Starr after he was searched on suspicion of being a witch.[10]

Like reading the Lord's Prayer, identifying the witch's teat was a test that could be (and was) ordered and conducted at court, not merely during the pre-trial investigation. For example, in 1621 Arthur Robinson, a Middlesex JP from Tottenham who had periodically questioned Elizabeth Sawyer on suspicion of witchcraft, learnt from Sawyer's neighbours during her Old Bailey trial that she had a "private and strange marke on her body". (Clearly no examination had been conducted prior to trial in this case). He immediately alerted the judges, and "sitting in the Court at that time of her triall, informed the bench thereof, desiring the bench to send for women to search her, presently before the jury did goe forth to bring in the verdict". The presiding judge agreed and ordered court officers to find three such women. One of them was Margaret Weaver, who kept the sessions house for the City of London, and was a widow of good reputation; the other two were "grave Matrons, brought in by the Officer out of the streete, passing by there by chance". Sawyer resisted the process, and behaved "sluttishly and loathsomely" towards them. The women appear to have used a degree of force to search her (as was common in such situations), and "nicenesse they laid aside". They subsequently informed the court that a little above Sawyer's buttocks they had found a teat the size of a little finger. Sawyer vigorously denied this, but the discovery was deemed to have given the trial jury some insight into her true character.[11]

Pricking and the Witch's Mark

Unlike belief in the witch's teat, that of the witch's mark, a spot on the witch's body devoid of feeling and denoting her diabolical allegiance, was widespread throughout Europe, not (relatively) special to England. According to some commentators, the witch's mark was a blemish left

---

10. Ewen, *Witchcraft and Demonism*, p. 440.
11. Tract 1621 p. 4.

by the devil's claws on his servant's body.[12] However, in 1616 the Reverend Alexander Roberts was reiterating already widespread opinion when he suggested that it was a relic of the sealing in blood of the diabolical covenant between the witch and the devil; the latter, once all terms of the contract had been agreed, gave her a scratch. The mark was said to acquire certain distinct properties, as the devil would "so benumme the same, that though it be pierced with any sharpe instrument, yet is without any sense of feeling, and will not yeelde one droppe of bloud at all".[13] These qualities became classic signs of the witch's mark. Thus Richard Bernard agreed that that they were "insensible, and being prickt will not bleede". Similarly, Matthew Hopkins thought they would "feele neither pin, needle, aule, &c., thrust through them".

If the suspected person had no physical reaction when such marks were pricked with a bodkin or other instrument, it would indicate that she was a witch. This belief gave rise to specialist "witch prickers", who identified and tested potential marks, in some parts of Europe, including Scotland. They were rarely seen in England and, when they were, often came from north of the border. For example, in 1649 a Scottish pricker dealt with women brought into Newcastle after accusations from their neighbours. They were stripped and "openly had pins thrust into their bodies". Nevertheless, during Matthew Hopkins' East Anglian campaign, two local women, Mary Phillips and Priscilla Briggs, seem to have played a major role in identifying marks as well as teats, and were well paid for their work.

Even so, in England, amateurs conducted most cases of 'pricking'. A tract from 1689 noted that a JP dealing with a female witch suspect had ordered that she be "searcht by a *jury* of Women, who found about her several purple Spots, which they prickt with a sharp Needle, but she felt no pain: She had about her other Marks and Tokens of a *Witch,* of which the Women upon Oath, gave an Account to the *Justice;* and some Swearing positively against her, she was sent to the County *Jayle,* where she is remaining to be Tryed the next *Assizes*".[14]

---
12. Heikki Pihlajamäki, "Swimming the Witch, Pricking for the Devil's Mark: Ordeals in the Early Modern Witchcraft Trials", *The Journal of Legal History,* v. 21, issue 2 (2000), p. 36.
13. Roberts, *Treatise,* p. 15.
14. Tract 1689 p. 1.

By the seventeenth century, the search for a witch's mark could last for several hours, and involve shaving suspects from head to toe and having every scar inspected by a surgeon to see if it was natural, although such thoroughness was rare in England.[15] Even so, prickers might test multiple potential marks on a suspect. To establish a genuine lack of sensitivity, and to prevent a suspected witch from feigning discomfort, Bernard thought it advisable to take them by surprise with a sharp instrument and "prick it suddenly and secretly so the witch could not dissemble".[16]

The process was open to abuse, as was seen with the Scottish pricker in Newcastle. It was later suggested that, to produce a suitably high number of positive results, he had resorted to trickery, as most of those tested were found to be witches. Ralph Gardiner noted that in one case he observed the woman involved had been disoriented and ashamed by her nakedness, so that blood had run away from her legs before the pin was put in, explaining an initial lack of reaction and bleeding. When, at the insistence of one Colonel Hobson, who was present at the test, the experiment was repeated on the same woman, in the same place, blood "gushed out".[17] Even worse, it was sometimes suggested that, to get the desired results, some fraudulent prickers used a specially designed tool which had a retractable needle, so that it gave the appearance of going deep into the witch without producing blood or pain.

Because of their similarity, the English mythology pertaining to marks and teats often became confused amongst contemporary observers, so that the terms were sometimes used interchangeably. For example, a pamphlet authored by Edmund Bower referred to a "certain mark or teat" on Anne Bodenham's shoulder. More properly, in 1712 the JP Sir Henry Chauncy eventually ordered a search of Jane Wenham's body for "any teats, or other extraordinary and unusual marks about her". (Four women failed to find any).[18]

At the Maidstone witch trial of 1652, both indicia were present in different suspects. One of the women accused had a mark on one of her

---

15. Pihlajamäki, "Swimming", p. 36.
16. Bernard, *Guide*, p. 215.
17. Ralph Gardiner, *England's Grievance Discovered, in Relation to the Coal Trade*, London, 1655. (Reprinted North Shields: Philipson and Hare, 1849), p. 169.
18. Darr, *Marks*, p. 117.

limbs, such that a "pin being thrust to the head into one of their arms, the party did not feele it, neither did it draw bloud from her". Another of the accused witches, Mary Read of Lenham, "had a visible Teat under her tongue".[19]

Natural Blemishes

Of course, in an era of very limited hygiene and medical treatment, many people, especially if elderly, had superficial blemishes, and it was not difficult for searchers to find a suitable spot. In 1646 John Gaule claimed that what were really ulcers and boils were being made into witch's marks and teats.[20] Similarly, Francis Hutchinson thought that some marks were piles, warts, moles, scurvy spots, or scars.[21] At Wenham's trial it was claimed that almost any physical excrescence or deformity was being attributed to the "Stamp of the Devil".[22]

Thomas Ady believed that all unusual bodily marks could be explained naturally, and even provided medical reasons for their properties. He had high-level support for such an analysis. Receiving news of the second large wave of Lancashire suspects in 1633, the sceptical King Charles I ordered the eminent physician William Harvey to examine Margaret Johnson and three other women in London. Assisted by a team of seven surgeons and ten midwives, Harvey found nothing on three of them, but Johnson proved more problematic, as she did have two blemishes that could potentially pass as teats. Even so, Harvey concluded that their origin was natural, merely being the "Skin of the Fundament drawen out as yt wil be after the pyles or applicacon of leeches".[23]

As this suggests, even William Harvey was not quite willing to reject the very notion of a witch's teat. Several less eminent medical men, such as the physician Richard Boulton, the author of a number of obscure medical treatises, and the apothecary William Drage, were strong believers

---

19. Tract 1652 (2) p. 5.
20. Gaule, *Select Cases*, pp. 4–6.
21. Hutchinson, *Historical Essay*, p. 140.
22. Tract 1712 (2) pp. 1–10.
23. Gaskill, "Witchcraft and Evidence", p. 45.

in their reality.[24] Furthermore, even the strongest believers appreciated that quite natural blemishes could be mistaken for marks or teats, as they usually claimed to have considered and rejected such a possibility. After the widow Coman's death in Essex in 1699, the midwife who examined her body and found two apparent nipples on the corpse stressed that they were "neither Piles nor Emrods (for she knew both)".[25]

Swimming

The swimming test for identifying a witch caught the popular imagination during the seventeenth century, and lingered long afterwards. Suspected witches would be thrown into ponds or rivers to see if the water would reject or accept them, i.e. they floated or they sank. The former indicated the presence of a witch, the latter an innocent person. According to John Stearne, who was something of an enthusiast for the test, when witches were thrown into a lake or stream they would "lye topling on the water, straining to get their heads, or themselves under the water, but cannot".[26]

James VI identified the rationale for this test in *Daemonologie* (1597); God had appointed that "the water shall refuse to receive them in her bosome, that have shaken off them the sacred Water of Baptisme, and wilfully refused the benefite thereof". However, even some of the most enthusiastic believers in witchcraft had doubts about the value of the procedure. As early as 1616, the physician John Cotta, attempting to introduce a more "scientific" method into the discovery of witchcraft, and to put paid to techniques that he found irrational, was very dismissive of swimming, which he thought ridiculous, albeit noting that it was vulgarly credited with being an infallible test.[27]

Perhaps strangely, given the enthusiasm with which it was eventually taken up, the swimming of witches was not a traditional English practice. Reginald Scot did not mention it in his major work of 1584, indicating

---

24. Darr, *Marks*, pp. 126–127.
25. Tract 1712 (1) p. 21.
26. Stearne, *Confirmation*, p. 19.
27. John Cotta, *The Triall of Witch-craft, Shewing the True and Right Methode of the Discovery: With a Confutation of erroneous wayes*, London, 1616, p. 104.

that it had yet to reach England. By then it was already well known in Germany, eventually being sanctioned, for example, by magistrates in Osnabruck and Munster, though banned by Phillip II in the Spanish Netherlands in 1595 and in France a few years later (many observers thought that it was sacrilegious).[28] It is sometimes suggested that swimming first arrived in England from Scotland, a view that is supported by a few manuscript sources, although this is by no means certain.[29]

The test may have been used on some suspects in Scotland in 1597, but appears to have fallen out of favour there almost immediately, so that there is little record of its being employed again, unlike the situation further south. Swimming might have arrived in England in the late 1590s, and was certainly used in 1613 to identify witches near Bedford, at the suggestion of a traveller who had "seen it often tried in the North Country".[30] This could be Scotland, but it is far more likely to refer to the northern counties of England.

However, ordinary people quickly adopted swimming as a reliable and convenient way of identifying a witch. As Francis Hutchinson noted in 1718, country people were as fond of it as they were of bullbaiting.[31] Its final, quasi-official use took place in Leicester as late as 1717, where the unfortunate accused, a mother and daughter, "swam like a cork, [or] a piece of paper or an empty barrel, though they strove all they could to sink". However, the test was not confined to country people. In 1701 Sarah Morduck, an alleged Southwark witch, was recognised while walking in Newgate Market in London. A large and unruly mob "flocked about her, and threatened to throw her into a horse pond". It took more than a century after 1736 before the practice was eradicated from popular usage (see below). Doubtless, the ease with which swimming could be conducted — it required only a body of water — and the malevolent pleasure that it provided helps explain its longevity.

To some enthusiasts, in the late-sixteenth and early-seventeenth centuries, swimming was supposed to be conducted with the right thumb

---

28. Gaskill, *Introduction*, p. 54.
29. Robert Bartlett, *Trial by Fire and Water: the Medieval Judicial Ordeal* (Oxford: Clarendon, 1986), pp. 146–147.
30. Rosen, *Witchcraft*, p. 342.
31. Hutchinson, *Historical Essay*, p. 135.

tied to the left big toe, and the left thumb connected to the right big toe, so that the limbs made a cross over the body; there were numerous well-evidenced cases of this occurring, both in England and on the Continent. However, in many cases, especially when the test was conducted informally (rather than under the supervision of a JP), the witch was simply heaved into the water. Those who sank would be recovered and not allowed to drown, unless by accident, although the mistaken modern belief that an alleged witch could only prove their innocence by meeting a watery death appears to have taken root fairly early.[32] Those being tested were often connected to a safety rope so that they could be hauled in. The degree of tension placed on this rope could also affect flotation; sometimes, it was claimed, deliberately.[33]

The circumstances in which swimming occurred varied enormously, as did its significance. Frequently it was carried out by those associated with the accusers, and the results reported later (if at all) to an examining magistrate when the accused person was committed to his custody. For example, in 1704, Sarah Griffiths, an elderly woman who lived in a garret in Rosemary Lane in London, had long been thought a bad person, with local children falling ill in her vicinity. Eventually, she was suspected of an identifiable act of serious malefic witchcraft. Coming across her near the River Thames, a group of three men decided to test whether she was a witch, and simply "tossed her in". She duly floated like a cork.[34]

If an accused person proved buoyant in these circumstances, further close examination, such as the search for a witch's mark or teat, might be thought justified. Thus, after Mary Sutton, the Bedford witch of 1613, floated despite the men holding the safety rope (allegedly) tossing her up and down in an effort to make her sink, she was searched and found to have a kind of teat on her left thigh. These tests having proved positive, she was then taken to a JP, where a formal accusation was made and questioning conducted.[35]

Sometimes, swimming was even ordered or supervised by examining magistrates. For example, in December 1645 the Mayor and Jurats of Rye

---

32. *The Gentleman's Magazine*, 1736, v. vi, p. 137.
33. *Daily Journal*, 15 January 1731.
34. Tract 1704 p. 1.
35. Rosen, *Witchcraft in England*, p. 343.

(*ex officio* JPs for the town) ordered that Martha Bruff, a married woman, and Anne Howsell, a widow, who were suspected to be witches, be tried by putting them into water.[36] As late as 1716, John Dineley (1680–1741), a JP in Hertfordshire, was removed from the bench for, *inter alia,* misconduct while present at a test for witchcraft. The accused woman had been thrown into a millpond to see if she would sink, apparently at the magistrate's instigation. After she was pulled out, the JP stripped off his own clothes, jumped into the water, and swam about on his back, "exposing his nakedness" to bystanders.[37] By then, it may have been thought that any involvement by a JP in such proceedings was slightly inappropriate.

However, swimming was not ordered by judges at Assizes (unlike the recitation of scripture or searches for marks and teats) and, even more pertinently, its legal status at trial, even by report, was virtually non-existent, unlike evidence of marks, teats, and faulty recitation of scripture. The judiciary were actively opposed to members of the public conducting the test, as were some JPs, if only because of the danger of disorder and mob violence; this was freely admitted by many proponents of the test.

For example, Serjeant John Godbold, a former Recorder of Bury St Edmunds and Chief Justice of the Isle of Ely, expressly prohibited swimming when sitting at Assizes in 1645, and Matthew Hopkins stressed that the test was never brought in against any of the people he accused "at their tryals as any evidence". Although his colleague John Stearne admitted that he swam some of those suspected of witchcraft early in the East Anglian campaign, during the warmer summer months, he, too, emphasized that swimming had been abandoned after judicial warnings and had never been adduced as formal evidence at trial: "neither was it ever given in or taken, that I know, as an evidence against any". Significantly, when, in 1712, Jane Wenham offered to submit to the swimming test at her examination, her questioners, being aware of the courts' antipathy to the procedure, rejected her request. [38]

---

36. Anon, *The Manuscripts of Rye and Hereford Corporations, Etc.* (London: Historical Manuscripts Commission, 1892), pp. 213–216.
37. Norma Landau, *The Justices of the Peace 1679–1760* (Berkeley and Los Angeles: University of California Press, 1984), p. 596; Elmer, *Witchcraft, Witch-hunting*, p. 279.
38. Jones, "Hertfordshire Trial", p. 283.

Eventually, in an effort to actively deter swimming, Lord Chief Justice Parker, sitting at the Essex Assizes at Brentwood in 1712, warned that "if any dare for the future to make use of that experiment, and the party lose her life by it, all they that are the cause of it are guilty of Wilful murder". The courts also tried to discourage the practice by prosecuting those who conducted it for assault.

Most early-modern Englishmen and women could not swim, but had to go near open water on a regular basis for washing and other reasons, as the era's appalling incidence of drowning bears out. More than 44 per cent of all accidental deaths in the London area were caused by water immersion in the years from 1654 to 1735.[39] This lack of familiarity with water may also help to explain popular faith in the test.

Nevertheless, as Thomas Ady observed, different levels of individual buoyancy could have entirely natural explanations. A lot would depend on physical variables, such as whether the tested person's lungs were full of air or whether she was fully dressed when she entered the water. Francis Hutchinson thought that the clothes commonly worn by those being tested meant that half the old women in the country would float, if only because of the inherent buoyancy of "woollen and sweaty petticoats". He, too, appreciated that natural "fatness and leanness" affected flotation.[40] In the 1650s, when a suspected witch in Bermuda was thrown into the sea (twice), because of the lack of a suitable body of fresh water, the warm salty water meant that she did not sink properly, even though "she did open her mouth and breathe".[41]

Even many proponents of swimming appreciated that its results could be mistaken. Some were sufficiently concerned about this risk to apply a degree of scientific method to the test as the seventeenth century advanced, with a view to reducing the possibility of false results. Most commonly, this was done by the increased use of a "control", a person who was not suspected of witchcraft who might be swum voluntarily, for payment, at the same time as the suspected witch. The use of several (up to three) tests, to confirm initial findings, and stripping those

---

39. Craig Spence, *Accidents and Violent Death in Early Modern London, 1650–1750*, (Woodbridge: Boydell Press, 2016), p. 79.
40. Francis Hutchinson, *Historical Essay*, p. 138.
41. Bernhard, "Religion, Politics", p. 693.

to be tested down to their shifts also played a role in producing a more scientific regime.

For example, in 1689 an elderly woman in Somerset, suspected of bewitching two young people, had been swum, and floated like a cork in front of a significant crowd. However, "[a]t the same time, also, there was put into the Water, a Lusty young Woman, who sunk immediately, and had been drown'd, had it not been for the help that was at hand. To satisfy the World, and to leave no Room for doubting, the old Woman was had down to the Water the third time, and being put in as before, she did still Swim".[42]

Similarly, three years later, in 1692, during a late and small scale witch-panic in Kent, the subjects of the swimming test, some of whom had volunteered to undergo the process so as to clear them from public suspicion (a regular phenomenon of the time), were each immersed on three occasions. Furthermore, a man who was not under suspicion was paid five shillings to serve as a control for the test. Apparently, he immediately sank and had ingested a considerable amount of water before he could be pulled out.[43]

---

42. Tract 1689 p. 1.
43. *Athenian Gazette*, 28 February 1693.

Crimen Exceptum

CHAPTER 8

Trial and Punishment

Introduction

A witch-trial followed the same general pattern as that for any other felony. Early in the morning on the first day of sessions, shackled prisoners from the local gaol would be brought to court, while those on bail would arrive there under their own steam, as would their prosecutors (and prosecution witnesses). The latter would normally produce appropriate bills of indictment written on slips of parchment, or preparatory drafts of such bills. These might have been drawn up with the help of examining JPs or the court clerk. They would then go for consideration by the grand jury.

The Grand Jury Hearing

Although JPs committed suspected witches to trial, whether at Assizes or (much less commonly) Quarter Sessions, a majority (and at least a dozen) of the 13 to 27 men normally found on a grand jury would first have to be satisfied that there was enough evidence to establish a prima facie case. They would reach this decision by hearing prosecution evidence in private. This would usually be oral testimony, supplemented by any recorded confession made by the accused person and *possibly* other depositions made to JPs.

If the grand jury produced an affirmative answer, they would mark the tendered bill of indictment *billa vera*, or "true bill'"; if not, it would be marked "no true bill", "not found", or *ignoramus*, and the suspect released by proclamation. Thus, when the Warboys witches came for trial at the Huntingdon Assizes in 1593, it was noted that their "Inditements being deliuered to the graund Jury, the evidence was given them privately, by Maister Dorington Doctor of Divinitie, and Parson of the towne of Warboyes aforesaide, by Gilbert Pickering of Tichemersh in the Countie of Northampton Esquire, by Robert Throckmorton Esquire, father of the said children [other names follow]". It was clearly a speedy process; the grand jury "made no great delay", and the matter was ready to proceed to trial by about 8 am, so they must have taken less than an hour, even allowing for a 7 am start.[1]

In the Elizabethan period, grand jurors were of a somewhat higher social status than the trial jurors found at the same forum, and by the Restoration they were markedly superior to those who sat on the petty jury. By then, those at Assizes were increasingly drawn from what might be termed the upper orders, some being knights and others justices of the peace. Even in 1622 the grand jury that considered the case against six women accused by the prominent gentleman Edward Fairfax at the York Assizes (and which called all the prosecution witnesses to give testimony before them) included six JPs, although this may have reflected the sensitivities of the case.

Because of its generally higher social and educational level, which distanced it from popular beliefs and local tensions and anxieties, the grand jury played a potentially vital function in giving measured consideration to witchcraft allegations. Its members might have been expected to be less credulous than those who sat on trial juries, who were usually drawn from the middling orders, especially as elite attitudes towards witchcraft started to depart from those of the wider population during the 1600s. Richard Bernard thought that it was incumbent on grand jurors not to leave the "simple men" of a trial jury to determine a difficult allegation like witchcraft, unless the evidence was very clear.[2] In Fairfax's case the trial judge sent a message expressly warning the grand jury of the need for special caution before finding a true bill, and "to be very careful in the matter of Witches".

---

1. Tract 1593 p. 108.
2. Herrup, *The Common Peace*, p. 68 and p. 114.

Clearly, some witch cases were thrown out by a finding of *ignoramus*. For example, at the Buckinghamshire Assizes in March 1615, Elizabeth Mason accused a widow named Alice Stevens of bewitching her baby to death. Stevens claimed that this accusation was made to avoid repaying a debt of £12 and to blackmail her into making a further payment of £20. There had been a delay of some five months between the death of the baby and Mason's going to law. Presumably the grand jury was made aware of the defence case in the JPs' depositions. They returned the bill of indictment *ignoramus*, and Stevens walked free. She subsequently took proceedings against Mason in the Court of Star Chamber.[3]

Nevertheless, in practice, and for whatever reasons, it seems that grand juries did not reject large numbers of witchcraft indictments, even in the closing decades of proscription, when many grand jurors must have entertained severe doubts about such proceedings, or even (occasionally) the very existence of witchcraft. For example, only nine out of 48 witchcraft indictments filed at the Home Circuit between 1660 and 1701 were rejected by the grand jury, even though the remaining 39 all resulted in acquittals at trial.[4]

Arraignment

The normal plea to a felony indictment was "not guilty", even if the evidence was strong, and by the Jacobean period many judges were actively encouraging such a response from defendants. This applied to witchcraft cases as much as any other crime. Only a handful of witches formally admitted the allegation against them, especially when it was a capital form of the offence. Pleas of guilty to non-capital forms of witchcraft were slightly more common, as they were with other crimes, and one of the last convictions under the 1604 Act was secured by such a plea in Kent in 1704.

However, and as with other felonies, some witches pleaded not guilty and then made little attempt to challenge the prosecution evidence against them. In 1682 the three Bideford witches who were capitally

---

3. Ewen, *Star Chamber*, p. 43.
4. Gaskill, "Witchcraft and Evidence", pp. 33–70.

indicted at the Exeter Assizes went further. They all pleaded not guilty but then freely admitted their crimes at trial.[5]

The Trial

Witch trials were unusual. They lasted far longer than most other criminal hearings, the majority of which were over in less than half an hour, and not a few in as little as 15 minutes. (They were not, however, unique in this: murder by poison also produced lengthy trials). For example, in an exceptional case, the trial of two witches at the Lent Assizes for Oxfordshire in 1605 lasted at least eight hours, with the jury not retiring to consider its verdict until 10 pm; they acquitted.[6] (Trials could not be adjourned overnight). One reason for the length of such cases was the unusually large number of witnesses who were often called to establish the crime. At Joan Buts's trial at the Surrey Assizes in 1682, up to 20 prosecution witnesses were called against her, so that the hearing was almost three hours long.[7] The trial of the Warboys witches in 1593 was eventually brought to an end by limitations of time and intimations from the tribunal that they had heard enough, after five hours without a break, when the "judge, justices, and jury saide openly that the cause was most apparant: their consciences were wel satisfied, that the said Witches were guilty, & had deserved death".[8]

Defendants could not be legally represented in felony trials, except on points of pure law, during the period of proscription, while it was rare, though not forbidden, for the prosecution to have legal representation. Nevertheless, and unusually, at Joan Peterson's Old Bailey trial in 1652, it was claimed that those pursuing the case attended with "three Councellors to prosecute the said *Peterson*". These lawyers called the "many women persons of mean degree (and of ill fame and reputation) [who] were produced against her, and interrogated by the said Councel,

---

5. Gent, *Bideford Witches*, p. 18.
6. Brian P. Levack, "Possession, Witchcraft, and the Law in Jacobean England", *Washington and Lee Law Review*, v. 52, issue 5 (1995), p. 1623.
7. Tract 1682 (3) pp. 1–2.
8. Tract 1593 p. 108.

according to the Briefs delivered unto them, wherein were all the witnesses testimonies, written before hand".[9]

The forensic atmosphere in witch trials could be notably lacking in decorum, not least because they attracted numerous spectators. John Aubrey noted that when one of his friends, Anthony Ettrick, a Middle Temple barrister, had observed Anne Bodenham's trial for witchcraft at Salisbury in 1652, the "crowd of spectators made such a noise that the judge, Chief Baron Wild, could not hear the prisoner, nor the prisoner the judge. Words were handed from one to another by Mr Chandler, and sometimes not truly reported".[10]

The Evidence Adduced at Trial

The three main witchcraft statutes created serious supernatural offences, but without giving any kind of indication as to how these were to be established in a forensic environment. This was to be a constant challenge between 1563 and 1736. Ultimately a hybrid system of evidence was used to convict witches, combining traditional methods of proof with specialist or even supernatural techniques. To the end of proscription, the relative importance and weight of these forms of evidence was disputed. At the trial of Joan Buts at the Surrey Assizes in 1682 it was noted, "The Jury having been some time out, returned and gave in their Verdict that she was not Guilty, to the great amazement of some who thought the Evidence sufficient to have found her Guilty; yet others who consider the great difficulty in proving a Witch, thought the Jury could do no less than acquit her".[11]

Witches might be convicted on the basis of, *inter alia*: confessions (admissions made to others, especially examining JPs); circumstantial evidence (usually cursing followed by unexpected misfortune); being seen to have congress with a familiar by an eyewitness; the physical presence of witch's teats or marks on their bodies; their inability to recite scripture accurately; common repute; and spectral evidence (the testimony

---
9. Tract 1652 pp. 1–8.
10. Oliver Lawson Dick (ed.), *Aubrey's Brief Lives*, (London: Secker and Warburg, 1949), p. 54.
11. Tract 1682 p. 2.

of a victim seeing the defendant witch attacking them in a dream or during a fit).

The last of these would extend to "The sick party in his fits naming the parties suspected, and where they be or have been, or what they do, *if truly*".[12] Sometimes it did not even require a fit. In the case of the Warboys' witches, when Alice Samuel visited one of her alleged victims, who was attended by her family, the child responded by saying, "Grandmother look where the old witch sitteth [pointing to Samuel] did you ever see one more like a witch than she is: Take off her black thrumbed cap, for I cannot abide to look on her". This was among the "proofes, presumptions, circumstances, & reasons" brought against Samuel at trial.[13]

However, a general trend can be discerned after about 1600, whereby the courts slowly came to require more clear-cut evidence of witchcraft than general rumour, hearsay, personal opinion, and the "voice of the country". These had sometimes been accepted as sufficient to found convictions during the Elizabethan period. Of course, such matters continued to be important. As was noted in 1645, a key indicator of a witch was the "Common report of their neighbours, especially if the party suspected be of kin, or servant to, or familiar with a convicted Witch".[14] Nevertheless, this was no longer enough. Unfortunately, this development also encouraged the use of novel tests and ordeals to provide the extra "evidence" needed to secure convictions, as discussed in *Chapter 7*.[15]

The Witnesses

The courts were fairly liberal about who they allowed to testify against alleged witches, more so than they usually were with other types of felony, and another illustration of the special status accorded to such hearings. In his *Daemonologie* of 1597, James VI had noted "Children, women and liars can be witnesses over high treason against God". This was used, *inter alia*, to justify allowing children to give evidence in such cases, even if they were younger than would usually be permitted. Famously, nine-year-old

---

12. Tract 1645 (1) pp. 1–8.
13. Tract 1593 p. 108.
14. Tract 1645 (1) pp. 1–8.
15. Gaskill, *Witchfinders*, 2006, p. 47.

Jennet Device gave vital testimony at the Pendle witch trial of 1612, held at the Lancashire Assizes, implicating her own family, and leading to the deaths of her mother, brother, sister, and several neighbours. It was not a new phenomenon even then. The large St Osyth witch trial of 1582 saw several small children testify against their parents, including Agnes Dowsing, at seven-years-old the youngest to give evidence, who claimed her mother kept familiars in the form of black birds. Children were to play prominent roles in several more of the era's witch trials, although the notion of giving evidence against parents was something that George Gifford thought quite "vile". Inevitably, this also encouraged manipulation by adults, including examining JPs.

Most prosecution witnesses belonged to one of three categories. In the first could be found victims, complainants and prosecutors (the same person was frequently all three) who would give evidence of how they had annoyed the alleged witch, the hurt they had subsequently suffered, the witch's general reputation, and frequently, it seems, the outcome of any tests suggested by cunning folk at their behest.

For example, in 1682 Jane Kent, a woman of about 60, was tried for witchcraft at the Old Bailey. It was alleged that she had bewitched five-year-old Elizabeth Chamblet and her mother; the child had died, and the mother fallen very ill. The main prosecution witness was the father/husband. He testified to Kent's "having bargained with him for two pigs, which he refused to deliver her without money". Subsequently, his child had become ill in a very unusual manner: "Swelling all over her Body, which was discoloured after a strange rate". After his wife also fell ill, he went to Dr Hanks, a cunning man in Spitalfields, who advised him to take a quart of his wife's urine, her nail parings, and some of her hair, and boil them. When he did this, he: "Swore he heard the Prisoners voice at his door, and that she Screimed out as if she were Murdered, and that the next day she appeared to be much swelled and bloated".

The second category of witness was made up of those who provided supporting allegations against the defendant, albeit that these had not formed the basis of the indictment. In Kent's case they included: "A Coach-man [who] likewise Swore, that upon his refusing to carry her and her Goods, his Coach overthrew". They, too, could give evidence of the accused person's general reputation in her/his neighbourhood.

The third category constituted those who had been involved in the post-arrest investigation. These might include the examining JP (or his clerk) giving evidence of the magistrate's questioning, and anyone who had been involved in searching the witch for marks, pricking her, etc. Thus, in the case of Jane Kent: "A Woman that searched her likewise Swore, that she had a Teat on her back, and unusual Holes behind her ears".

It was much less common for defendants to call witnesses, although not unheard of, and they could not give sworn testimony until 1706. Even so, not a few accused witches called good character evidence. Jane Kent produced "[e]vidence that she had lived honestly, and was a great pains-taker, and that she went to Church". She was found "not guilty".[16] The following year, at the same forum, Jane Dodson, accused of using witchcraft to lame one Mary Palmer, "called divers Persons appearing to Testifie her Life and Conversation, [and] she was Acquitted".[17] However, a few defendants, such as Joan Peterson in 1652, called witnesses to both fact and reputation, although, in Peterson's case, they were not well received by the Old Bailey. She gave the court a list of witnesses that she wished to call. Some were allowed to testify, saying that they had known her a long time, that she had done much good by curing her neighbours, and that they had never known her to do any harm. Unfortunately, it was claimed that the officers of the court interrupted them in a taunting manner, and even cut some short, asking, "[A]re you for a Witch? And is this all you can say?"[18]

Whether called for the prosecution or defence, early-modern witnesses, including those in witch cases, were not fettered by a rigid hearsay rule of exclusion. Typically, during the trial of the Warboys witches at the Huntingdon Assizes in 1593, unexpected witnesses came forward, offering to testify for the prosecution, who "spake som things of their owne knowledge, and some of the reporte: the first was Robert Poulter vicar

---

16. OBSP, Trial of Jane Kent, 1 June 1682: t16820601a-11.
17. OBSP, Trial of Jane Dodson, 12 July 1683: t16830712-7.
18. Tract 1652 pp. 1–11.

& Curat of Brampton aforesaid, who said openly that one of his parishioners called Iohn Langley, at that instant being very sicke in his bed, had tolde him, that ...".[19] The testimony of the person hurt by a witch "upon his death" (i.e. a deathbed allegation) was considered particularly significant. [20]

Nevertheless, by the closing decades of proscription, the hearsay rule can be seen emerging, albeit primarily going to weight rather than admissibility. It was a criticism of many of the prosecution witnesses in Joan Peterson's case that they could swear only to "generalities, hear-says, and most absurd and ridiculous impertinences".[21]

Inevitably, to modern readers, the fantastic nature of some of the testimony given raises questions as to the sincerity of witnesses. It is perhaps germane in this context to remember the distress and even hysteria that could be caused by a fear of witchcraft. As late as 1726, a newspaper correspondent noted a case from Kent in which an elderly and very unhygienic woman, widely reputed to be a witch, had passed lice on to a well-to-do lady sitting near her on a bench. Once the latter learnt of the source of her infestation she experienced terrible agonies, and became convinced that she was bewitched, feeling pins and needles prick her all over her body. She fainted several times, and thought every louse was an imp. The lady had "screwed her imagination to that extravagant height, that she is now under the operation of a violent fever".[22]

Expert Evidence

Well before 1563, it was accepted that expert testimony might be adduced at common law trials to help a jury understand a matter outside their normal competence. As Sir Edward Saunders, a judge of the Court of Common Pleas, said in 1554, "If matters arise in our law which concern other sciences or faculties we commonly apply for aid of that science or faculty which it concerns".[23] Many such cases involved civil matters, but

---
19. Tract 1593 p. 110.
20. Tract 1645 (1) p. 8.
21. Tract 1652 p. 8.
22. *Weekly Journal, or The British Gazetteer* 18 June 1726.
23. *Buckley v Rice-Thomas* (1554) 1 Plowd 118, at 124.

the principle extended to criminal trials. The highly arcane and recondite nature of witchcraft meant that it was quickly recognised that such expertise could be valuable, both for the prosecution and the defence; however, the power dynamics of early-modern trials meant that it was more common for the former.

In the modern era, a key question for the admissibility of expert evidence is whether the proposed expert is deemed to be *perens* or especially knowledgeable in the relevant field. In witchcraft cases this was difficult to establish, and a variety of physicians and self-identified experts testified on the issue. For example, in a notorious case in 1602, Mary Glover, a 14-year-old girl became ill after a bitter verbal exchange with an old woman named Elizabeth Jackson. At the latter's trial for witchcraft at the Old Bailey, the most significant evidence was the testimony of medical and other experts, given for both sides, on whether the girl's symptoms were supernatural in origin. Edward Jorden (1569–1632), a distinguished physician, argued that Mary was merely suffering from a form of what would now be termed hysteria, which could produce fits and other physical manifestations, something that was occasioned by female biology rather than diabolical influence. (More commonly, at this time, symptoms resembling bewitchment were ascribed to the psychological effects of "melancholy"). Another member of the College of Physicians, John Argent, and an eminent divine, Dr. James Meadowes, supported him. In response the prosecution called two noted physicians, Francis Herring and one Dr Spencer, to testify that Mary's symptoms went beyond any normal female malady and "proceeded of some cause supernaturall".[24]

Unfortunately, Lord Chief Justice Anderson was presiding over the trial, albeit sitting with others on the Old Bailey's collegiate bench. A strong believer in witchcraft, he was quite overt in rebutting Jorden's evidence: "Divines, physicians, I know they are learned and wise, but to say this natural, and tell me neither the cause nor the cure of it — I care not for your judgement".[25] This somewhat humiliating experience prompted Jorden to write a book on female hysteria, *A briefe discourse of*

---

24. MacDonald, *Witchcraft and Hysteria*, pp. xiv–xvi.
25. Maxwell-Stuart, "The New King", p. 43.

a disease called the Suffocation of the Mother ("mother" was an old-fashioned term for the uterus), which was published in 1603. He noted that such naturally occurring manifestations of human biology were often so frightening that even some physicians were "often times deceyued, imagining such manifolde straunge accidents … to proceed from some metaphysicall power".[26]

Defence experts might be called to establish that ill-health allegedly brought about by witchcraft was entirely natural. This was reported with regard to one of Joan Peterson's supposed victims in 1652. Two physicians, Dr Bates and Dr Colledon, together with two surgeons, testified that the dead woman's sickness was a combination of the: "Dropsie, the Scurvey, and the yellow Jaundies, and that they wondred how she was able to live so long, having most of those diseases growing on her for many years before".[27] Peterson was still convicted.

In the case of the two witches accused before Matthew Hale at Bury St Edmunds, in 1662, the prosecution called Sir Thomas Browne (1605–1682), who had been present throughout trial. Browne, a prolific scholar and writer (on a variety of themes), had travelled extensively and studied medicine. His citation of a similar trial in Denmark to suggest that the women were guilty may have influenced the jury. Less eminent experts were called by the prosecution in the case of Margaret Landis, one of four witches tried at the Worcester Assizes in 1647. She was indicted as the result of an incident in which a girl had publicly accused her of witchcraft. Landis had responded to this allegation by telling the child that she would "smart for it". Unfortunately, the child fell sick that night and died three weeks later; as she lay gravely ill, she accused Landis of having bewitched her. Medical testimony was adduced in court to support the girl's charge: the "Child's doctor also deposed that she dyed of a Distemper, which was more than meerly Natural, and that she was

---

26. MacDonald, *Witchcraft and Hysteria*, p. x; Carroll Camden, "The Suffocation of the Mother", *Modern Language Notes*, v. 63, no. 6 (1948), p. 393; Philip C. Almond, "The puritan martyr: The story of Mary Glover". In *Demonic Possession and Exorcism in Early Modern England*, Almond (ed.) (Cambridge: Cambridge University Press, 2004), pp. 287–330.
27. Tract 1652 pp. 1–11.

under the Torture of some Diabolical Agent".[28] Of course, such a diagnosis would absolve the doctor of any allegation of negligence.

Conviction and Execution Rates for Witchcraft

The majority of accused witches were acquitted at trial, while some of the minority who were convicted of capital witchcraft were reprieved or successfully pleaded pregnancy. Conviction followed by execution was by no means a certainty, or even likely. Indeed, Thomas Potts felt that his 1613 publication was necessary to explain why some of the Pendle witches had been acquitted. According to L'Estrange Ewen about half of those who were capitally indicted for witchcraft in England during proscription were executed, although other assessments might place the figure at a somewhat lower level, and it was, in any event, inflated by some of the trials held during Matthew Hopkins' East Anglian campaign. For most years in which witchcraft was a criminal offence the figure was well below half. Of the 258 people indicted at Assizes on the Home Circuit, under the new Elizabethan Witchcraft Act, between 1563 and 1600, 59 (23 per cent) were found guilty.[29] During its peak (ignoring the Civil War), and even after including the effect of post-conviction reprieves, it seems that, in the last six years of Elizabeth's reign and the first four of that of James I, only 41 per cent of those tried on the Home Circuit went to the gallows.[30]

Even at the height of Matthew Hopkins' campaign, when unprecedentedly large numbers of people were accused of witchcraft, a significant proportion were still being acquitted, although there were a few localised exceptions where most of those indicted were executed. For example, in the first wave of trials at Great Yarmouth, in September 1645, eleven people appeared before the town's powerful Quarter Sessions after being accused of witchcraft. Five were acquitted, and six convicted. Of the latter, five were executed but Johanna Lacey was reprieved, at least

---

28. Tract 1670 pp. 2–3.
29. Gaskill, "Witchcraft and Evidence", p. 40.
30. Ewen, *Witch Hunting*, p. 31.

temporarily.[31] Five more people were indicted for witchcraft at the same forum the following April, but all were acquitted.[32]

A conviction and execution rate of 50 per cent would have been about par for Europe as a whole, with some places, such as Scotland and Luxembourg, seeing 80 per cent of those prosecuted being put to death, countries like Poland about 42 per cent, and others far less.[33] For example, only 16 per cent of prosecuted witches in early-modern Finland were executed.[34]

Post-Conviction Reprieves

Throughout the early-modern period, judges could seek a pardon for those convicted before them, including witches. This was usually done because they were concerned about the strength of the case against the alleged witch or, in the closing decades of proscription, because they did not believe in witchcraft.

In these situations, the judge would temporarily reprieve the convicted witch, usually after passing sentence of death on her, and then raise her case in their post-circuit report to the Crown, which would make the final decision (often through the Privy Council). For example, in 1587 Agnes Morris of Stevenage in Hertfordshire was temporarily reprieved from execution after being found guilty of a murder by witchcraft, allegedly committed some four years earlier, as the trial judge thought that the "evidence was weak". This would give the Crown time to consider a pardon.[35]

Sometimes, it seems, a senior local JP might become involved in the reprieve process. In March 1573 a man named Morris was capitally convicted of invoking spirits at the Bury Assizes. He appears to have been temporarily reprieved from execution. Sir Ambrose Jermyn (1511–1577), a Suffolk landowner and JP, wrote to Sir Nicholas Bacon (senior), the Lord Keeper, who hailed from the county, asking for a pardon. He claimed

---
31. NRO Yarmouth Sessions Book Y/S 1/2.
32. NRO Yarmouth Sessions Book Y/S 1/2.
33. Wyporska, *Witchcraft in Early Modern Poland*, p. 23.
34. Gaskill, *Witchcraft: A Very Short Introduction*, pp. 76–77.
35. Cockburn, *Hertfordshire Indictments*, p. 421.

that the guilty verdict was "somewhat too straight [strict] a proceeding in law", and noted that Morris was extremely repentant about his behaviour. Sir Nicholas then wrote to his identically named son, asking whether he had attended the Assizes (as, being a local JP, he should have), and whether the county thought Morris was worthy of death. He also noted that he had heard that Morris was comparatively wealthy, and might be expected to pay for a pardon (still a common practice).[36]

The award of such pardons in witchcraft cases was by no means a rare occurrence, even in the late-sixteenth century. During her reign, Queen Elizabeth I granted at least 36 pardons to people who were convicted under the 1563 Act.[37] Pardons continued to be issued during the Interregnum, albeit not in the name of the monarch. For example, in March 1653 the House of Commons resolved that Johan Price, who had been found guilty of being a witch, should be pardoned because the evidence in the case was doubtful. They also resolved that Mary Heckington, who had also been convicted of witchcraft, should be pardoned (the reasons were not enunciated). The Clerk of the Commonwealth in Chancery prepared such pardons, which were issued under the Great Seal of England.[38]

Although temporary reprieves normally turned into permanent clemency, this was not quite invariably the case. A very rare (if oblique) exception is the case of Thomasine Short, who was tried for capital witchcraft under the 1563 Act at the County of Exeter Quarter Sessions in 1581. It was alleged that in September 1580 she had threatened the family members of a local weaver, several of whom had subsequently died. Short was accused of murdering them by witchcraft and committed to prison by the mayor in his capacity as an *ex officio* justice for the city. The sessions' grand jury returned all three allegations against her as true bills. The prosecution called 12 witnesses at trial, and the petty jury convicted. Short was sentenced to hang. However, perhaps nervous of passing a death sentence at such a forum, the bills were also marked

---

36. David L. Jones, *The Ipswich Witch* (Stroud: The History Press, 2015), pp. 75–76.
37. Kesselring, *Pardon and Punish*, p. 105.
38. Anon, *Journal of the House of Commons: Volume 7, 1651–1660* (London: HMSO, 1802), pp. 265–266.

reprehensa sine judicio (re-imprisoned without judgment). Even so, it is clear that no reprieve was granted, as Short was subsequently executed.[39]

A very few witches were even able to benefit from general pardons granted to all convicted felons to mark national events, such as a coronation, provided that they did not exclude witchcraft from their terms (as was usually the case with serious felonies by the Tudor era). In 1607 a woman was capitally convicted of witchcraft at the Rye Borough Sessions. Her indictment was based on the then recent witchcraft statute of 1604, which made it a felony to "consult covenant with … feede or rewarde any evill and wicked Spirit to or for any intent or purpose". It was alleged that she had done this to find treasure. She was duly sentenced to death, which was unusual in a case that did not involve damage to persons or goods. Even so, the sentence was not carried out; she was kept in prison, and eventually released under a general pardon in 1611.[40]

In practice, trial judges did not have an entirely unfettered discretion to recommend pardons: they had to consider the likely popular reaction. This, in part, explains the execution of the three Bideford witches convicted before Sir Thomas Raymond in 1682, certainly the penultimate (and possibly the final) such hangings to take place in England, and surprising even at the time, given their scale. In a letter to Sir Leoline Jenkins, the Secretary of State, sent from Exeter in August that year, Sir Francis North considered the implications of a pardon. He noted that there was great popular animosity towards the women. Although he accepted that the "virtuosi" might think they were suffering from the effects of melancholy and delusion, the consequences of mercy might be severe, as "wee cannot repreive them without appearing to denye the very being of witches, which, as it is contrary to law, so I think it would be ill for his Majesties service, for it may give the faction [later to be known as the Whigs] occasion to set afoot the old trade of witchfinding that may cost many innocent persons their lives."[41] He was also concerned that a pardon might lead to local disorder because of the level of popular zeal over the case.

---

39. Stoyle, "'Olde Wytche Gonne'", p. 144.
40. Gregory, "Witchcraft, Politics", p. 37.
41. Paul Q. Karkeek, "Devonshire Witches", *Transactions of the Devonshire Association*, v. 6, part 2 (1874), pp. 736–763.

Crimen Exceptum

Pregnancy

Women (i.e. most witches) who had been capitally convicted, whether for witchcraft or any other felony, might escape execution (at least in the short-term) by "pleading their bellies" (claiming to be pregnant). If found to be "quick with child", they would be given a temporary reprieve and held in custody until they gave birth or could be shown to have pleaded falsely. Any claim to pregnancy would be determined by a "jury of matrons", made up of 12 older females with personal experience of childbirth, who would conduct an intimate examination, in private, in the same way that smaller groups of women might search for the witch's mark or teat prior to, or at, trial.[42] Such a claim could be made as of right. At the Huntingdon Assizes in 1593, considerable public amusement was occasioned after Alice Samuel, a convicted witch of almost 80-years-of-age, insisted on pleading pregnancy. However ludicrous, this was seen as an entitlement, even though it swiftly produced a negative result. Her daughter and co-defendant, Agnes, had more self-respect. When she was asked whether she had anything to say before judgment was passed; another prisoner, standing nearby, urged her to say she was with child, but she refused: "Nay, said she, that will I not do: It shall never be said, that I was both a Witch and a whore".[43]

Claims of pregnancy were slightly elastic; tacit encouragement might be given to the jury of matrons to find a woman "quick with child" where the court was reluctant to see death imposed. Where a record of the determination of this issue on the Home Circuit survives, it appears that five women in witchcraft cases were found to be pregnant, and two not pregnant, suggesting that, as in other types of felony, the benefit of the doubt was normally given to the defendant.[44]

After giving birth, or proving not to be with child, the convict's sentence would, in theory, be carried out. Thus, Agnes Crockford, from Chertsey in Surrey, was hanged in 1575 for murdering a six-year-old child by witchcraft, her sentence having been postponed for a year after

---

42. William Blackstone, *Commentaries on the Laws of England*: Vol. IV (Oxford: Clarendon Press, 1769), p. 388.
43. Tract 1593 p. 112.
44. Ewen, *Star Chamber*, pp. 104–105, p. 132 and p. 174.

conviction due to suspected pregnancy. However, it seems that a considerable proportion of women in this situation were permanently reprieved or quietly released after a year or so in prison.[45]

For example, a Kentish witch, Alice Daye, was sentenced at the Dartford Assizes in March 1574 to hang for murdering three people by witchcraft in her home village of Boxley. She was reprieved when the jury of matrons found her to be pregnant. It appears that the original sentence of death was never carried out, and that she was released fairly speedily from custody, as her name comes up again at the Summer Assizes of 1578, held in Maidstone, accused of killing two heifers and making one John Collins ill by witchcraft (both then non-capital forms of the crime). Unfortunately for Daye, Collins died shortly after her conviction for making him ill. She was kept in prison, and retried for capital murder by witchcraft at the Lent Assizes in 1579; this time she was convicted and sentenced to death.[46]

Execution of Witches

Capitally convicted English witches were normally hanged, like other felons; they were not burned. A witch would be executed by burning only if she had killed her master or husband using witchcraft, making it petty treason. Burning was the penalty for this crime, whether the killing was committed by witchcraft or a conventional means. In these situations, after about 1660 the condemned woman was often first strangled with ropes and a pulley.

A rare example of this disposal being used for witchcraft can be seen in the execution of a Suffolk witch, Mother Lakeland, who was burned at Ipswich on 9 September 1645. Amongst her "victims" had been her spouse, who died after a lingering illness supposedly induced by her familiars, for which she was "condemned to die, and in particular to be burned to death, because she was the death of her husband".[47] She was burnt with the aid of pitch barrels, at a cost of £3 3s 6d (three times that

---

45. J.M. Beattie, *Crime and the Courts in England 1660–1800* (Oxford: Clarendon Press, 1986), p. 431.
46. Cockburn (ed.), *Kent Indictments*, p. 127, p. 158 and p. 161.
47. Tract 1645 (1) p. 8.

of a normal hanging).[48] Mary Oliver, who killed her husband using witchcraft was, it seems, also executed in this manner at Norwich in 1559.[49]

The normal lack of differentiation between execution for witchcraft and that for other felonies troubled some observers. Brian Darcy, a witch-hunting JP in Elizabethan Essex thought that witches deserved a death "much the more horrible" than that meted out to ordinary felons.[50]

Despite the rarity of witch burnings, the belief that this was normal practice appears to have been well-established in England, even at the time. The reasons are not totally clear. It may have been a folk memory of the traditional punishment for all forms of heresy, or an awareness of foreign, especially Scottish, practice in this regard. Reports of witch trials from north of the border made popular reading in England. Nevertheless, even James VI (and I) stressed that the actual manner of executing witches was not important: "It is commonly used by fire, but that is an indifferent thing to be used in every cuntrie, according to the Law or custome thereof".[51]

Execution would usually be carried out quickly after a guilty verdict if the judge did not decide to temporarily reprieve the convict. In an extreme case, the three Essex witches convicted at Chelmsford in July 1589 were returned to prison for just two hours before being conducted to the place of execution.

In early-modern England, an essential part of public hanging was the ritual and ceremony that accompanied executions. Pressure from attendant clerics played a major role in producing certain forms of approved behaviour at the gallows. The execution of Mary Smith, hanged for witchcraft in Norfolk in 1618, provides an illustration: she asked for a psalm to be sung and confessed openly at the place of execution, in front of the "multitudes of people gathered together (as is usual at such times) to be beholders of her death".[52] However, contrition was not universal. In 1612 Jennet Preston died "impenitent and void of all feare or grace". In 1653 Anne Bodenham, demanded beer from houses on the route to

---

48. Gaskill, *Witchfinders*, p. 177.
49. G. K. Blyth, *The Norwich Guide and Directory* (London: R. Hastings, 1842), p. 34.
50. Rosen, *Witchcraft in England*, p. 106.
51. James VI, *Daemonologie In Forme of a Dialogue*, Edinburgh, 1597, p. 77.
52. Roberts, *Treatise*, p. 60.

the gallows, becoming truculent on those occasions when it was refused. Her conduct continued to be scandalous at the place of execution. She tried to jump off the scaffold prematurely, so as to break her neck and avoid the normal slow strangulation, and then refused to confess in public, holding that she was "wronged and abused". When the executioner placed the noose round her neck he begged forgiveness, as was customary, to which she snapped, "Forgive thee? A pox on thee, turn me off".[53]

Executed witches would often be buried in unconsecrated ground, especially if unrepentant, and were frequently interred in unmarked graves, sometimes dug near or under the gallows. However, this was not quite invariably the case; a few, such as Thomasine Shorte, ended up in local graveyards. After being hanged as a witch in 1581 she was buried in the churchyard of St Sidwell's parish in Exeter.[54]

---

53. Tract 1653 (1) p. 8; Gaskill, "Witchcraft, Politics", p. 301.
54. Stoyle, "'Olde Wytche Gonne'", p. 144.

Crimen Exceptum

CHAPTER 9

Late-Jacobean and Caroline Prosecutions

Introduction

By the time King James came south in 1603, his enthusiasm for witch-hunting was probably already on the turn.[1] His attitude towards such prosecutions gradually softened further in the decade after his arrival in England, where he was exposed to an Anglican religious establishment whose upper ranks were, by then, sometimes less than enthusiastic about pursuing witches. Although the King still formally adhered to his earlier ideas about witchcraft, he became much more sceptical about its manifestation in specific cases, and assiduous about exposing fraud, sometimes even becoming personally involved in the latter process. Looking back a few years, the Reverend Thomas Fuller (1608–1661), a prolific author and church historian, was convinced, albeit with some exaggeration, that the frequency of fraudulent cases that the monarch encountered: "… wrought such an alteration upon the judgement of King James that he, receding from what he had written in his *Daemonologie*, grew first diffident of, and then flatly to deny the workings of witches and devils, as but falsehoods and delusions".[2] It has even been suggested that, by the time he had been in England for over a decade, deer-hunting was of more interest to him than witch-hunting,

---

1. Jenny Wormald, *Court, Kirk, and Community: Scotland 1470–1625* (London: Edward Arnold, 1981), pp. 168–169.
2. P.G. Maxwell-Stuart, "King James's Experience Of Witches, And The 1604 English Witchcraft Act", 2008, p. 45.

although many of his subjects may not have appreciated this, given his earlier concern and interest.[3]

A Turning Point

A turning point in witch prosecutions seems to have occurred in 1616. In July of that year, nine of a group of 15 alleged witches from Husbands Bosworth, a small village not far from Leicester, were convicted at the Assizes, and then executed, for bewitching (but not killing) John Smith, the young grandson of Erasmus Smith, Lord of the Manor of Bosworth. The boy had fallen into a series of very violent fits, during which he made strange noises and beat himself. He also provided extensive details on the alleged witches' familiars; bizarrely (but not uniquely), one of them was a fish. Sometimes the noises he made in his fits were those appropriate to the animal familiars allegedly attacking him. John's juvenile testimony was crucial at trial, although largely unsupported. The other six women were sent to prison to await their hearings at the following Lent Assizes.

By chance, about a month after the initial trials, James I visited Leicester, during a royal progress. Although the King remained there for only one night, he became aware of the six witches awaiting their hearings, and found time to examine John Smith. He quickly became suspicious or, in the words of the essayist Francis Osborne, "discovered a Fallacy" in the case. The King sent the boy to Archbishop Abbot for further investigation at Lambeth Palace, where he eventually confessed to trickery. Abbot then sent him back to the King, before whom he made a clean breast of his imposture. A royal pardon was issued to the surviving witches who were still in custody. In a letter that October, Robert Heyrick observed to his brother, Sir William, that the "under-sherive, by a warrant directed to the highe-sherive, hathe set the 5 witches at liberty; the sixth is ded in the gayle".

The reputations of the two judges associated with the Leicester cases, Justice Humphrey Winch (1545–1625), a judge of the Court of Common Pleas, and Serjeant Ranulph Crew, were badly damaged. Ben Jonson

---

3. Gaskill, *Witchfinders*, p. 31.

openly mocked them in a satirical comedy based on the trials.[4] They fell into a degree of judicial disfavour, which was even termed "disgrace", for their conduct, although not enough to be removed from the bench.[5] However, they were effectively reprimanded.[6] This was important. The judges and serjeants-at-law who sat at Assizes regularly met while presiding over, or appearing at, the main common law courts in Westminster Hall. Furthermore, the dozen or so full-time members of the judiciary periodically met at Serjeants Inn to discuss complicated questions of law that had been reserved by lower courts for their consideration.

In these circumstances, it would quickly have been understood that the level of credulity manifest by Winch during this trial was not to be repeated. This new level of caution on the part of judicial authorities was compounded by several other well-publicised cases of fraud. That these lessons had been learnt became apparent over ensuing years, as can be seen in the "Bilston boy" case of 1620, and that involving Edward Fairfax's daughters in 1622.

In the spring of 1620, in Bilston, Staffordshire, 13-year-old William Perry, the son of a local yeoman, refused to go to church and began having fits and vomiting bent pins, straw, thread, and bits of rag. William told his parents that Jane Clarke, an elderly neighbour who already had a bad reputation, had bewitched him. She was summoned to the boy's bedside, her presence prompting another fit. Clarke was taken into custody and then brought before the Assizes. However, the judges were cautious about the matter, and turned the boy over to Bishop Morton, who was present, for further investigation. The bishop, assisted by his secretary, set out to test William, their suspicions being aroused when he failed to recognise St John's gospel—the recitation of which in English had induced fits—in the original Greek. (The devil would have had no problem with a classical language). He was secretly watched, and the careful preparations for his deceptions eventually exposed. He was then persuaded to admit that he was a cheat in court, in front of Sir Peter

---

4. G. L. Kittredge, "King James I and 'The Devil Is an Ass'", *Modern Philology*, v. 9, no. 2 (1911), p. 201.
5. J. S. Cockburn, *A History of English Assizes, 1558–1714* (Cambridge: Cambridge University Press, 1972), p. 120; Edward Foss, *Biographica Juridica* (Boston: Little, Brown, 1870), p. 748.
6. Gaskill, "Witchcraft and Evidence", p. 43.

Warburton and Sir Humphrey Winch (the judge who had sat on the 1616 case), and to beg the forgiveness of Clarke.[7]

Another indication of a new climate of judicial scepticism can be seen in the handling of a witch case at the York Assizes in August 1622. The prominent northern gentleman Edward Fairfax accused six women of bewitching his daughters and the daughter of a neighbour named Jeffrays. When the matter came for trial the children took turns at falling into trances; they were physically carried out of the court. However, several judges and JPs then made some fairly blunt "experiments to prove if they counterfeited or not". As a result, the case was dismissed, on the grounds that it "reached not to the point of the statute". Jeffray's daughter was eventually persuaded by her parents to admit to dissembling. It was suggested that Fairfax's daughters may have been influenced by this girl.[8]

Caroline Prosecutions

There was a further marked decline in the number of witchcraft trials after about the middle of the 1620s. It has been argued that witchcraft almost went into "hibernation" during the pre-Civil War reign of Charles I (1625–1642). This is a slight exaggeration; allegations continued to be made and to come to court. On one analysis, from 1628 to 1637 there were eleven prosecutions for witchcraft on the Home Circuit alone; four in Kent, five in Essex, and two in Surrey, albeit that none of them produced an execution.[9] On the same circuit, during the 1630s, just 13 women were indicted for witchcraft; of whom only four were convicted but then reprieved.[10]

Although it has been suggested that Jane Wiggins was capitally convicted for witchcraft at the Chelmsford Assizes in 1634, and probably hanged, this is by no means certain. Undoubtedly, Wiggins had a bad reputation in her hometown of Harwich, allegedly even sinking a ship at sea because its master had refused her request for free fish. She seems to have been accused before the Borough Court there in 1633 for the

---

7. Notestein, *History of Witchcraft*, pp. 141–142.
8. *Ibid.*, p. 145.
9. Gaskill, "Witchcraft Trials", p. 293.
10. Gaskill, "Witchcraft and Evidence", p. 46.

mischief occasioned ashore by her "imps" (familiars), some of which were similar to rats "with great staring eyes", others like black birds but about the "bignes of two penny chikins". It was claimed that they killed and injured both humans and horses.[11] However, the evidence for any ensuing conviction and execution at Assizes is unclear, and would be unusual for Essex at this time.[12]

Nationally, a handful of alleged witches were still convicted and executed during this period. For example records in Sandwich, a Cinque Port with power of gaol delivery independent of Assizes (and its professional judges) mention that in 1631 Goodwife Reynold was hanged after being swum as a witch. However, Charles I was personally sceptical of witchcraft. Furthermore, in the politically very strained environment leading to the Civil War, the King was not minded to support disproportionately Puritan preoccupations, such as witch prosecutions.

The monarch intervened to prevent a witch panic that broke out near Pendle in 1634 from following the path of its local predecessor just over two decades earlier. In this case, Edmund Robinson, an eleven-year-old boy who lived in Pendle Forest with his father of the same name, claimed to have encountered two greyhounds on All Saints' Day which he tried to set on a hare. When they failed to run, he beat them, and the dogs turned into one Mother Dickinson (a local woman) and a small boy. The former tried to buy his silence for a shilling, and, when he refused to take the money, turned the little boy into a white horse, which she used to take Robinson to a large witches' Sabbath that was being held in a barn. He eventually managed to escape, albeit hotly pursued, and later reported the matter to a pair of rather gullible local JPs. The boy and his father appear to have been paid for identifying further witches, and Mother Dickinson and 17 others from nearby parishes were arrested and thrown into gaol. At the subsequent Lancashire Assizes in March 1634, 17 were convicted. It was reported to the court in London that, along with this "huge pack of witches", at least 60 others had been identified, with more being reported every day.[13]

---

11. Peter C. Brown, *Essex Witches* (Stroud: The History Press, 2014), pp. 106–107.
12. I am grateful for a communication from Alison Rowlands on this issue.
13. John Bruce (ed.), *Calendar of State Papers Domestic: Charles I, 1634–5*, 1864, pp. 23–48.

However, judicial attitudes had changed since 1612, and the presiding judge was less credulous (or more career conscious) than the jurors and JPs thus far involved in the case. He granted a temporary reprieve to the accused, who were remanded in custody, so that the matter could be referred for further investigation. Four of the supposed witches were sent to London, where seven court physicians, including the eminent William Harvey, and ten midwives, examined their bodies for signs of the witch's mark.[14] After deciding that the matter was fraudulent, the King pardoned all the accused, although by then three had died in prison. In the meantime, Dr John Bridgemans, the Bishop of Chester, had also conducted an inquiry into the case, separating the boy from his father, lodging him on his own, and questioning him closely. Eventually, the youth confessed that he had fabricated the whole story, with paternal encouragement and assistance.[15]

In July 1634 George Long, a Middlesex JP, formally examined Edmund Robinson Sr, the alleged instigator of the case, at the behest of Francis Windebank, the Secretary of State. Although Robinson had a major motive to conceal his role in the affair, he revealed some of its dynamics. He claimed that at first he had strongly discouraged his son from reporting the matter to the authorities. However, the boy continued to maintain the truth of what had occurred, leading his father to assume that he had indeed seen something. Robinson stressed that he had not personally prosecuted the suspects but had received a warrant to bring his son before two JPs, who then bound him over to produce the boy at the next Assizes. He further claimed that, when he went there, the grand jury and several other people expressly told him to prefer an indictment against Frances Dickinson for bewitching his son, but that he initially refused, not least because he had previously had an amicable relationship with her, and thought Frances and her husband to be harmless people.[16]

By the 1630s many members of the judiciary were probably quite doubtful about witchcraft, while those who were not were aware of the likely professional consequences of excessive enthusiasm. Another

---

14. Malcolm Gaskill, "Witchcraft Trials in England", 2013, p. 293.
15. Montague Summers, *A Popular History of Witchcraft*, 1937, pp. 294–295.
16. John Bruce (ed.), *Calendar of State Papers Domestic: Charles I, 1634–1635*, (London: HMSO, 1864), p. 141.

indication of this new level of judicial concern, if not outright hostility, towards such prosecutions occurred in March 1636, at the Chard Assizes in Somerset. Lord Chief Justice Finch assigned four experienced junior barristers and an attorney to act for a poor widow, Elizabeth Stiles, who had been acquitted on a charge of witchcraft. Her free counsel would have enabled her to bring a civil action for malicious prosecution against Nicholas Hobbes and the other complainants in the case.[17] This would most likely have had a major deterrent effect on such prosecutions.[18]

The climate of royal, religious, legal, and medical opinion meant that, by the end of the decade, it might have been thought that witch prosecutions were slowly dying a natural death. However, and very significantly, it is apparent that there was still a popular demand "from below" for action. In 1630, 33 people from Reigate in Surrey unsuccessfully prosecuted a suspected witch for murdering a local child.[19] This helps explain why the descent into civil war after 1640 (conflict broke out in 1642) would see a rapid re-engagement with the phenomenon, particularly in East Anglia, the heartland of the Parliamentarian (and Puritan) cause.

---

17. J.S. Cockburn (ed.), *Western Circuit Assize Orders 1629–1648: A Calendar* (London: Royal Historical Society, 1976), p. 99.
18. Andrew Pickering, *The Witches of Selwood Forest: Witchcraft and Demonism in the West of England 1625–1700* (Newcastle: Cambridge Scholars, 2017), p. 77.
19. Gaskill, "Witchcraft and Evidence", p. 46.

Crimen Exceptum

CHAPTER 10

The Civil War and Interregnum

Introduction

The campaign against witches in Essex and East Anglia during the 1640s was the nearest England came to a full-scale "craze", despite its coming out of a background of near *de facto* abolition of executions for witchcraft. It involved more than 250 arrests in seven counties and 100 hangings, possibly many more.[1] A number of factors contributed to this sudden upsurge, but two in particular are worthy of note.

As a very general (but European-wide) rule, the further a witch was tried from the place where he or she had been accused, the more likely he or she was to be acquitted. The influence of local passions and persons abated with distance. In those early-modern states, such as the duchies of Bavaria and Wurttemberg or the kingdoms of France and Spain, that enjoyed a well-centralised judicial apparatus, jurists were more likely to look down on the "superstitious" accusations that emanated from villages as a product of ignorance, and were more willing to resist their demands for witch prosecutions and convictions. By contrast, the closer they were to the local conflicts that prompted such allegations, and the village elders who brought them, as was the case in the prince-bishoprics of Augsburg, Bamberg, Trier, and Cologne, and in the Channel Islands (with their singular local legal systems), the more likely they were to share the beliefs of commoners and to countenance official charges of

---
1. Monter, "Re-contextualizing", p. 108.

witchcraft.[2] Many of the most intense witch-hunts in Europe occurred in tiny legal jurisdictions, where achieving such distance was impossible.

For example, Guernsey had no more than 8,000 inhabitants in its 64 square kilometres of land during the late-sixteenth century; even so, between 1563 and 1649, some 103 people (76 of them women) were accused of witchcraft before its Royal Court. These hearings produced 50 executions and 26 banishments (for a period of several years to life). Jersey was only slightly better. In the sixteenth century, its ten parishes and 118 square kilometres had a population of more than 10,000 people. Even so, 65 witch trials (57 involving women) came before its Royal Court between the 1560s and 1660s; although several ended at the indictment stage, 33 led to execution, and another eight people were sentenced to perpetual banishment.[3]

In the years between 1651 and 1655, Bermuda, the smallest and most isolated of England's colonies, with a total area of just 21 square miles, and a multi-racial population of about 3,000 people, saw five people hanged for witchcraft, and many others investigated. Although these were the only executions for the crime in the history of the colony, there are records of eight more witchcraft cases over the remainder of the seventeenth century; they produced one guilty verdict, in 1671, but the governor pardoned the convicted witch.[4] Even in Scotland, it seems that a frequently decentralised judicial system, encouraging local determination, contributed to the high incidence of executions.[5]

Furthermore, and again as a very general rule, the less professional the judges involved in a witch trial, the more likely it was that convictions and executions would ensue. The experience of Sweden from 1668 to 1676 shows that even a country with generally low levels of prosecution might suffer an intense craze if anxiety was high and judicial restraint weak.[6] Thus, in the Bermuda witch trials, the court was presided over by

---

2. Erik Midelfort, "Witch Craze?: Beyond the Legends of Panic," *Magic, Ritual and Witchcraft*, v. 6, no. 1 (2011), p. 15.
3. Darryl Ogier, "Glimpses of the Obscure: the witch trials of the Channel Islands". In *The Extraordinary and the Everyday in Early Modern England*, Angela McShane and Garthine Walker (eds.) (Basingstoke: Palgrave Macmillan, 2010), pp. 177–191.
4. Bernhard, "Religion, Politics", p. 706.
5. Larner, "Witch Beliefs", pp. 32–36.
6. Gaskill, "Witchcraft and Evidence", p. 35.

the governor and members of his council. Its secretary was clerk of the Assizes and responsible for keeping the register book of all verdicts and judgments as well as delivering them to the sheriff (which role he also filled) to execute. None had any significant legal training.[7]

Both these phenomena, localism and amateurism, were present in Civil War East Anglia, at least to some extent. Indeed, they were closely linked, because they arose from the temporary loss of the normal Assize system. Although held fairly locally (at specific towns in each county), the Assizes were centrally staffed courts, presided over by the relatively urbane, worldly, professional, highly experienced Westminster judges, who often had relatively few local connections on their Circuits. Such men had normally absorbed a cautious approach to witch-hunting during the 1630s.

In the run-up to the conflict, between the summers of 1641 and 1642, most Assize circuits lost one of their two judges to impeachment for sanctioning the Personal Rule of Charles I. As a result, in July 1642 Justice Thomas Malet (1582–1665), who had been called to the Bar by Middle Temple in 1606, and had strong royalist sympathies, rode the Home Circuit alone. At Chelmsford in Essex he presided over the trial of an alleged witch who was duly acquitted (as had been common practice over the previous decade). However, he was sent to the Tower of London shortly afterwards, and remained there for two years. In the autumn of the same year, war broke out, and in July 1643 the normal schedule of Assizes was suspended. Instead, commissions of gaol delivery were issued by Parliament for those areas where it held sway, on an ad hoc basis, including one for Essex that was authorised in June 1645.[8] The ecclesiastical courts ceased to operate altogether, depriving complainants of an alternative and less draconian forum to address their concerns about witchcraft.

The breakdown in the proper functioning of the normal English system of local government and law enforcement contributed greatly to the unprecedented extent of the East Anglian witch campaign. As a result, when 23 women were accused of witchcraft and tried at Chelmsford in 1645, their hearings were conducted not by Assize judges but by local JPs

---

7. Bernhard, "Religion, Politics", p. 694.
8. Gaskill, "Witchcraft and Evidence", pp. 33–70.

presided over by Edward Montagu (1602–1671), the Earl of Manchester; he had been an influential Parliamentarian, but had almost no formal legal training and no more experience of such matters than any other county magistrate. The effect on convictions and executions was dramatic.

Such hearings lasted until 1646. In February that year, Parliament ordered Assize judges to return to their normal circuits. However, this order did not come into force until June. As a result, the witches tried at the Huntingdon Assizes in May still had their cases heard before a bench of JPs (sitting with a jury) rather than before professional judges.[9] This meant that local, often Puritan, gentlemen presided over capital witch trials (with a jury), although prior to the Civil War they would rarely have determined cases more serious than petty larceny, even if they had been JPs during that decade (often not the case).

Nevertheless, although the number of witch prosecutions, convictions, and executions in East Anglia was extraordinary, the cases themselves were not. They were remarkably similar to those of the previous 80 years, with many of the same allegations being made, albeit with a slightly greater emphasis on diabolism.

Matthew Hopkins and John Stearne

Like several other major European witch-hunts, the East Anglian campaign of 1644–1647 involved itinerant witch-finders who claimed expertise in the identification of suspects. Teams of witch-finders had fuelled France's largest witch panic from 1643 to 1645, prompting at least 650 arrests in Languedoc alone, before royal authorities caught those involved and sent them to the galleys or the gallows.[10] Matthew Hopkins and John Stearne, along with their male and female associates, played a vital role in the panic in East Anglia.

Hopkins was the younger son of a Suffolk clergyman of Puritan leanings. He shared his father's theology, but was not, in that sense, an extremist (probably less so than Stearne); furthermore, he did not take an overt position in the struggle between King and Parliament. Hopkins

---

9. Gaskill, *Witchfinders*, p. 225.
10. Monter, "Re-contextualizing", p. 110.

had a modest inheritance, but serious prospects in the church or law appeared closed to him, not least because he had not been to one of the ancient universities or enrolled at an Inn of Court. Nevertheless, he seems to have been engaged in some form of low-level legal work in his adopted town of Manningtree when his witch-hunting began. There he had also made the acquaintanceship of his future partner, John Stearne, a man some ten years older than the youthful Hopkins, who would be dead at 27.

Hopkins later claimed that his interest in witches developed after he discovered that he lived close to where a coven met every six weeks.[11] He became actively involved when a Manningtree tailor, John Rivet, consulted a wise woman about his wife's apparently strange illness, and she implicated 80-year-old Elizabeth Clarke. Clarke (whose mother had been hanged as a witch) was stripped, searched, and pricked by Hopkins and his colleagues, and found to have three witch's teats. She eventually made extensive admissions, identifying many others as witches. Ultimately, Hopkins questioned more than 100 people. Some 23 were accused of witchcraft at Chelmsford in July 1645, and 19 convicted and condemned to death (several others had died in prison in the meantime), some being hanged in the town and others elsewhere in the county.

After news of the success of the Chelmsford trials spread, Hopkins became sought after as a witch-finding expert. As a result, a wave of witchcraft accusations spread from Essex into neighbouring Suffolk.[12] It seems that Hopkins and Stearne divided the latter county, roughly along the route of the road between Ipswich and Norwich, Stearne taking the area to the west and Hopkins that to the east (he reached Dunwich), so as to cover more territory. Several assistants and female searchers, such as Priscilla Briggs, accompanied them.[13] By the end of 1645, magistrates, constables, accusers, and jailors were working with the witch-finders to produce fairly swift and efficient prosecutions and trials for witchcraft. By the autumn of 1646, Hopkins and Stearne had taken their campaign

---

11. Matthew Hopkins, *The Discovery of Witches* (London, 1647), p. 1.
12. Garland, "Great Witch Hunt", pp. 1152–1180.
13. Gaskill, *Witchfinders*, pp. 80–81.

beyond Essex and Suffolk and into some of the other nearby counties, such as Norfolk.

However, the quite unprecedented nature of the campaign, not least its very large number of executions, rapidly occasioned concern. John Gaule, a Puritan minister from Great Staughton in Huntingdonshire, preached openly against Hopkins and started collecting evidence of his allegedly abusive methods of investigation and interrogation. He eventually went into print on the subject. Just as significantly, the authorities became alarmed. A number of queries regarding Hopkins' techniques were presented at the Norfolk Assizes to judges who questioned both Hopkins and Stearne about their alleged use of torture and the remuneration that they claimed for their work. Conviction rates fell as caution started to re-emerge. A second wave of prosecutions at Great Yarmouth produced not guilty verdicts for all accused, and Hopkins may not even have been paid for his services on this occasion. By late-1646 a Parliamentary newspaper, *The Moderate Intelligencer*, had also begun to question the witch-finders' methods, while Parliament itself took notice of their activities. A special commission was appointed to monitor them. Furthermore, the considerable financial cost of holding witches in gaol prior to their hearings was also occasioning concern, especially after it was passed on to the communities identifying them.[14]

Hopkins was eventually forced into print, writing *The Discovery of Witches*, to deal with some of the criticisms in a systematic manner. Noting the changing climate, he retired to Manningtree, where he died of tuberculosis in August 1647. A few months later John Stearne also went home, and the East Anglian campaign petered out. Even so, a year later, in his own literary effort, *A Confirmation and Discovery of Witchcraft*, Stearne stressed that Hopkins had died without any regrets for what had occurred.

Despite his *soi-disant* title of Witchfinder-General, it is important to note that Hopkins had no official position, clerical or legal. He constantly liaised with local JPs and borough magistrates, and fed the witches he identified into the ordinary criminal justice system. Even more important,

---

14. *Ibid.*, p. 163.

and like his French counterparts from a couple of years earlier, he was usually invited into East Anglian communities to find witches. The towns and villages involved voluntarily paid him (or promised to pay him) for his services, very generously, but not absurdly so, given his retinue, which included three horses, assistants, and need for good accommodation (he viewed himself as a minor gentleman). Although Hopkins only admitted to receiving 20 shillings a town, he was paid £6 by Aldeburgh and as much as £23 by Stowmarket. Nevertheless, not many years after the campaign, Stearne was in considerable financial difficulties, suggesting that he had not made vast sums from the enterprise.

Where Hopkins sensed or was told (sometimes after specific inquiry) that he would not be welcome, he usually kept away. For example, in a letter to a Huntingdonshire JP he asked whether the magistrate's town would be willing to afford his group "good welcome and entertainment, as other where I have been, else I shall wave your Shire (not as yet beginning in any part of it myself) and betake to such places, where I doe, and may persist without controle, but with Thanks and Recompense". Indicative of this, an entry in the Great Yarmouth Assembly Book from August 1645 notes that it was agreed that "Mr Hopkins imployed in the countie for discovering & finding out of witches shall be sent for hither to come to Towne; to make search for such wicked p[er]sons if any be here". Similarly, the following May, the King's Lynn Hall Book records that one Alderman Revitt was requested to "sende for Mr. Hopkins the witch discoverer to come to Lynne and his charges & Recompence to be borne by the Towne". The Chamberlain's account book for the town contains entries for expenses to cover the cost of sending messengers to Hopkins and also an order that he be paid £15.[15]

Many people appear to have actively welcomed the willingness of Hopkins and his associates to deal with their long-rumoured and often strongly resented local witches. Once the witch-finders arrived in a community, they voluntarily brought forward suspects from amongst their neighbours for testing. Hopkins did not normally have to search for them; he acted as a catalyst for their active prosecution, although the

---

15. NRO KLBA, KL/C39/102 and KL/C 7/10.

indictment of the Reverend John Lowes, in which Hopkins and Stearne went around Brandeston encouraging witnesses to come forward, was something of an exception. They were convinced that the clergyman was "naught but a foul witch".

Subsequent Campaigns

The collapse of the East Anglian witch-hunt in 1647 did not spell the end of what might be described as the Civil War upsurge in such prosecutions, which increased generally from the very low level of the 1630s. Two further intense, if very much more limited, campaigns would occur, in the North and Southeast of the country, in 1649 and 1652, respectively.

Newcastle and Northumberland

In March 1649, the inhabitants of Newcastle petitioned the city's common council, asking that those suspected of witchcraft should be apprehended and brought to trial.[16] Ralph Gardner later noted that, in response, Newcastle-upon-Tyne's magistrates (with whom he was then at loggerheads) had sent Thomas Shevil and Cuthbert Nicholson, two of the city's serjeants, north of the border to invite an unnamed but skilled Scottish witch-finder and pricker to their city, offering 20 shillings for each witch he identified. This may have been the same man summoned for a similar service by Berwick-upon-Tweed that same month.[17] It is possible that it was John Kincaid, a famous Scottish witch-pricker who was active in his native country in 1649. For example, records disclose a payment of 20 marks by Dunfermline parish to Kincaid that year, after he came and "tried the witch mark on Bessie Mortoun". He was also paid £6 Scots for similar work in Burntcastle.[18] (George Cathie has also been mentioned as a possible candidate).[19]

---

16. Eneas Mackenzie, *Historical Account of Newcastle-Upon-Tyne Including the Borough of Gateshead* (Newcastle-upon-Tyne: Mackenzie and Dent, 1827), pp. 23–46.
17. Maureen Anderson, *Executions and Hangings in Newcastle and Morpeth* (Barnsley: Wharncliffe, 2005), p. 44.
18. MacDonald, "Torture", p. 104.
19. I am grateful for communications from Julian Goodare and Peter Maxwell-Stuart on this topic.

In Newcastle, a bellman paraded through the town, asking local people to bring the pricker any suspected witches for testing. Thirty women were brought to the Town Hall by their neighbours, and partially stripped for examination. Some 27 were initially identified as witches, after being stuck with pins and bodkins, although it seems that the physical circumstances in which the test was administered were very conducive to positive results and may have included blatant trickery. Many of these people were set down for trial at the forthcoming Assizes. In the meantime the witch finder went into County Durham and Northumberland to continue his work, this time receiving up to £3 for each witch identified. Fortunately Henry Ogle (1600–1669), a former MP and a county JP, eventually intervened and had the Scotsman bound over to appear at sessions, prompting him to flee home with his earnings. Without such action it was feared that he "would have made most of the women in the North, witches, for money". Allegedly (it has not been substantiated in any form), the witch-finder was ultimately prosecuted in Scotland for his activities in that country, convicted, and executed, begging forgiveness and claiming at the gallows to have hanged 220 witches north and south of the border for financial gain.

Nevertheless, in 1650 at least 15 of the witches he had identified in Newcastle (all but Matthew Bulmer being women) were produced from gaol, convicted at the Assizes in the city, and executed on Town Moor, despite resolutely refusing to confess to anything; several others were tried but acquitted. One woman, Margaret Brown, apparently begged God to give some sign of her innocence and, at her execution, Gardiner recorded that as soon as she was turned off the ladder "her blood gushed out upon the people to the admiration of the beholders". Gardner did not question the trial or punishment itself, but asked by what law the magistrates of Newcastle could send for a foreign "mercenary" to establish that some of the town's women were witches, have a bellman call for them to be brought forward, and give the former 20 shillings apiece to condemn them. It is not known how much of the witch-finder's pre-trial testing was revealed to the trial jury to become evidence in the case, but the conviction level suggests that it must have been very substantial.[20]

The use of a Scottish witch-pricker at this time is unsurprising. A major witch-hunt raged in the Lowlands in 1649 and 1650, producing several hundred executions and, undoubtedly, a number of self-proclaimed experts. It might also be expected that the anxieties that underlay such activity would have something of a ripple effect, and might even cross the border. Indeed, it has been observed that the Northern campaign, along with those in East Anglia and Kent (before and afterwards), almost give the impression that Scottish-type witch-hunting had entered England for a short period.[21]

Kent

The third and final major Civil War/Interregnum witch-hunt took place in Kent in 1652; as a result, 18 people, including (unusually) six men, were sent to the Maidstone Assizes for trial. Of these, some 16 were indicted (two cases being thrown out by the grand jury), and all but two of the remaining 14 were convicted after trial before Sir Peter Warburton, one of the Justices of Common Pleas (a Civil War appointment).[22] The events in East Anglia five years earlier, and those in the North in 1650, may have influenced what occurred in Kent. However, the cases did not flow from a single event, or from the same area, and varied considerably in nature. For example, eight of the accused came from Cranbrook and another four from the rather isolated Isle of Grain in the north of the county. Thomas Wilson and his wife, labourers from the island, apparently confessed to the non-capital offence of ruining 33 quarters of wheat belonging to a farmer and bewitching sheep.[23] They were sentenced to the standard year in prison. However, at least six others were hanged for murder by bewitchment.

---

20. Gardiner, *England's Grievance*, pp. 169–171.
21. Brian P. Levack, *Witch-hunting in Scotland: Law, Politics and Religion* (London: Routledge, 2007), pp. 69–71.
22. Tract 1652 (2) p. 4.
23. Zell, *Early Modern Kent*, pp. 245–247.

Other Regions

No other parts of England produced anything comparable to the witch-hunts in Northumberland and Kent, let alone East Anglia, during the Civil War and early-Interregnum. Nevertheless, in several other places the number of convictions and executions for witchcraft picked up significantly from the tiny figures seen in the 1630s. For example, in Middlesex, no capital conviction has been preserved for the years from 1625 until October 1650. During this period, seven people were prosecuted for witchcraft and six acquitted, while one suspect's indictment was found *ignoramus* by the grand jury. However, in the autumn of 1650 Joan Allen was convicted and hanged. Joan Paterson followed in April 1652, and Elizabeth Newman at the end of 1653, after which capital convictions petered out again.[24]

Late-Interregnum

After the Kent trials, something closer to the pre-war pattern of witch prosecution gradually resumed throughout England. Indeed, the level of concern occasioned by witchcraft appears to have declined markedly, and fairly swiftly. Laurence Price's farcical and scatological chapbook, *The Witch of the Woodlands,* published in 1655, proved very popular, and was reissued regularly throughout the rest of the seventeenth century.[25] Many of the witch cases that were brought to trial resulted in acquittals. Thus, in September 1657, a true bill was found against Katherine Evans, a widow from Fulham in Middlesex, who was believed to be a "common witch" for bewitching an infant so that "his body was wasted pined and consumed". Even so, she was found not guilty at the Old Bailey.[26] Just a handful of people, such as Judith Sawkins in Kent, were convicted and executed for witchcraft in England during the mid-to-late-1650s.

---

24. Ewen, *Demonism,* p. 434.
25. Davies, *Witchcraft and the Book Trade,* p. 175.
26. Jeaffreson, *Middlesex County Records,* pp. 256–268.

Crimen Exceptum

CHAPTER 11

From the Restoration to Abolition

Introduction

By the end of the middle third of the seventeenth century, a critical mass of political leaders and judges throughout Western Europe, including England, had lost their belief in the prevalence and threat posed by malefic witchcraft. Even more important, whatever their views on its reality, they had become concerned about the practicality of identifying witches in specific cases in a forensic environment.[1] This, combined with the start of a very slow retreat from the notion of confessional states and enforced religious orthodoxy, as well as a generally reduced level of religious "enthusiasm", began to turn opinion against witchcraft as a prosecutable crime.[2]

At the same time, some of the harsh economic conditions of the late-sixteenth and early-seventeenth centuries, which may have created an environment that was conducive to witch-hunting, began to ease. More generally, Professor Elmer has suggested, after the Restoration of 1660, witchcraft swiftly became a more politicised issue than it had been before the war; it became caught up in emerging party politics, with nonconformists more likely to retain a belief in it than the well-educated and influential men found at the highest levels of the established church. This confessional divide even appears to have extended, to some degree, beyond clergymen to senior physicians. By the late-seventeenth and

---
1. Bever, "Witchcraft Prosecutions", pp. 263–264.
2. Gaskill, "Pursuit of Reality", p. 1077.

early-eighteenth centuries, ruling elites in England were ignoring the claims of witch-hunters and demonologists.[3]

As a result, the Restoration did not merely continue the late Interregnum pattern of witch trials, but brought about a return to the status quo ante. Nevertheless, as in the 1630s, witch trials continued on an occasional basis, albeit in rapidly declining numbers. They had greatly increased in Kent during the Civil War: there were 45 cases (most in the late-1640s and early-1650s) from 1640 to 1659, but only 15 from 1660 to 1679, and ten in the final 20 years of the seventeenth century.[4] Similarly, of the 35 people indicted in Yorkshire for witchcraft in the second half of the seventeenth century, a majority were prosecuted in the 1650s, prior to the Restoration, and all but four were charged before 1675.[5]

However, there was also considerable regional variation in the incidence of prosecutions after 1660. In some parts they lingered into the 1690s and beyond; in others they largely petered out in the 1670s. This appears to have been the case in the City of London and Middlesex. Only two cases can be identified at their shared Old Bailey Court after 1680, though the loss of records means that one or two more may have been missed.

In 1682 Jane Kent, a 60-year old woman, was indicted and acquitted for bewitching a child to death.[6] The last trial for witchcraft at the Old Bailey appears to have occurred in 1683, when the elderly Jane Dodson was accused of using "divers Hellish Arts and Inchantations" to lame one Mary Palmer and, if one witness is to be believed, kill another person. However, because no evidence was given as to what means she used to carry out this crime, and in light of her apparent good character, she was acquitted.[7]

Even so, Dodson's case was not the last (serious) allegation of witchcraft to be made at the Old Bailey, merely the last to be indicted. In 1699 Mary Poole, a gypsy from St Giles-in-the-Fields, was prosecuted for stealing more than £7 from Richard Walburton, who lived near Lincolns Inn

---

3. Elmer, *Witchcraft, Witch-Hunting*, pp. 12–13.
4. Pollock, "Social and Economic", p. 38.
5. Barbour-Mercer, *Prosecution And Process*, p. 135.
6. OBSP, Trial of Jane Kent, 1 June 1682: t16820601a-11.
7. OBSP, Trial of Jane Dodson, 12 July 1683: t16830712-7.

From the Restoration to Abolition

Fields. She had pretended to have a magical (i.e., cunning woman) ability to find buried treasure while taking the opportunity to steal from him. Poole had a history of such crimes. However, one of the prosecution witnesses was convinced that she genuinely had occult powers. He claimed that some seven years earlier he had been riding between Gravesend and Rochester when he met the defendant, gave her a cut with his whip for impertinence, and rode on. He had not gone 40 yards when his horse fell, and she overtook him, so that "he thought she was a witch, and had bewitched him and his Horse". Poole was convicted of the theft.[8]

Throughout England a handful of witches were not merely prosecuted but convicted and hanged in the quarter-century after the Restoration. For example, in September 1660, what may have been the last execution for witchcraft on the Home Circuit took place, when Joan Neville was convicted at the Surrey Assizes held in Kingston-on-Thames and (probably) hanged, although 40 or so more people would be tried for some form of the crime in the ensuing decades. Three years later, Julian Cox (a woman) followed her to the gallows after being found guilty at the Somerset Assizes (on the Western Circuit) of bewitching a servant maid who had refused her alms.[9]

The conviction and execution of two women in a well-reported case from 1662, at the Bury St Edmunds Assizes (on the Norfolk Circuit), probably played a major role in helping to prevent the de facto end to witchcraft trials in the immediate Restoration period. In part this was because it was presided over by Matthew Hale, a prestigious and influential judge; he was slightly unusual amongst the senior judiciary of the time in having a strong belief in both the reality of witchcraft and the possibility of proving it in a satisfactory manner.[10] It is possible that had Hale taken an overtly sceptical approach to the evidence in this case, the tiny number of women who died for the crime over the next two decades might have avoided their fates. Certainly, Serjeant John Kelynge, Hale's fellow Assize judge, who appears to have been present in court (he may

---

8. OBSP, Trial of Mary Poole, 13 December 1699: t16991213a-2.
9. Pickering, *Witches of Selwood*, pp. 58–59.
10. Matthew Hale, *A Collection of Modern Relations of Matter of Fact, Concerning Witches & Witchcraft upon the Persons of People*, London, 1693, pp. 1–4.

have sat on the *nisi prius* civil cases earlier), was unsatisfied with the evidence and thought that it was "not sufficient to convict the prisoners".[11]

In August 1674 the elderly Ann Foster was executed at Northampton, after being indicted for employing her "malice and witchcraft" to set fire to barns and corn and to kill sheep belonging to Joseph Weeden, a local grazier. Learning that Weeden had slaughtered a sheep for his family, Foster appeared at his door asking for some of the meat. Weeden refused her request, and Ann left muttering threats. A few days later, Weeden found 30 of his sheep dead in their pasture. A few weeks after this, his house and barns caught fire.[12] Arson, however caused, was always considered a very grave crime, an attitude that would have told heavily against Foster.

In April 1675 Mary Baguley from Wildboarclough, in Cheshire, was indicted for using witchcraft to kill a married schoolmaster named Robert Hall in nearby Wincle. It was claimed that she had caused him to sicken for ten days, while sweating and spitting blood, and, although absent from the deathbed, had eventually "crushed his heart in pieces". Baguley was convicted at Chester, sentenced to death, and hanged.[13]

Alice Molland (or Wellend) was, it is claimed, the last witch executed in England and Wales, having been convicted at the Devon Assizes held at Exeter in March 1685. Few details have been preserved of her trial and execution, the latter of which has sometimes been doubted. This is unlike the fate of the three Bideford witches hanged in the same place in 1682, who were the last to go to the gallows in England whose deaths can be verified.[14] Theirs was an unusual case, not least because of the number of convicts at such a late time. Sir Thomas Raymond, a judge of the King's Bench, who presided at the Exeter Assizes, was in a difficult position, as the three women not only looked the part, they had made extensive out-of-court admissions when questioned by a JP and then (largely) repeated them in court. Temperance Floyd, the eldest of the three (and alleged ringleader), admitted the accusation, acknowledged that she had

---

11. Tract 1682 (4) p. 16.
12. Tract 1674 p. 2.
13. C. L'Estrange Ewen (ed.), *Witch Hunting and Witch Trials* (London: Kegan Paul, Trench, Trubner, 1929), p. 43; Garthine Walker, *Crime, Gender and Social Order in Early Modern England* (Cambridge: Cambridge University Press, 2003), p. 85.
14. Carole Levin et al., *A Biographical Encyclopedia of Early Modern Englishwomen: Exemplary Lives and Memorable Acts, 1500–1650* (London: Routledge, 2016), pp. 334–335.

been in league with the devil for more 20 years, and conceded that she had "afflicted both Man and Beast". This included sinking ships at sea with the loss of many sailors' lives. (She was not indicted for this crime). The other two were slightly more "pensive" and circumspect in their testimony, but still admitted that they had spent five years as apprentices in witchcraft to Temperance, and carried out many acts of *maleficium*.[15] Short of the judge persuading the jury that they were deranged (very possibly the case), so that their admissions were not to be believed, convictions were always likely, while his failure to reprieve the three from execution has been explained elsewhere in this book.

The Final Fifty Years

The death penalty had not been imposed for witchcraft for more than half a century when the 1604 legislation was finally repealed in 1736. Even so, the 1604 statute was periodically invoked until the 1720s, albeit at a steadily declining rate. However, no-one was convicted after 1712, or reached court after 1717, despite popular (rather than elite) belief in witchcraft remaining strong. In the 31 years between 1686 and 1717, more than 20 people (most of them women) were prosecuted for witchcraft but had their cases thrown out by the grand jury or received an acquittal from the petty jury after trial. For example, Mary Hanson was acquitted of witchcraft at the York Assizes in 1691. On a larger scale, and hinting at something of a panic, the Kent Assizes record that, in 1692, three women were unsuccessfully tried for witchcraft. It was indicative of changing times that a report of this case, published in the *Athenian Gazette* early the following year, noted that the allegations had met with a degree of open disbelief in some quarters. (Ironically, the same edition of this journal contained an advertisement for Cotton Mather's account of the Salem witch trials, which had also taken place in 1692, and which had had a very different outcome.)[16]

At the Bury Assizes in 1694, a resident of Hartest known as old Mother (Philippa) Munnings was accused of witchcraft but acquitted because

---

15. Tract 1682 (2) p. 6.
16. *Athenian Gazette*, 28 February 1693.

the evidence against her was deemed too thin. It was alleged that several local people, when on their deathbeds, had blamed her for their medical conditions, and that she was also suspected of bewitching cattle. Furthermore, she had apparently threatened her landlord, who died shortly afterwards, and it was claimed that she had been seen in her Suffolk cottage with familiars, including one that appeared as a polecat. That Lord Chief Justice Holt, the presiding judge at her trial, was a noted sceptic undoubtedly assisted Munnings' defence (none of his eleven witchcraft trials resulted in a conviction). It was one of two such cases heard in Suffolk that year.[17] In 1695 Mary Guy was also tried before Chief Justice Holt at Launceston Castle in Cornwall (he had moved circuit in the meantime) for bewitching another woman who, allegedly, vomited pins, straws, and feathers. Again, Holt steered the trial jury to an acquittal.

In 1696 Elizabeth Horner was indicted and acquitted of witchcraft before the same judge in Devonshire. She had been accused of bewitching three children, one of whom had died, as well as of having a toad familiar and a teat on her shoulder.[18] Details of this trial are preserved in a letter written shortly afterwards by Archdeacon Blackburne to the Bishop of Exeter. The children's parents were the chief prosecution witnesses, reporting the strange ailments of their offspring, including the vomiting of pins and stones. Several other people also testified, including one who reported driving a red-hot nail into the witch's footprint, after which she apparently went lame until the nail was pulled out of the earth. However, in court the alleged witch "denied all" and bared her shoulder, showing that the supposed teat or mark was "nothing but a mole or wart". She also managed to repeat the Lord's Prayer and the Creed accurately, after a little hesitation. Although content with the verdict, Blackburne was slightly troubled by Holt's overt scepticism, noting that he "seemed to believe nothing of witchery".[19] In 1700 Anne Grantley and Margaretta Way were acquitted of a similar crime in Dorset.

However, at least three "witches" were capitally convicted, albeit reprieved, during this period. In March 1687 Sir John Reresby was present

---

17. Hollingsworth, *Stowmarket*, p. 172.
18. Ashton, *Devil in Britain*, p. 294.
19. Barry, "The Passing of the Act", p. 205.

at the York Assizes when Serjeant Powell (a future Lord Chief Justice and another noted sceptic) presided over the trial of an old woman for witchcraft. It seems that this was Isabella Bowling, a widow from Leeds, accused of bewitching a boy named John Ingram, who had languished for some time. She was found guilty, Reresby noting, "Those who were more credulous in Points of this Nature than my self, conceived the Evidence to be very strong against her".[20] Ingram fell down in court when he saw Bowling, and then came to and related the injuries she had done to him. Even so, perceptive observers noted the boy did not foam at the mouth when having fits, which also seemed to leave him in an instant. The clear inference was that they were feigned "so that, upon the whole, the Judge thought it proper to reprieve her; in which he seemed to act the Part of a wise man".[21]

This was probably the last conviction for capital witchcraft secured on the Northern Circuit. However, it was not the last nationally. In 1694, it was reported that Ann Hart, from Sandwich in Kent (a Cinque Port), had been convicted of witchcraft but was able to claim the benefit of a general pardon, so that she went free.[22] Most significantly of all, Jane Wenham was tried and convicted in 1712 (see below).

The 1700s

Witch cases survived well into the eighteenth century. One that originated from Southwark, in Surrey, just south of the River Thames and London, prompted a trial at the county's Assizes in July 1701. A blacksmith's apprentice named Richard Hathaway started to experience regular fits, and was hospitalised for the condition. He may have suffered from epilepsy. One of the attendants suggested that his medical problems might have a non-natural cause. Eventually, he accused Sarah Morduck, a sharp-tongued local fruiterer, of bewitching him, and fabricated evidence against her (even if he genuinely believed her to be guilty). A warrant for her arrest was issued and enforced in April 1701. She was

---

20. Ewen (ed.), *Witchcraft and Demonism*, p. 406.
21. Reresby, *Memoirs*, pp. 237–8.
22. Notestein, *History*, pp. 419–420.

questioned and committed to prison "till such time as it shall appear, what proof can be brought against her". Several examinations relating to the affair, from a variety of potential witnesses, were taken on oath.[23] Hathaway's allegations were viewed sufficiently seriously for Morduck to be tried for capital witchcraft at the Surrey Assizes at Guildford in July 1701, accused of having "bewitched Richard Hathaway, who was wasted, consumed, etc.". (She was tried along with a lunatic who had killed his child and a waterman who had negligently caused his clients to drown). After a lengthy hearing, in which up to eleven men and six women gave evidence against her, she was acquitted, which was an unsurprising verdict by that date.[24]

However, this was not the end of the matter: despite Morduck's legal vindication, she faced the constant threat of popular violence from those who thought her guilty. A London alderman (a de facto magistrate for the Square Mile) refused to protect her from attacks by the mob when she crossed the river into the City. It eventually became necessary to prosecute Hathaway as a person that "pretends to be bewitched" to deter others, an information being laid in October 1701.[25] He was ultimately tried for being a cheat and imposter, and for riot, allegedly committed during the protests against Morduck.[26] The case was presided over by Lord Chief Justice Holt, and Hathaway duly convicted. It appears likely that the prosecution was also aimed at ending such cases on the Home Circuit.

Despite the results of the Hathaway prosecution, a few further cases of capital witchcraft went to trial in the early-1700s; all produced acquittals. It seems that Susanna Hanover was tried at the Devonshire Assizes in 1702, as was Joanna Tanner at the Wiltshire Assizes the following year. Finally, it appears that in 1707 Maria Stevens was tried at the Somerset Assizes.[27] Informed observers may well have thought that this would be the last witch trial in England. However, five years later a case went to trial, and produced a capital conviction for witchcraft, probably the first for almost two decades.

---

23. *London Post*, 23–25 April 1701.
24. Tract 1702 (2) p. 3; *London Post*, 1–4 August 1701.
25. *Post Boy*, 1–4 November 1701.
26. Tract 1702 (1) p. 691.
27. Notestein, *History*, p. 317.

Final Conviction

The trial and conviction of Jane Wenham at the Hertford Assizes in March 1712 went so much against the trend in such matters that it warrants special consideration. The previous month, Jane, an elderly and unpopular widow long suspected in the village of Walkern of being a witch, had confessed to bewitching Anne Thorne and to entering into a pact with the devil some 16 years earlier, just before her husband's death.

Wenham's trial, presided over by Sir John Powell, was such a novelty that a "vast" number of people were present. Several neighbours gave evidence against her, mentioning, inter alia, strange visitations by various cats, including one that had Wenham's face. Powell was openly sceptical throughout the trial, almost sneering at some prosecution witnesses, and treating much of the evidence in a flippant manner. This may well have been counter-productive. The jury deliberated for two hours before finding Wenham guilty. However, Powell granted her a temporary reprieve from the death sentence, and later obtained an unconditional pardon from Queen Anne.

Even so, it quickly became apparent that the popular hostility towards Wenham in Walkern meant that it was not safe for her to return there. Francis Hutchinson later noted that Captain John Plummer gave protection to her in another village, so that she was not "torn to peeces". Jane lived there quietly until 1720, when her benefactor died. She then lived another ten years under the supervision of William Cowper, the first Earl Cowper, dying at the stately age of 90 in 1729, and receiving a well-attended funeral.[28]

The Pamphlet War

Francis Bragge, the vicar of Hitchin, who had taken an active role in the Wenham prosecution, was clearly angered at the decision not to execute Jane, and wrote a pamphlet on the topic. It went into five editions, four of them within a month of the trial, suggesting that there was still a fairly

---

28. Hutchinson, *Historical Essay*, p. 130: *Fog's weekly journal*, 3 January 1730.

substantial literate audience that was sympathetic to such legal actions. Although it was titled *A Full and Impartial Account*, it included a harsh attack on Jane's character, suggesting that even her close relations thought she deserved to die. This work prompted a pamphlet "war" about the case, with at least nine tracts being published, for and against Jane. A riposte to Bragge, condemning the prosecution, was unequivocally titled *The Impossibility of Witchcraft*. Even so, no witchcraft cases appear to have come to court between 1712 and 1717.

Final Prosecution

In 1717 the elderly Jane Clerk and her son and daughter, all from Great Wigston, were prosecuted for witchcraft at the Leicester Assizes. This was the last concerted attempt in England to secure convictions for the crime and, apparently, the last case to end up at Assizes, albeit that it was thrown out by the grand jury there, without going for trial. The accusation against the three defendants involved mysterious illnesses amongst local people, and the alleged vomiting of stones and bees by their victims. All the accused had been subjected to robustly administered traditional witch identification techniques, the results of which appear to have been recounted to the grand jury. Despite a warning at the Wenham trial that it was illegal, the three suspects had also been thrown into water by local villagers, with their fingers and toes bound in approved fashion, where they apparently "swam like a cork, a piece of paper or an empty barrel, though they strove all they could to sink". The two females had also been searched by a group of women, and several apparent teats identified, as well as being repeatedly and forcibly scratched to draw their power. The trio were "so stubborn, that they [investigators] were often forced to call the constable to bring assistance of a number of persons to hold them by force to be blooded". Twenty-five of their neighbours attended court to give evidence against them, albeit to no avail.[29]

---

29. O. Davies, *Witchcraft, Magic*, p. 90; Pickering, *Witch Hunt*, pp. 120–121; R. T. Davies, *Four Centuries*, p. 183; Notestein, *History*, p. 233.

Last Formal Allegations

Even so, this was not the final case of witchcraft to be put before legal authorities; it seems that a handful of cases went in front of JPs during the 1720s, though they were speedily dismissed. For example, in April 1726 there were reports of an old woman from Brent Pelham in Hertfordshire being apprehended as a witch by virtue of a JP's warrant; when she was brought before another magistrate for examination he apparently "acquitted her at first sight", mocking the process by claiming she was too old and plain to be a witch.[30]

Repeal and the 1736 Act

After largely falling into desuetude for a generation, the 1604 Act was repealed in June 1736 (9 Geo., 2, c.5). The Witchcraft Act of that year also repealed the Scottish Act of 1563, the countries having been combined in 1707. The statute decreed: "No Prosecution, Suit or Proceeding, shall be commenced or carried on against any Person or Persons for Witchcraft, Sorcery, Inchantment or Conjuration or for charging another with such an offence, in any Court whatsoever in Great Britain".[31] (In Ireland the 1586 Witchcraft Act would linger on the Statute Book until 1821, although, by then, no cases had been brought for generations). James Erskine, Lord Grange (1679–1754) whose Presbyterian faith and beliefs were founded in the Scottish experience, led the tiny amount of parliamentary opposition to the bill, but was subjected to some ridicule for doing so, Sir Robert Walpole allegedly discounting him as a political threat as a result.

The repealing statute expressly created a new offence aimed at deterring any "Pretences to such Arts or Powers as are before mentioned, wherby ignorant persons are frequently deluded and defrauded". Under its terms anyone claiming magical powers, or "practising" witchcraft, was guilty of acting fraudulently and liable to be imprisoned for one year and to stand in the pillory for an hour every quarter. In effect the law reverted

---
30. *Mist's Weekly Journal*, 30 April 1726.
31. O. Davies, "Spell", pp. 7–13.

to the position reached by the high medieval church: witchcraft was a deception practised by people on the ignorant and gullible rather than a genuine display of power gained through consorting with the devil.

In some respects, this statutory change merely reflected existing practice in several places by the 1730s. For example, in July 1731 a woman was tried at the Middlesex Quarter Sessions at Hicks Hall for defrauding one Mrs Newton of £12 13s on pretence of being a cunning person, capable of procuring three men to fall in love with her. (After a long hearing, the defendant was acquitted).[32]

In England, reaction in the press to the 1736 Act was muted. In the decades after 1736, several Anglican clergymen, a number of them from the West Country, registered disapproval in private conversations and diary entries, but almost none went public with their views.[33] However, some 30 years later, John Wesley, one of the founders of Methodism, would complain that: "The giving up of witchcraft is, in effect, giving up the Bible".

Survival of Popular Witch Beliefs

Repeal of the 1604 statute largely reflected changes in attitudes among the elite and "middling" social orders rather than in the beliefs of ordinary people. In September 1730, just six years before the repeal of laws against witchcraft, a case of witch swimming occurred at Frome in Somerset; a prescient report in the *Daily Journal* suggested that the "old notions of witchcraft are not so nearly extinguish'd as some people imagine, especially in the remote parts of the country".[34] Despite the Enlightenment, various scientific advances, and even the first onset of industrialisation, popular belief in witchcraft remained, and continued to manifest itself in various ways.[35]

---

32. *Grub-street Journal*, 22 July 1731.
33. Monod, *Solomon's Secret Arts*, p. 237.
34. *Daily Journal*, 15 January 1731.
35. O. Davies, "Spell", pp. 7–13.

Post-Repeal Incidents

In November 1736, just a few months after the 1604 Act had been repealed, a dispute broke out in Baildon, a remote West Yorkshire parish, between members of the Goldsbrough and Hartley families, leading to members of the latter being bound over to keep the peace. According to one witness, Mary Hartley claimed that Bridget Goldsbrough had entered her house in the shape of two grey cats.[36] Witchcraft continued to prompt incidents of popular action long after 1736. Witches were illegally swum in Bedfordshire in 1737, Norfolk in 1748, Hertfordshire in 1751, Suffolk in 1752, Leicestershire in 1760, Cambridgeshire in 1769, Essex in 1774, Leicestershire (again) and Suffolk (again) in 1776.[37] Doubtless, far more cases went unrecorded. Many more suspected witches were scratched, pricked or beaten.

For example, in 1762, the wife of John Pritchers of West Langdon in Kent was pulled from her house by a mob and dragged for about a mile along a dirt track. When they reached the home of a 13-year-old boy whom she was supposed to have bewitched, she was pricked in order to find a "devil's spot". The crowd was about to swim her when a local JP intervened. The two ringleaders of the mob were ultimately convicted of assault.[38] Similarly, one evening in July 1776, at Farnham in Suffolk, a poor man suspected of being a wizard was swum in the River Deben in front of a large crowd of people. He immediately "sunk to the bottom and had it not been for the assistance of a humane spectator the experiment would have terminated in a manner shockingly to it's protectors."[39]

The turn of the century did not see the end of such incidents. In 1808 three young women in the village of Great Paxton in Huntingdonshire began to suffer from unexplained convulsions, fits, and bouts of depression.[40] A cunning man appears to have identified Ann Izzard, apparently a "harmless, inoffensive" woman of almost 60, as the source of their misfortunes, which had, it was claimed, been effected via malefic witchcraft.

---

36. WYRO Quarter Sessions Rolls, QS1/76/2/File 3.
37. Montague Summers, *A Popular History of Witchcraft* (New York: E.P. Dutton, 1937), p. 237.
38. *Dover Mercury*, 16 September 2004.
39. *The Ipswich Journal*, 20 July 1776.
40. Simpson, "Witchbusters", p. 5.

Panic spread through the community, both amongst the local poor and some of the area's farmers, who were quickly persuaded of Ann's malign status. One Sunday evening in May a crowd broke into the cottage where she lived with her husband. Ann was dragged from bed, near naked, and pulled into the yard, where a mob of men and women beat her in the face and stomach with a club. Others scratched her arms to draw blood, and so break her powers.[41] The crowd subsequently dispersed, but the following evening Ann was attacked again, and it was reported that she was to be swum. Prudently, she fled to a neighbouring village and brought legal proceedings through local magistrates. A year later nine villagers were found guilty at the county Assizes of assaulting the couple. Even so, the attackers would not accept that their behaviour was wrong, despite the judge's suggesting that their behaviour was primarily motivated by personal malice.[42]

The last recorded swimming of a wizard in Suffolk appears to have occurred as late as July 1825. Several villagers from Wickham Skeith blamed a 67-year-old man named Isaac Stebbings for their ailments after a farmer paid a local cunning man to identify the source of their maladies. Stebbings was swum in a large pond, albeit with his agreement. Hundreds of people from the area attended, the parish constable keeping them in order, and another man of similar size to Stebbings being used as a "control". Clergymen from the area eventually intervened to prevent any recurrence.[43]

Another, more tragic, example can be identified in Essex as late as 1863. An 80-year-old deaf-mute known as "Dummy", who was locally reputed to be a witch or, at least, a cunning man, made a modest income in Sible Hedingham from reading fortunes and advising young people on their romances. (He was able to communicate). He lived in a wattle and daub hut in the village. One day he went to nearby Ridgewell and drank in a tavern there. The evening drawing on, he asked to spend the night at the establishment. The wife of the patron, one Emma Smith,

---

41. *The Ipswich Journal*, 28 May 1808.
42. Stephen Mitchell, "A case of witchcraft assault in early nineteenth-century England as ostensive action". In *Witchcraft Continued: Popular Magic in Modern Europe*, Willem de Blécourt and Owen Davies (eds.) (Manchester: Manchester University Press, 2004), pp. 1–28.
43. *The Times*, 19 July 1825.

refused to allow this, and Dummy became annoyed, apparently making what were deemed to be threatening gestures, and striking his stick on the ground before leaving. Emma became ill shortly afterwards. In a late illustration of the "charity-refused" model, she became convinced that Dummy had bewitched her.

Some ten months later, still not properly recovered, Smith, together with a man named Stammers, found herself in *The Swan* tavern, along with Dummy and up to 50 other people. Smith appears to have been keen to appease her alleged tormentor. She begged him to sleep in her house, so as to remove the curse, and even offered him three gold sovereigns to do so. Dummy refused, as he thought his life would be in danger if he went with her. At closing time, appreciating that she was getting nowhere, and encouraged by the presence of a crowd of up to 80 people, Smith threatened and then struck the old man with a stick and dragged him to a nearby brook, where she and Stammers pushed him into the water. He was subsequently pulled out, but spent the night in wet clothes in his hut before being taken to a workhouse, where he swiftly died of pneumonia, despite medical attention.[44]

Both Smith and Stammers were prosecuted at the behest of a public-spirited gentleman from Sible Hedingham. Although witnesses to the events were reluctant to give evidence against the pair, a jury "immediately" convicted them of manslaughter at the Chelmsford Assizes. They were sentenced to six months' imprisonment with hard labour. The modest punishment apparently reflected the genuineness of Smith's belief, and Stammers' having pulled the old man out of the stream. The rector of Sible Hedingham subsequently wrote to *The Times* to say that many people in the parish regarded what had occurred with horror.[45]

In another incident that was indicative of surviving attitudes, in 1857 a troubled yeoman farmer even sought a magistrate's warrant to have a suspected witch swum, unaware that this would be impossible. It became apparent to the astonished JP that many of the farmer's fellow villagers shared his opinion of the woman concerned. He felt that for a "more

44. *The Newcastle Courant etc.*, 18 March 1864.
45. *Bury and Norwich Post*, 22 March 1864.

radical cure [to such attitudes] we must look to education".[46] Arguably, this came in the form of the Elementary Education Act 1870 that established compulsory schooling for all children between the ages of five and 12, and which dealt a huge blow to such beliefs.

---

46. *The Times*, 7 April 1857.

CHAPTER 12

Conclusion

The vast majority of prosecuted felonies in early-modern England—murder, rape and theft, etc.—are still considered serious crimes. With very occasional exceptions, such as the cruentation test that was used to see whether a victim's body would bleed in the presence of their murderer and sometimes employed in early-modern homicide cases, the means used to prove such crimes—eyewitness testimony, confessions, circumstantial evidence—would be readily recognisable in the modern era. Present-day lawyers might be concerned at the speed of proceedings and the lack of institutional safeguards, but would rarely find the fact-finding process illogical. Witchcraft was a glaring exception. Those found guilty of the crime were convicted of something that (modern observers would think) could not have occurred, sometimes using methods of proof that were palpably valueless, if not downright absurd.

It is, perhaps, slightly reassuring that, compared to some parts of continental Europe and Scotland, this occurred on relatively few occasions in England, albeit much more frequently than it did in Ireland or even Wales. Most of those executed for witchcraft had either been enormously unlucky or had foolishly courted attention, sometimes both. Thousands of English women and men were, at some point in their lives, labelled as, or rumoured to be, witches, at least to some degree, without being formally accused. The vast majority of those who *were* reported to a JP could expect to escape death, and most even to avoid trial, as many hurdles had to be overcome by complainants and prosecutors before a rope was put around a suspected witch's neck.

Crimen Exceptum

At numerous stages in the prosecution process, a formally reported witch might be diverted away from the gallows. This might be done by an examining JP's dismissing the case against her; a prosecutor failing to appear at trial; a grand jury failing to find a true bill against her; a petty jury failing to convict (for a capital form of the crime); a reprieve being granted to a convicted witch, or such a person being found to be pregnant.

However, the bad luck that led to the gallows did not strike at random. The concatenation of circumstances that put people at risk can readily be identified. Such diverse factors as time and place—Essex in the 1590s was totally different from Sussex in the 1690s—gender, social class, personal appearance, the behaviour of the suspect, and the presence of believers in witchcraft amongst JPs on the local commission of the peace and the judges presiding over the Assizes all played a significant role in the trial outcome. Even so, the majority of those most at risk *still* escaped the gallows.

The active pursuit of witches was the product of a very limited period of time, little more than a century, and reflected a unique combination of religious, social, economic, cultural, and intellectual circumstances. It would have puzzled Englishmen at the start of the Tudor era, just as it did their successors at the beginning of the Georgian period. By the middle of the 1700s it appeared quite bizarre to educated men looking back just a few decades.

There were many reasons for this change, but one explanation can be found in the greatly increased degree of professionalisation found in the country's criminal-justice system by the eighteenth century, and the higher level of professionalism present amongst its legal personnel. It became progressively harder to "prove" a delusion. John Cotta was mistaken in believing that witchcraft could be established without recourse to special procedural, evidential and investigative techniques.[1] When witchcraft ceased to be *crimen exceptum*, it ceased to be a viable crime of any description.

---

1. Cotta, *The Triall of Witch-Craft*, p. 21.

Select Bibliography

Citations for Contemporary Tracts

1566 (1), Anon, *The Examination and Confession of Certain Witches at Chelmsford in the County of Essex, before the Queen's Majesty's Judges, the XXVI Day of July Anno 1566.* London.

1566 (2), Anon, *The examination of John Walsh before Maister Thomas Williams, commissary to the Reuerend father in God William bishop of Excetter, upon certayne Interrogatories touchyng Wytchcrafte and Sorcerye.* London.

1579 (1), Richard Galis, *A brief treatise containing the most strange and horrible cruelty of Elizabeth Stile alias Rockingham and her confederates, executed at Abingdon.* London.

1579 (2), Anon, *A Rehearsall both straung and true, of hainous and horrible actes committed by Elizabeth Stile alias Rockingham, Mother Dutten, Mother Deuell, Mother Margaret, Fower notorious witches, apprehended at winsore in the countie of Barks. and at Abbington arraigned, condemned, and executed, on the 26 daye of Februarie laste 1579.* London.

1582, Anon, *A true and just Recorde, of the Information, Examination and Confession of all the Witches, taken at S. Oses in the countie of Essex: whereof some were executed, and other some entreated according to the determination of lawe.* London.

1591, Anon, *Newes from Scotland, Declaring the Damnable Life of Doctor Fian a notable Sorcerer.* London.

1593, Anon, *The most strange and admirable discouerie of the three Witches Of Warboys.* London.

1599, Samuel Harsnett, *A Discovery of the Fraudulent practises of John Darrel.* London.

1603, Stephen Bradwell, *Marie Glovers late woefull case, together with her joyfull deliverance written upon occasion of Doctor Jordens discourse of the Mother.* Reproduced in Rosen, Barbara (ed.) (1972) *Witchcraft in England 1558–1618.* New York: Taplinger.

1619, Anon, *The Wonderful Discoverie of the Witchcrafts of Margaret and Phillip Flower, daughters of Joan Flower neere Beuer Castle: Executed at Lincolne, March 11, 1618.* London.

1621 (1), Edward Fairfax, *Daemonologia: A Discourse on Witchcraft as it was Acted in the Family of Mr. Edward Fairfax of Fuyston in the County of York, in the year 1621.* London.

1621 (2), Henry Goodcole, *The Wonderfull Discoverie of Elizabeth Sawyer a Witch, late of Edmonton.* London.

1643, Anon, *A Most Certain, Strange, and true Discovery of a Witch.* London.

1645 (1), Anon, *The lawes against witches, and conjuration And Some brief Notes and Observations for the Discovery of Witches.* London.

1645 (2), Anon, *A True and Exact Relation Of the severall informations, Examinations, and Confessions of the Late Witches, arraigned and executed in the County of Essex. Who were arraigned and condemned at the late Sessions, Holden at Chelmesford Before the Right Honourable Robert, Earle of Warwicke, and severall of his Majesties Justices of Peace, the 29 of July, 1645.* London.

1645 (3), Anon, *The Examination, Confession, Triall, and execution, of Joane Williford, Joan Cariden and Jane Hott: who were executed at Feversham, in Kent, for being Witches, on Munday the 29 of September, 1645.* London.

1652 (1), Anon, *The Witch of Wapping. Or, An exact and Perfect Relation, of the Life and Devilish Practises of Joan Peterson, that dwelt in Spruce Island, near Wapping.* London.

1652 (2), E. G., *A Prodigious & Tragicall History of the Arraignment, Tryall, Confession, and Condemnation of six Witches at Maidstone, in Kent, at the Assizes there held in July, Fryday 30, this present year, 1652.* London.

1652 (3) Anon, *A declaration in answer to several lying pamphlets concerning the witch of Wapping being a more perfect relation of the arraignment, condemnation, and suffering of Jone Peterson, who was put to death on Munday the 22 of April, 1652. Shewing the bloudy plot and wicked conspiracy of one Abraham Vandenbernde, Thomas Crompton, Thomas Collet, and others.* London.

1653 (1), James Bower, *Doctor Lamb's Darling: Or, Strange and terrible News from Salisbury; being a true, exact, and perfect Relation, of the great and wonderful Contract and Engagement made between the Devil, and Mistris Anne Bodenham.* London.

1670, Anon, *The Full Tryals, Examination and Condemnation of Four Notorious Witches, at the Assizes held at Worcester, on Tuesday the 4th March.* London.

1674, Anon, *The Full and True Relation of the Tryal, Condemnation, and Execution of Ann Foster.* London.

Select Bibliography

1682 (1), Anon, *A True and impartial relation of the informations against three witches, viz., Temperance Lloyd, Mary Trembles, and Susanna Edwards.* London.

1682 (2) Anon, *The tryal, condemnation, and execution of three witches viz. Temperace [sic] Floyd, Mary Floyd, and Susanna Edwards. Who were arraigned at Exeter on the 18th. of August, 1682.* London.

1682 (3), Anon, *An Account of the Tryal and Examination of Joan Buts, For being a Common Witch and Inchantress, before the Right Honourable Sir Francis Pemberton, Lord Chief Justice, at the Assizes holden for the Burrough of Southwark and County of Surrey, on Monday, March 27. 1682.* London.

1682 (4), Anon, *A Tryal of Witches, at the Assizes held at Bury St. Edmond's, for the County of Suffolk, on the tenth day of March 1664. Taken by a Person then attending the Court.* London.

1685, Anon, *The Strange News from Shadwell, Being a True and Just Relation of the Death of Alice Fowler, who had for many years been accounted a witch; together with the manner how she was found dead with both her great toes ty'd together, and laid out on the floor having a blanket flung over her.* London.

1689, Anon, *Great News from the West of England. Being a True Account of Two Young Persons Lately Bewitch'd in the Town of Beckenton in Somerset-shire.* London.

1702 (1), Anon, *A short Account of the Trial held at Surrey Assizes; in the Borough of Southwark: on an Information, against Richard Hathaway...for a Riot and Assault*, from *Cobbett's State Trials*, 1812.

1702 (2), Anon, *The Tryal of Richard Hathaway, Upon an Information For being a Cheat and Impostor, For endeavouring to take away The Life of Sarah Morduck, for being a Witch, at Surry Assizes, Begun and held in the Burrough of Southwark, March the 24th, 1702.* London.

1704, Thomas Greenwell, *A full and true account of the discovering, apprehending and taking of a notorious witch, who was carried before Justice Bateman in Well-Close, on Sunday, July the 23. Together with her examination and commitment to Bridewel,* London

1712 (1), J. Boys, *The Case of Witchcraft at Coggeshall Essex, in the year 1699.* London.

1712 (2), Anon, *A Full Confutation of Witchcraft: More particularly of the Depositions Against Jane Wenham, Lately Condemned for a Witch; at Hertford....In a Letter from a Physician in Hertfordshire, to his Friend in London.* London.

1736, Joseph Juxon, *A sermon upon witchcraft. Occasion'd by a late illegal attempt to discover witches by swimming. Preach'd at Twyford, in the county of Leicester, July 11, 1736.* London.

Bibliography

Ady, Thomas (1656) *A Candle in the Dark: Or, a Treatise Concerning the Nature of Witches And Witchcraft: Being Advice to Judges, Sheriffes, Justices Of The Peace And Grand Jury-men, what to do, before they passe Sentence on such as are Arraigned for their Lives, as Witches.* London.

Ady, Thomas (1661) *A Perfect Discovery of Witches. Shewing The Divine Cause of the Distractions of this Kingdome, and also of the Christian World.* London.

Alm, Torbjørn (2003) "The Witch Trials of Finnmark, Northern Norway, during the 17th Century: Evidence for Ergotism as a Contributing Factor". *Economic Botany*, vol. 57, no. 3, pp. 403–416.

Almond, Philip C. (2004) "The puritan martyr: The story of Mary Glover", in Almond (ed.). *Demonic Possession and Exorcism in Early Modern England: Contemporary Texts and their Cultural Contexts*, Cambridge: Cambridge University Press, pp. 287–330 .

Anderson, Maureen (2005) *Executions and Hangings in Newcastle and Morpeth.* Barnsley: Wharncliffe.

Anon (1599) *The Triall of Maist. Dorell.* London.

Anon (William Drage) (1665) *Daimonomageia: A Small Treatise of Sicknesses and Diseases from Witchcraft, and Supernatural Causes.* London: J. Dover.

Anon (1802) *Journal of the House of Commons: Volume 7, 1651–1660.* London: His Majesty's Stationery Office.

Anon (1892) *The Manuscripts of Rye and Hereford Corporations, Etc. Thirteenth Report, Appendix: Part IV.* London: Historical Manuscripts Commission.

Apps, Lara and Gow, Andrew (2003) *Male Witches in Early Modern Europe.* Manchester: Manchester University Press.

Ashton, John (1896) *The Devil in Britain and America.* London: Ward and Downey.

Bailey, Michael D. (2001) "From Sorcery to Witchcraft: Clerical Conceptions of Magic in the Later Middle Ages". *Speculum*, v. 76, no. 4, pp. 960–990.

Bailey, Michael D. (2006) *Magic and Superstition in Europe: A Concise History from Antiquity to the Present.* Lanham: Rowman & Littlefield.

Baker, J.H. (1977) "Criminal Courts and Procedure in England". In J.S. Cockburn (ed.), *Crime in England 1550–1800.* London: Methuen.

Barbour-Mercer, Sarah Anne (1988) *Prosecution And Process: Crime And The Criminal Law In Late Seventeenth-Century Yorkshire*. Ph.D. thesis, University of York.

Barry, Jonathan et al. (eds.) (1996) *Witchcraft in Early Modern Europe*. Cambridge: Cambridge University Press.

Barry, Jonathan (2008) "The Passing of the Act: The Politics of *Pandaemonium*". In John Newton and Jo Bath (eds.), *Witchcraft and the Act of 1604*. Leiden: Brill, pp. 181–206.

Barry, Jonathan (2012) *Witchcraft and Demonology in South-West England, 1640–1789*. Basingstoke: Palgrave Macmillan.

Bartlett, Robert (1986) *Trial by Fire and Water: The Medieval Judicial Ordeal*. Oxford: Clarendon Press.

Baxter, Richard (1691) *The Certainty of the Worlds of Spirits*. London: T. Parkhurst.

Beattie, J.M. (1986) *Crime and the Courts in England 1660–1800*. Oxford: Clarendon Press.

Behringer, Wolfgang (1999) "Climatic Change and Witch-hunting: The Impact of the Little Ice Age on Mentalities". *Climatic Change*, v. 43, no. 1, pp. 335–351.

Bellamy, John (1973) *Crime and Public Order in England in the Later Middle Ages*. London: Routledge and Kegan Paul.

Bernard, Richard (1629) *A Guide to Grand-Jury Men* (2nd. edn.) London.

Bernhard, Virginia (2010) "Religion, Politics, and Witchcraft in Bermuda, 1651–1655". *The William and Mary Quarterly*, v. 67, no. 4, pp. 677–708.

Bever, Edward (2002) "Witchcraft, Female Aggression, and Power in the Early Modern Community". *Journal of Social History*, v. 35, no. 4, pp. 955–988.

Bever, Edward (2009) "Witchcraft Prosecutions and the Decline of Magic". *The Journal of Interdisciplinary History*, v. 40, no. 2, pp. 263–293.

Black, Stephen F. (1986) "The Courts and Judges of Westminster Hall During the Great Rebellion, 1640–1660". *The Journal of Legal History*, v. 7, no. 1, pp. 23–52.

Blackstone, William (1769) *Commentaries on the Laws of England*: Vol. IV. Oxford: Clarendon Press.

Borman, Tracy (2013) *Witches: A Tale of Sorcery, Scandal and Seduction*. London: Jonathan Cape.

Boulton, Reginald (1722) *The Possibility and Reality of Magick, Sorcery, and Witchcraft, Demonstrated*. London: J. Roberts.

Bovet, Richard (1684) *Pandaemonium, or the Devils Cloyster*. London: J. Walthoe.

Breuer, Heidi (2009) *Crafting the Witch: Gendering Magic in Medieval and Early Modern England.* Abingdon: Routledge.

Briggs, Robin (1996) *Witches and Neighbours.* London: HarperCollins.

Briggs, Robin (1996) "'Many reasons why': witchcraft and the problem of multiple explanation'. In Jonathan Barry et al. (eds.), *Witchcraft in Early Modern Europe.* Cambridge: Cambridge University Press, pp. 49–63.

Brown, Peter C. (2014) *Essex Witches,* Stroud: The History Press.

Bruce, John (ed.) (1858) *Calendar of State Papers Domestic: Charles I, 1625–1626.* London: Her Majesty's Stationery Office.

Bruce, John (ed.) (1864) *Calendar of State Papers Domestic: Charles I, 1634–1635.* London: Her Majesty's Stationery Office.

Cambers, Andrew (2009) "Demonic Possession, Literacy and 'Superstition' in Early Modern England". *Past & Present,* v. 202, no. 1, pp. 3–35.

Camden, Carroll (1948) "The Suffocation of the Mother". *Modern Language Notes,* v. 63, no. 6, pp. 390–393.

Cockburn, J.S. (1972) *A History of English Assizes, 1558–1714.* Cambridge: Cambridge University Press.

Cockburn, J.S. (ed.) (1975) *Calendar of Assize Records: Hertfordshire Indictments, Elizabeth I.* London: Her Majesty's Stationery Office.

Cockburn, J.S. (ed.) (1977) *Crime in England 1550–1800.* London: Methuen.

Cockburn, J.S. (ed.) (1976) *Western Circuit Assize Orders 1629–1648: A Calendar.* London: Royal Historical Society.

Cockburn, J.S. (ed.) (1978) *Calendar of Assize Records: Essex Indictments, James I.* London: Her Majesty's Stationery Office.

Cockburn, J.S. (ed.) (1979) *Calendar of Assize Records: Kent Indictments, Elizabeth I.* HMSO, London.

Cockburn, J.S (ed.) (1980) *Calendar of Assize Records: Surrey Indictments, Elizabeth I.* London: Her Majesty's Stationery Office.

Cockburn, J.S. (ed.) (1982) *Calendar of Assize Records: Essex Indictments, James I.* London: Her Majesty's Stationery Office.

Cooper, Thomas (1617) *The Mystery of Witch-Craft.* London.

Cotta, John (1616) *The Triall of Witch-craft, Shewing the True and Right Methode of the Discovery: With a Confutation of erroneous wayes.* London.

Dalton, Michael (1618) *The Country Justice, Containing the Practise, Duty and Power of The Justices of the Peace As well in as out of their Sessions.* London.

Darr, Orna Alyagon (2011) *Marks of an Absolute Witch: Evidentiary Dilemmas in Early Modern England*. Farnham: Ashgate.

Davies, Owen (1997) "Cunning-Folk in England and Wales during the Eighteenth and Nineteenth Centuries". *Rural History*, v. 8, no. 1, pp. 91–107.

Davies, Owen (1997) "Urbanization and the Decline of Witchcraft: An Examination of London". *Journal of Social History*, v. 30, no. 3, pp. 597–617.

Davies, Owen (1999) "Witchcraft: The Spell that Didn't Break". *History Today*, v. 49, no. 8, pp. 7–13.

Davies, Owen (1999) *Witchcraft, Magic and Culture, 1736–1951*. Manchester: Manchester University Press.

Davies, Owen (2002) "Methodism, the Clergy, and the Popular Belief in Witchcraft and Magic". *History*, v. 82, no. 266, pp. 252–265.

Davies, Owen (2003) *Cunning-folk in English History*. London: Hambledon.

Davies, R. Trevor (1947) *Four Centuries of Witch Beliefs*. London: Methuen.

Davies, Simon Francis (2013) *Witchcraft and the Book Trade in Early Modern England*. Ph.D. thesis, University of Sussex.

Davies, S.F. (2013) "The Reception of Reginald Scot's Discovery of Witchcraft: Witchcraft, Magic, and Radical Religion". *Journal of the History of Ideas*, vol. 74, no. 3, pp. 381–401.

Dean, David (1996) *Law-Making and Society in Late Elizabethan England: The Parliament of England 1584–1601*. Cambridge: Cambridge University Press.

Dekker, T., Rowley, W. & Ford, J. (1658) *The Witch of Edmonton*. London: Edward Blackmore.

Dick, Oliver Lawson (ed.) (1949) *Aubrey's Brief Lives*. London: Secker & Warburg.

Dobson, Clifford (1996) *The Jewel of Salisbury*. Much Wenlock: RJK Smith.

Douglas, Mary (ed.) (1970) *Witchcraft Confessions and Accusations*. London: Routledge & Kegan Paul.

Drage, William (1668) *Physical experiments: being a plain description of the causes, signes, and cures of most diseases incident to the body of man, to which is added a discourse of diseases proceeding from witchcraft*. London: Simon Miller.

Duncan, Kirsty (1993) "Was ergotism responsible for the Scottish witch-hunts?" *Area*, v. 25, no. 1, pp. 30–36.

Durston, Gregory (2000) *Witchcraft and Witch Trials: A History of English Witchcraft and its Legal Perspectives, 1542–1736*. Chichester: Barry Rose.

Elmer, Peter (2016) *Witchcraft, Witch-Hunting, and Politics in Early Modern England*. Oxford: Oxford University Press.

Elton, G. R. (1986) *The Parliament of England, 1559–1581*. Cambridge: Cambridge University Press.

Ewen, C. L'Estrange (ed.) (1929) *Witch Hunting and Witch Trials: The Indictments for Witchcraft from the Records of 1373 Assizes Held for the Home Circuit AD 1559–1736*. London: Kegan Paul, Trench, Trubner.

Ewen, C. L'Estrange (ed.) (1933) *Witchcraft and Demonianism*. London: Heath Cranton.

Ewen, C. L'Estrange (1938) *Witchcraft in the Star Chamber*. Printed privately for the author.

Filmer, Robert (1653) *An Advertisement to the Jury-Men of England Touching witches, together with a Difference between an English and Hebrew witch*. London: Richard Royston.

Forsyth, Miranda (2016) "The Regulation of Witchcraft and Sorcery Practices and Beliefs". *Annual Review of Law and Social Science*, v. 12, pp. 331–351.

Foss, Edward (1870) *Biographia Juridica: A Biographical Dictionary of the Judges of England from the Conquest to the Present Time, 1066–1870*. Boston: Little, Brown.

Fudge, Thomas A. (2006) "Traditions and Trajectories in the Historiography of European Witch Hunts". *History Compass*, v. 4, issue 3, pp. 488–527.

Freeman, Jessica (2004) "Sorcery at Court and Manor: Margery Jourdemayne, the Witch of Eye next Westminster". *Journal of Medieval History*, v. 30, pp. 343–357.

Gairdner, James (ed.) (1892) *Letters and Papers Foreign and Domestic: Henry VIII, Volume 13, Part 1, January-July 1538*. London: Her Majesty's Stationery Office.

Gairdner, James and Brodie, R.H. (eds.) (1900) *Letters and Papers Foreign and Domestic, Henry VIII, Volume 17, 1542*. London: Her Majesty's Stationery Office.

Gardiner, Ralph (1655) *England's Grievance Discovered, in Relation to the Coal Trade*. North Shields: Philipson and Hare (1849).

Garland, Anna (2003) "The Great Witch Hunt: The Persecution of Witches in England, 1550–1660". *Auckland University Law Review*, v. 9, no. 4, pp. 1152–1180.

Gaskill, Malcolm (2000) *Crime and Mentalities in Early Modern England*. Cambridge: Cambridge University Press.

Gaskill, Malcolm (2007) "Witchcraft, Politics, and Memory in Seventeenth-Century England". *The Historical Journal*, v. 50, no. 2, pp. 289–308.

Gaskill, Malcolm (2008) "The Pursuit of Reality: Recent Research into the History of Witchcraft". *The Historical Journal*, v. 51, no. 4, pp. 1069–1088.

Gaskill, Malcolm (2008) "Witchcraft and Evidence in Early Modern England". *Past & Present*, v. 198, no. 1, pp. 33–70.

Gaskill, Malcolm (2008) *Witchfinders: A Seventeenth-Century English Tragedy.* London: John Murray.

Gaskill, Malcolm (2010) *Witchcraft: A Very Short Introduction.* Oxford: Oxford University Press.

Gaskill, Malcolm (2013) "Witchcraft Trials in England". In Brian P. Levack (ed.), *The Oxford Handbook of Witchcraft in Early Modern Europe and Colonial America.* Oxford: Oxford University Press, pp. 283–299.

Gaule, John (1646) *Select Cases of Conscience Touching Witches and Witchcrafts.* London.

Geis, Gilbert and Bunn, Ivan (1997) *A Trial of Witches: A Seventeenth-Century Witchcraft Prosecution.* London: Routledge.

Gent, Frank J. (2001) *The Trial Of The Bideford Witches.* Crediton.

Gere, Cathy (2001) "William Harvey's Weak Experiment: The Archaeology of an Anecdote". *History Workshop Journal*, v. 51, no. 1, pp. 19–36.

Gibson, Marion (2000) *Early Modern Witches: Witchcraft Cases in Contemporary Writing.* London: Routledge.

Gifford, George (1593) *A Dialogue concerning Witches and Witchcraftes.* London.

Giuseppi, M.S. (ed.) (1938) *Calendar of the Cecil Papers in Hatfield House: Volume 17, 1605.* London: His Majesty's Stationery Office.

Glanvil, Joseph (1681) *Saducismus Triumphatus, or Full and Plain Evidence Concerning Witches and Apparitions.* London.

Gleason, J.H. (1969) *The Justices of The Peace in England, 1558 to 1640,* Oxford: Clarendon Press.

Goodare, Julian (2005) "The Scottish Witchcraft Act". *Church History*, v. 74, no. 1, pp. 39–67.

Green, Mary Anne Everett (ed.) (1864) *Calendar of State Papers Domestic: Charles II, 1665–6.* London: Her Majesty's Stationery Office.

Gragg, Larry (2015) "Witchcraft in the Early Modern West". *Comparative Civilizations Review*, v. 72, no. 72, pp. 137–148.

Gregory, Annabel (1991) "Witchcraft, Politics, and 'Good Neighbourhood' in Early Seventeenth-Century Rye". *Past & Present,* v. 133, issue 1, pp. 31–66.

Guskin, Phyllis J. (1981) The Context of Witchcraft: The Case of Jane Wenham (1712). *Eighteenth-Century Studies*, v. 15, no. 1, pp. 48–71.

Hale, Matthew (1693) *A Collection of Modern Relations of Matter of Fact, Concerning Witches & Witchcraft upon the Persons of People.* London.

Harris, Marvin (1974) *Cows, Pigs, Wars, and Witches: The Riddles of Culture*, New York: Random House.

Harrison, G.B. (ed.) (1929) *The Trial of the Lancaster Witches, 1612.* London: Peter Davies.

Helmholz, Richard Henry (ed.) (1985) *Select Cases on Defamation to 1600.* London: Selden Society.

Henderson, Lizanne (2006) "The Survival of Witchcraft Prosecutions and Witch Belief in South-West Scotland". *The Scottish Historical Review,* v. 85, part 1, no. 219, pp. 52–74.

Herrup, Cynthia B. (1987) *The Common Peace: Participation and the Criminal Law in Seventeenth-Century England.* Cambridge: Cambridge University Press.

Holland, Henry (1590) *A Treatise Against Witchcraft.* Cambridge: University of Cambridge.

Hollingsworth, Arthur George Harper (1844) *The History of Stowmarket: The Ancient County Town of Suffolk.* Ipswich: F. Pawsey.

Holmes, Clive (1993) "Women: Witnesses And Witches". *Past & Present,* v. 140, no. 1, pp. 45–78.

Hopkins, Matthew (1647) *The Discovery of Witches: In Answer to Severall Queries, Lately Delivered to the Judges of Assize for the county of Norfolk, And now Published By Matthew Hopkins, Witch-finder, for the Benefit of the whole Kingdom.* London.

Howard, Sharon (2008) *Law and Disorder in Early Modern Wales: Crime and Authority in the Denbighshire Courts, c. 1660–1730.* Cardiff: University of Wales Press.

Hudson, Chris (2016) *Witch Trials: Discontent in Early Modern Europe*, working paper no. HEIDWP11–2016. Geneva: Graduate Institute of International and Development Studies.

Hunter, Michael (2012) "The Decline Of Magic: Challenge And Response In Early Enlightenment England". *The Historical Journal,* v. 55, no. 2, pp. 399–425.

Hussey, Arthur (1904) "Visitations Of The Archdeacon Of Canterbury". *Archaeologia Cantiana,* v. 26, pp. 17–50.

Hutchinson, Francis (1718) *An Historical Essay Concerning Witchcraft.* London.

Hutton, Ronald (2017) *The Witch: A History of Fear, from Ancient Times to the Present.* New Haven: Yale University Press.

Hyde, Patricia and Michael Zell (2000) "Governing the Country". In Michael Zell (ed.), *Early Modern Kent.* Woodbridge: Boydell Press.

Ingram, Martin (1987) *Church Courts, Sex and Marriage in England 1570–1640*. Cambridge: Cambridge University Press.
Jackson, Louise (1995) "Witches, Wives and Mothers: witchcraft persecution and women's confessions in seventeenth-century England". *Women's History Review*, v. 4, no. 1, pp. 63–84.
James VI (1597) *Daemonologie, In Forme of a Dialogue*. Edinburgh.
Jansson, Maija (1988) "Matthew Hale on Judges and Judging". *Journal of Legal History*, v. 9, pp. 201–213.
Jeaffreson, John Cordy (ed.) (1887) *Middlesex County Records: Volume 2, 1603–25*. London: Middlesex County Record Society.
Jeaffreson, John Cordy (ed.) (1888) *Middlesex County Records: Volume 3, 1625–67*. London: Middlesex County Record Society.
Jeaffreson, John Cordy (ed.) (1892) *Middlesex County Records: Volume 4, 1667–88*. London: Middlesex County Record Society.
Johnson, Noel D. and Koyama, Mark (2014) "Taxes, Lawyers, and the Decline of Witch Trials in France". *The Journal of Law & Economics*, v. 57, no. 1, pp. 77–112.
Jones, Charles (1929) "A Hertfordshire Trial for Witchcraft", *St Albans & Hertfordshire Architectural & Archaeological Society Transactions*, pp. 279–286.
Jones, David L. (2015) *The Ipswich Witch: Mary Lackland and the Suffolk Witch Hunts*. Stroud: The History Press.
Jones, Karen and Zell, Michael (2005) "'The divels speciall instruments': women and witchcraft before the 'great witch-hunt'". *Social History*, v. 30, no. 1, pp. 45–63.
Jorden, Edward (1603) *A Briefe Discourse of a Disease Called the Suffocation of the Mother*. London: John Windet.
Kamerick, Kathleen (2008) "Shaping Superstition in Late Medieval England". *Magic, Ritual, and Witchcraft*, v. 3, no. 1, pp. 29–53.
Karkeek, Paul Q. (1874) "Devonshire Witches". *Transactions of the Devonshire Association for the Advancement of Science, Literature and Art*, v. 6, part 2, pp. 736–763.
Kent, E.J. (2005) "Masculinity and Male Witches in Old and New England", 1593–1680. *History Workshop Journal*, v. 60, issue 1, pp. 69–92.
Kesselring, Krista (2000) *To Pardon and to Punish: Mercy and Authority in Tudor England*. Ph.D. thesis, Queen's University, Kingston (Ontario).
Kesselring, K.J. (2015) "Bodies of Evidence: Sex and Murder (or Gender and Homicide) in Early Modern England, c. 1500–1680". *Gender & History*, v. 27, no. 2, pp. 245–262.

Kittredge, G.L. (1911) "King James I and 'The Devil Is an Ass'". *Modern Philology*, v. 9, no. 2, pp. 195–209.

Klaits, Joseph (1985) *Servants of Satan: The Age of the Witch Hunts.* Bloomington: Indiana University Press.

Kors, Alan Charles and Peters, Edward (1972) *Witchcraft in Europe 1100–1700: A Documentary History.* Philadelphia: University of Pennsylvania Press.

Lambarde, William (1599) *Eirenarcha, or Of the Office of the Justices of Peace, in foure Bookes.* London.

Landau, Norma (1984) *The Justices of the Peace 1679–1760.* Berkeley and Los Angeles: University of California Press.

Langbein, John H. (1976) *Torture and the Law of Proof: Europe and England in the Ancien Régime.* Chicago: University of Chicago Press.

Larner, Christina (1980) "'*Crimen Exceptum?* The Crime of Witchcraft in Europe". In V. A. C. Gatrell et al. (eds.), *Crime and the Law: The Social History of Crime in Western Europe since 1500.* London: Europa Press, pp. 49–75.

Larner, Christina (1981) *Enemies of God: The Witch-hunt in Scotland.* London: Chatto & Windus.

Larner, Christina (1981) "Witch Beliefs and Witch-hunting in England and Scotland". *History Today*, v. 31, issue 2, pp. 32–36.

Larner, Christina (1984) *Witchcraft and Religion: The Politics of Popular Belief.* Oxford: Basil Blackwell.

Leeson, P.T. and Russ, J.W. (2018), "Witch Trials", *Economic Journal*, v. 28, pp. 2066–2105.

Le Hardy, William (ed.) (1937) *County of Middlesex. Calendar to the Sessions Records: New Series, Volume 3, 1615–16.* London: Ernest Hart.

Levack, Brian P. (1995) "Possession, Witchcraft, and the Law in Jacobean England". *Washington and Lee Law Review*, v. 52, issue 5, pp. 1613–1640.

Levack, Brian P. (1987) *The Witch-Hunt in Early Modern Europe.* London: Pearson Education.

Levack, Brian P. (ed.) (2001) *New Perspectives on Witchcraft, Magic, and Demonology: Volume 4, Gender and Witchcraft.* London: Routledge.

Levack, Brian P. (ed.) (2004) *The Witchcraft Sourcebook.* London: Routledge.

Levack, Brian P. (2007) *Witch-hunting in Scotland: Law, Politics and Religion.* London: Routledge.

Levin, Carole et al. (2016) *A Biographical Encyclopedia of Early Modern Englishwomen: Exemplary Lives and Memorable Acts, 1500–1650*. London: Routledge.

Lipscomb, Suzannah (2019) *The Voices of Nimes: Women, Sex, and Marriage in Reformation Languedoc*. Oxford: Oxford University Press.

MacDonald, Michael (ed.) (1991) *Witchcraft and Hysteria in Elizabethan London: Edward Jorden and the Mary Glover Case*, London: Routledge.

MacDonald, Stuart (2002) "Torture and the Scottish Witch-hunt: A Re-examination". *International Review of Scottish Studies*, v. 27, pp. 95–114.

Macfarlane, Alan (1970) *Witchcraft in Tudor and Stuart England: A Regional and Comparative Study*. New York: Harper & Row.

Macfarlane, Alan (1970) "Witchcraft in Tudor and Stuart Essex". In Mary Douglas (ed.), *Witchcraft Confessions and Accusations*. London: Tavistock, pp. 81–99.

Mackenzie, Eneas (1827) *Historical Account of Newcastle-upon-Tyne Including the Borough of Gateshead*. Newcastle-upon-Tyne: Mackenzie and Dent.

McGinnis, Scott (2002) "'Subtiltie' Exposed: Pastoral Perspectives on Witch Belief in the Thought of George Gifford". *The Sixteenth Century Journal*, v. 33, no. 3, pp. 665–686.

Machielsen, Jan (2016) "New College of Magic and Wizardry: A Second Note on the 1566/7 Visitation". *New College Notes,* issue 7, pp. 1–5.

Machielsen, Jan (2016) "'Moved and Seduced by the Instigation of the Devil': Witchcraft and the Law, 1450–1701". In Russell Sandberg, Norman Doe, Bronach Kane, and Caroline Roberts (eds*.), The Research Handbook on Interdisciplinary Approaches to Law and Religion* (forthcoming).

Maxwell-Stuart, P.G. (2008) "The New King and the Crucible of the Act: King James's Experience of Witches and the 1604 English Witchcraft Act". In John Newton and Jo Bath (eds.), *Witchcraft and the Act of 1604*. Leiden: Brill, pp. 29–46.

Melling, Elizabeth (ed.) (1969) *Crime and Punishment, Kentish Sources VI,* Maidstone: Kent County Council.

Midelfort, Erik (2011) "Witch Craze? Beyond the Legends of Panic". *Magic, Ritual and Witchcraft*, v. 6, no. 1, pp. 11–33.

Middleton, Thomas (1778) *The Witch*. London.

Millar, Charlotte-Rose (2017) *Witchcraft, the Devil, and Emotions in Early Modern England*. London: Routledge.

Mitchell, Stephen (2004) "A case of witchcraft assault in early nineteenth-century England as ostensive action". In Willem de Blécourt and Owen Davies (eds.),

Witchcraft Continued: Popular Magic in Modern Europe. Manchester: Manchester University Press, pp. 14–28.

Monod, Paul Kléber (2013) *Solomon's Secret Arts: The Occult in the Age of Enlightenment.* New Haven: Yale University Press.

Monter, E. William (1969) *European Witchcraft.* New York: Wiley.

Monter, William (2004) "Review: Re-contextualizing British witchcraft". *Journal of Interdisciplinary History*, v. 35, issue 1, pp. 105–111.

Newton, John, and Jo Bath (eds.) (2008) *Witchcraft and the Act of 1604.* Leiden: Brill.

North, Roger (1826) *The Lives of the Right Hon. Francis North, Baron Guildford, the Hon. Sir Dudley North, and the Hon. and Rev. Dr. John North,* Volume 1. London: Henry Colburn.

Notestein, Wallace (1911) *A History of Witchcraft in England from 1558 to 1718.* Washington, D.C.: American Historical Association.

Ogier, Darryl (2010) "Glimpses of the Obscure: The Witch Trials of the Channel Islands". In Angela McShane and Garthine Walker (eds.), *The Extraordinary and the Everyday in Early Modern England: Essays in Celebration of the Work of Bernard Capp.* Basingstoke: Palgrave Macmillan, pp. 177–191.

Oldridge, Darren (ed.) (2002) *The Witchcraft Reader.* Abingdon: Routledge.

Oldridge, Darren (2016) *The Supernatural in Tudor and Stuart England,* Abingdon: Routledge.

O'Brien, Sheilagh Ilona (2016) "The discovery of witches: Matthew Hopkins's Defense of his Witch-Hunting Methods". *Preternature: Critical and Historical Studies on the Preternatural*, v. 5, no. 1, pp. 29–58.

Oster, Emily F. (2004) "Witchcraft, Weather and Economic Growth in Renaissance Europe". *Journal of Economic Perspectives*, v. 18, no. 1, pp. 215–228.

Parkin, Sally (2006) "Witchcraft, Women's Honour and Customary Law in Early Modern Wales". *Social History*, v. 31, no. 3, pp. 295–318.

Parry, Keith (2011) "Witchcraft in seventeenth-century Norfolk". https://keithparry.org. Last accessed 14 February 2019.

Pavlac, Brian Alexander (2009) *Witch Hunts in the Western World: Persecution and Punishment from the Inquisition through the Salem Trials.* Westport: Greenwood Press.

Pearl, Jonathan L. (1999) *The Crime of Crimes: Demonology and Politics in France, 1560–1620,* Waterloo: Wilfrid Laurier University Press.

Perkins, William (1608) *A Discourse of the Damned Art of Witchcraft*. In I. Breward (ed.) (1970) *The Work of William Perkins*. Abingdon: Sutton Courtenay Press.

Pickering, Andrew and Pickering, David (2013) *Witch Hunt: The Persecution of Witches in England*. Stroud: Amberley Publishing.

Pickering, Andrew (2017) *The Witches of Selwood Forest: Witchcraft and Demonism in the West of England 1625–1700*. Newcastle: Cambridge Scholars.

Pihlajamäki, Heikki (2000) "'Swimming the Witch, Pricking for the Devil's Mark': Ordeals in the Early Modern Witchcraft Trials". *The Journal of Legal History*, v. 21, issue 2, pp. 35–58.

Poland, Peter S. (2014) "A Matter of Life, Death, and Legal Procedure: What every Texas lawyer should know about the European witch hunts". *Texas Bar Journal*, v. 77, no. 9, pp. 784–787.

Pollock, Adrian (1979) "Social and Economic Characteristics of Witchcraft Accusations in sixteenth- and seventeenth-century Kent". *Archaeologia Cantiana*, v. 95, pp. 37–48.

Poska, Allyson M. (2005) *Women and Authority in Early Modern Spain: The Peasants of Galicia*. Oxford: OUP.

Potts, Thomas (1613) *The Wonderfull Discoverie of Witches in the Countie of Lancaster*. London.

Purkiss, Diane (1996) *The Witch in History: Early Modern and Twentieth-Century Representations*. London: Routledge.

Raine, J. (ed.) (1845) *Depositions and Other Ecclesiastical Proceedings from the Courts of Durham, Volume 21*. Durham: Surtees Society.

Rennison, Eileen (2009) *Yorkshire Witches*. Stroud: Amberley.

Reresby, John (1734) *The Memoirs of the Honourable Sir John Reresby, Bart. and Last Governor of York*. London: Samuel Harding.

Roberts, Alexander (1616) *A Treatise of Witchcraft*. London.

Roberts, R. A. (ed.) (1904) *Calendar of the Cecil Papers in Hatfield House: Volume 10, 1600*. London: His Majesty's Stationery Office.

Roper, Lyndal (2006) *Witch Craze: Terror and Fantasy in Baroque Germany*. New Haven: Yale University Press.

Rosen, Barbara (ed.) (1972) *Witchcraft in England 1558–1618*. New York: Taplinger.

Ross, Richard S. (2017) *Before Salem: Witch Hunting in the Connecticut River Valley, 1647–1663*. Jefferson, N.C.: McFarland.

Rowlands, Alison (2003) *Witchcraft Narratives in Germany: Rothenburg, 1561–1652*. Manchester: Manchester University Press.

Rowley, W., Dekker, T., and Ford, J. (1621; first published 1658) *The Witch of Edmonton*. London.

Rushton, Karen (2014) "History of the Ecclesiastical Courts of the Diocese of Canterbury, 1566–86". *Archaeologia Cantiana*, v. 134, pp. 263–281.

Rushton, Peter (1982) "Women, Witchcraft, and Slander in Early Modern England: Cases from the Church Courts of Durham, 1560–1675". *Northern History*, v. 18, issue 1, pp. 116–132.

Ryrie, Alec (2008) *The Sorcerer's Tale: Faith and Fraud in Tudor England*. Oxford: Oxford University Press.

Scot, Reginald (1584) *The Discoverie of Witchcraft*. Facsimile reprint (1973). Wakefield: E. P. Publishing.

Seitz, Jonathan (2011) *Witchcraft and Inquisition in Early Modern Venice*. Cambridge: Cambridge University Press.

Sharpe, J.A. (1987) *Early Modern England: A Social History, 1550–1760*. London: Edward Arnold.

Sharpe, J.A. (1991) "Witchcraft and women in seventeenth-century England: Some Northern evidence". *Continuity and Change*, v. 6, issue 2, pp. 179–199.

Sharpe, J.A. (1992) *Witchcraft in Seventeenth-Century Yorkshire: Accusations and Counter Measures*. York: University of York (Borthwick Papers).

Sharpe, J.A. (1994) "Women, Witchcraft and the Legal Process". In Jennifer Kermode and Garthine Walker (eds.), *Women, Crime and the Courts in Early Modern England*. London: University College London Press, pp. 125–141.

Sharpe, J.A. (2000) *The Bewitching of Anne Gunter: A Horrible and True Story of Deception, Witchcraft, Murder, and the King of England*. London: Routledge.

Sharpe, J.A. (2007) "Witchcraft in the Early Modern Isle of Man". *Cultural and Social History*, v. 4, issue 1, pp. 11–28.

Sharpe, James (1997) *Instruments of Darkness: Witchcraft in Early Modern England 1550–1750*. London: Penguin.

Sharpe, James (2013) "In Search of the English Sabbat: Popular Conceptions of Witches' Meetings in Early Modern England". *Journal of Early Modern Studies*, no. 2, pp. 161–183.

Simpson, Jacqueline (1996) "Witches and Witchbusters". *Folklore*, vol. 107, issue 1–2, pp. 5–18.

Sinclair, George (1685) *Satan's Invisible World Discovered.* Glasgow.

Sneddon, Andrew (2012) "Witchcraft belief and trials in early modern Ireland". *Irish Economic and Social History,* v. 39, issue 1, pp. 1–25.

Sneddon, Andrew (2013) *Possessed by the Devil: The Real History of the Islandmagee Witches and Ireland's only Mass Witchcraft Trial.* Dublin: The History Press Ireland.

Sneddon, Andrew (2015) *Witchcraft and Magic in Ireland.* London: Palgrave Macmillan.

Spence, Craig (2016) *Accidents and Violent Death in Early Modern London.* Woodbridge: Boydell Press.

Sprenger, Jacob and Kramer, Heinrich (1487) *Malleus Maleficarum.* (1996) translated by Montague Summers. London: Bracken Books.

Stearne, John (1648) *A Confirmation and Discovery of Witch Craft.* London

Stockdale, Eric (1977) *A Study of Bedford Prison, 1660–1877.* Luton: Bedfordshire Historical Record Society.

Stoyle, Mark (2011) "'It Is But an Olde Wytche Gonne': Prosecution and Execution for Witchcraft in Exeter, 1558–1610". *History,* v. 96, issue 322, pp. 129–151.

Stoyle, Mark (2017) *Witchcraft in Exeter: 1580–1660.* Exeter: The Mint Press.

Summers, Montague (1928) *The Discovery of Witchcraft: A Study of Master Matthew Hopkins.* London: Cayne Press.

Summers, Montague (1926) *The History of Witchcraft and Demonology.* London: Kegan Paul, Trench, Trubner.

Summers, Montague (1937) *A Popular History of Witchcraft.* New York: E. P. Dutton.

Sweetinburgh, Sheila (ed.) (2010) *Later Medieval Kent, 1220–1540.* Martlesham: Boydell Press.

Syme, Holger Schott (2012) *Theatre and Testimony in Shakespeare's England: A Culture of Mediation.* Cambridge: Cambridge University Press.

Thomas, Keith (1971) *Religion and the Decline of Magic.* London: Weidenfeld & Nicolson.

Tourney, Garfield (1972) "The Physician And Witchcraft In Restoration England". *Medical History,* v. 16, no. 2, pp. 143–155.

Trevor-Roper, H. R. (1990) *The European Witch-Craze of the Sixteenth and Seventeenth Centuries.* Harmondsworth: Penguin.

Tyler, Philip (1969) "The Church Courts at York and Witchcraft prosecutions, 1567–1640". *Northern History,* v. 4, issue 1, pp. 84–110.

Valletta, Frederick (2000) *Witchcraft, Magic and Superstition in England, 1640–70.* Farnham: Routledge.

Walker, Garthine (2003) *Crime, Gender and Social Order in Early Modern England.* Cambridge: Cambridge University Press.

Weyer, Johann (1563) *De praestigiis daemonum.* (1991) Translated by John Shea. Binghamton, N. Y.: Medieval and Renaissance Texts and Studies.

Wilkinson, Peter M. (ed.) (2017) *Chichester Archdeaconry Depositions 1603–1608.* Lewes: Sussex Record Society.

Willis, Deborah (2013) "The Witch-Family in Elizabethan and Jacobean Print Culture". *Journal for Early Modern Cultural Studies,* v. 13, no. 1, pp. 4–31.

Winzar, Patricia (1995) "Witchcraft Counter-Spells in Charing". *Archaeologia Cantiana,* v. 115, pp. 23–28.

Wormald, Jenny (1981) *Court, Kirk, and Community: Scotland 1470–1625.* London: Edward Arnold.

Wyporska, Wanda (2013) *Witchcraft in Early Modern Poland, 1500–1800.* Basingstoke: Palgrave MacMillan.

Young, Alan R. (1972) "Elizabeth Lowys: Witch and Social Victim", 1564. *History Today,* v. 22, issue 12, pp. 879–85.

Contemporary Journals and Newspapers Cited

Athenian Gazette
Bury and Norwich Post
Daily Journal
Fog's Weekly Journal
Ipswich Journal
Mercurius Britanicus; Communicating the Affaires of Great Britaine
Mist's Weekly Journal
Original Weekly Journal
Post Boy
The Faithful Scout
The Gentleman's Magazine
The Grub-Street Journal
The London Post
The Spectator
The Times
The Weekly Journal, or British Gazetteer

Index

A

absurdity *209*
abuse *80, 144, 171, 186*
accumulation of complaints *115*
accusatorial/adversarial system *71, 111*
acquittal (examples) *64, 67, 105, 108, 156, 181*
admissions *72, 118, 157*
age *64*
aggressive questioning *128*
allegations *115*
amateurism *183*
amulets *28*
Anderson, Sir Edmund *103*
appeasement *82*
arraignment *155–156*
Assizes *38, 52, 153*
attainder *93*
attempts *106*

B

bail *131*
banishment *20, 99, 182*
banquets, etc. *71*
Bartmann jugs *83*
Bavaria *26, 181*
beliefs *91, 210*
benefit of clergy *93*
benign activities, etc. *26*
Bermuda *14, 140, 182*
bewitchment *15–16, 33, 37, 132, 133, 190*
   animals, of *54*
Bideford witches *116*
   last verified hanging *196*
"Bilston boy" case *175*
binding-over *205*
   to prosecute *132*
bishops *95–96, 175*
black
   black birds *177*
   black mass *72*
blemishes *145*
blindness *86*
blood *76, 86*
   blood sacrifice *70*
   "fetching the blood" *87*
Burgundy *61*
burning to death *169*
Bury St Edmunds *195*

C

Calvinism *95*
Canterbury *21, 60, 88*
"carnal copulation" *72–74*
Carolina Code *92*
Catholics *36, 46, 95*

Catholic strongholds *50*
Channel Islands *181*
character *66*, *160*, *194*
charity *82*, *83*
  "charity-refused" model *115*, *207*
Charles I *145*, *176*, *183*
charms *20*, *27*, *83*
Chaucer, Geoffrey *21*
Chauncy, Sir Henry *119*
Chelmsford *62*, *183*
church *20*, *27*, *173*
circles
  "book of circles" *88*
Civil War *15*, *42*, *89*, *177*, *181–191*
  Civil War upsurge *188*
Clarke, Elizabeth *185*
class *50*, *210*
clemency *166*
Clerk, Jane and others
  final prosecution *202*
cognitive impairment *126*
coincidence *35*
complainants *159*
confessions *94*, *120*, *122–124*, *153*
  to the impossible *123*
Confirmation and Discovery of Witchcraft *186*
conjuring *28*, *89*, *93*. See also *magic*
constables *138*, *206*
conviction rates *164*
convulsions *49*
coroners *64*
counsellors, abettors, and procurers *94*
counterfeit *18*, *37*, *176*
Country Justice *122*

courts
  Assizes (examples) *12*, *15*, *99*
  ecclesiastical courts *21*, *34*, *70*, *80*, *87*, *183*
  King's/Queen's Bench *80*, *97*
  Quarter Sessions *124*, *132*, *153*
covenant *69*
covens *72*, *185*
cozening *97*
credulity *34*
Creed *139*, *198*
"crime apart" *18*, *210*
criminal justice system *111–136*
criminal procedure *18*
croanes *59*
crop failures *49*, *69*
cruentation *209*
cunning folk *21*, *26–28*, *88*, *94–101*, *139*, *159*
cursing *62*, *66*, *157*

D

Daemonologie *103*, *146*, *158*, *173*
Darcy, Brian *119*
death
  deathbed allegations *161*
  death penalty *197*
debauchery *66*
deception *61*, *204*
defamation *80*
defence
  active defence *85*
  passive defence *83*
deformity *55*, *59*
delusion *173*
demons *36*, *70*

demonic possession *50*
demonic witchcraft *46*
depositions *122*
depression *129*
detention *135*
deviance *66*
devil *15*, *23*
  "devil's mark/spot" *63*, *205*
  pact with the devil *69*
Devon *94*
diabolism *23*, *24*, *70*, *91*, *184*
  as a criminal offence *104*
disasters *43*
  disasters at sea *69*
Discovery of Witches *186*
doctors *162*
Dodson, Jane *194*
ducking *67*
Durham *189*

E

East Anglia (examples) *30*, *55*, *127*, *149*, *183*
effigy *92*
Elementary Education Act 1870 *208*
Elizabeth I *95*, *166*
enchantment *77*
Enlightenment *34*
ergotism *49*
Essex (examples) *63*, *88*, *108*, *119*, *183*
Estonia *61*
Europe *25*, *91*, *111*, *142*, *165*, *181*, *193*, *209*
evidence *137*, *157–159*
  circumstantial evidence *19*, *157*
  hybrid system of evidence *157*

juvenile testimony *174*
  lack of tangible evidence *122*
  valueless proof *209*
examining witches *118*, *121*
execution *26*, *39*, *42*, *76*, *98*, *169*, *190*
  Channel Islands, in *182*
  effective abolition *181*
  execution rates *164*
  ritual *170*
Exeter *94*
  Exeter Quarter Sessions *133*
experts *161–163*, *184*
  self-proclaimed experts *190*

F

fairies *46*, *88*
familiars *33*, *63*, *70*, *73–75*, *174*
fear *24*, *161*
felony *92*
  felony trials *153*
  secular felony *11*
female malady *162*
feminism *51*
Finland *61*, *165*
Finnmark *39*, *49*
fits *86*, *158*, *162*, *174*
flying through the air *71*
folk aspects *20*
forfeiture *93*
fortune-telling *206*
France *20*, *147*, *181*
fraud *35*, *37*, *93*, *173*

G

gaol
    gaol calendars *12*
    gaol delivery *183*
gender *59*, *210*
Germany *20*, *50*, *147*
Great Yarmouth *134*
grievances *112*
Guernsey *71*, *182*
Gunter, Anne *37*

H

hair *83*, *159*
Hale, Matthew *195*
hallucinations *49*
hanging *169*, *181*
harm *71*, *98*, *107*, *130*
Hart, Ann
    late conviction for witchcraft *199*
healers *28*
hearsay *160*
Henry VIII *92*
Hertfordshire *52*
hoaxes *38*
Hobbes *34*
Holt, Lord Chief Justice *198*, *200*
Hopkins, Matthew *42*, *59*, *107*, *126*, *164*, *184–186*
    remuneration *187*
Horne, Janet *45*
horseshoe *53*
House of Lords *103*
Huntingdon Assizes *122*
hurt. See *harm*
Husbands Bosworth *174*

hysteria *86*, *161–162*
    female hysteria *162*
    mass hysteria *127*

I

Iceland *61*
ignoramus *155*
illusions *35*
imprisonment *98*
"imps" *73*, *177*
incantations *77*
indictment *153*
inquisition *50*, *111*
Interregnum *65*, *89*, *166*, *181–191*
interrogation *13*
    abusive methods *186*
    deep interrogation *126*
investigation
    specialist investigative techniques *118*
Ipswich *62*, *169*, *185*
Ireland *16*, *22*, *46*, *50*, *203*, *209*
    Islandmagee witch case *138*
Isle of Man *47*

J

Jacobean period *53*, *155*, *173–179*
James I/VI *102*, *146*, *158*, *174*
Jersey *182*
Joan of Arc *22*
Jonson, Ben *174*
judges *40*, *120*, *133*, *167*, *174*, *210*
    judicial scepticism *176*
    weak judicial restraint *182*
jurisdiction *21*, *42*, *88*, *96*
    tiny *182*

jury *43–44*, *137*
　grand jury *153*

K

Kent (examples) *97*, *190*
Kincaid, John *188*
King's Lynn *113*, *134*, *187*

L

labelling *91*, *209*
lameness *86*
Lancashire *119*
　Lancaster Assizes *122*
Languedoc *184*
Leeds *199*
legal
　legal aspects *11*, *14*
　legal records *43*
　legal representation *92*, *156*
legislation *91–109*
　repeal *203*
　　post-repeal incidents *205–208*
Leicester *174*
　Leicester Assizes *202*
lewdness *66*
localism *183*
London *22*, *53*, *92*, *102*, *133*, *145*. See also *Old Bailey*
Lord's prayer *137*, *138*, *198*
　Lord's Prayer backwards *73*
love
　"unlawfull love" *106*
luck *210*
Luxembourg *165*

M

magic *19*, *23*, *25*, *26*
　"black/white" magic *26*
　counter-magic *82*, *83*
　image magic *77*
　indivisibility of magic *32*
　"magic and conjuration" *96*
　magic ring *94*
magistrates *14*, *31*, *86*, *99*, *116*, *118*, *120*, *160*, *188*
　investigating magistrates *71*
Maidstone Assizes *190*
maleficium *91*
　acts of *maleficium* *69*
Malet, Thomas *183*
malice *33*, *56*, *196*, *206*
malignancy *20*
Malleus Maleficarum *25*
Malmesbury *120*
Manningtree *185*
marginalisation *55*, *91*
marital status *64*
medieval times *19*
melancholy *129*, *162*
mental illness *35*
"mercenaries" *189*
mercy *99*
Middle East *48*
Middlesex *191*
misfortune *113*, *157*
misogyny *61*
Molland, Alice
　last hanging *196*
Montagu, Edward *184*
muteness *86*

N

nail parings *83*, *159*
Netherlands *147*
net-widening *55*
Newcastle *55*, *144*, *188–190*
Newgate Prison *141*
nipples *76*, *146*
Norfolk *186*
Normandy *61*
Northumberland *73*, *188–190*
Norwich *21*
Nowel, Roger *119*
Nutter, Alice *56*

O

occult *28*
Old Bailey *64*, *101*, *133*, *159*, *162*
   last witchcraft trial at *194*

P

pagans *48*
pamphlets *201*
panic *75*, *177*, *184*
   Kent near-panic *130*
pardon *101*, *109*, *165*, *174*, *201*
   general pardon *167*, *199*
   paying for a pardon *166*
Peacock, Samuel *126*
penance *27*, *87*
Pendle *56*, *72*, *105*, *122*, *159*, *177*
persecution *39*
personal appearance *210*
pillory *64*, *96*
pins *92*
Poland *165*
popular lore *77*
potions *20*, *78*
   love potions *88*
Potts, Thomas *13*
poverty *55*
pregnancy *89*, *93*, *109*, *164*, *168–169*
"presumptions" *66*, *140*
pretences *203*
previous allegations *63*
pricking *137*, *142*, *185*, *189*
   "witch prickers" *143*
Privy Council *125*, *165*
professionalisation *210*
profiling *69*
propaganda *50*
property
   lost/stolen property *93*
proscription *11*
prosecution *25*
   Caroline prosecutions *173*
   dangers of *81*
   decision to prosecute *131*
   Elizabethan prosecutions *100*
   Jacobean prosecutions *108*
   malicious prosecution *82*
   prosecutors *159*
Protestants *45*, *46*, *50*, *95*
psychology *129*
punishment *153*
Puritans *184*
   Puritan preoccupations *177*

Q

quarrelling *55*

Index

R

rack *126*
recognisances *80, 131–132*
Reformation *50*
religion *19, 48, 173, 193*
reprieve *165–166*
reputation *80, 157, 160, 175*
Restoration *53, 119, 193*
revenge *81*
ripple effect *190*
ritual *12*
Roman law *12*
rumour *209*
Russia *61*
rye *49*

S

sacrifice *12, 70*
"sadducism" *34*
Salisbury *56*
Satan *23, 61*
    consorting with Satan *71*
    covenant with *70*
    Prince of Darkness *24*
    satanic Sabbath *23*
Scandinavia *39*
scare tactics *83*
scepticism *34*
science *146, 161*
    quasi-science *138*
    Scientific Revolution *34*
scolds *59, 67*
Scotland *16, 27, 44, 61, 71, 104, 147, 165, 182, 209*
    Scottish Witchcraft Act of 1563 *27*

scratching *85, 86, 137, 139, 202*
scripture
    reciting scripture *138*
serjeants-at-law *175*
sexual activity *71*
sinking ships at sea *197*
social status *66*
sorcery *23, 54, 95*
Southampton *140*
Spain *181*
spectators *157*
spells *77, 94*
spinsters *65*
spirits
    entertaining spirits *108*
    feeding evil spirits *105*
sprites *74*
Staffordshire *175*
Star Chamber *38, 57, 81, 85*
statements *122*
statutes *91–109*
Stearne, John *184–186*
stereotypes *58, 63*
stocks *75, 82*
St Osyth witch trial *159*
subversion *51, 69*
Suffolk (examples) *56, 124, 127, 169, 184–186, 198*
suggestibility *130*
superstition *21, 22, 181*
surgeons *145*
Surrey (examples) *42, 54, 99, 156, 199–200*
suspicion *55, 137*
Sweden *182*
swimming *16, 137, 146*

"control" *206*
illegal swimming *205*
Switzerland *23, 26*

T

teat
  witch's teat *76, 137, 139, 185, 202*
testing *16, 137–151*
torture *13, 44, 125, 186*
  Scotland, in *127*
treason *18, 22, 71, 92, 158, 169*
treasure *93, 98, 167, 195*
  hidden treasure *58*
treatises *92*
trial *153–171*
trickery *32, 174, 189*
  to obtain confessions *128*
triggering events *112*

U

ugliness *55*
Ukraine *61*
"unnatural" climatic phenomena *48*
unpopularity *55, 66*
urine *83, 84, 137, 159*

V

vagabonds *89*
vexatious accusations *38*
victims *62, 85, 114, 159*
  victim-complainant *71*
"voice of the country" *158*
vomiting *202*
  vomiting pins, etc. *175, 198*

W

Wales *42, 209*
"walking" *126*
Wapping
  Witch of Wapping *57, 65*
"warding" *127*
warrants *116, 207*
"watching" *126*
Waterhouse, Agnes *76*
Wenham, Jane *82, 86, 115, 138*
  last conviction for witchcraft *199–201*
West Country *75, 133*
widows *65, 179, 201*
Winchester *21*
Windsor *117*
witchcraft
  abolition of crime of *193*
  black witches *29*
  blood relatives *63*
  "bookish" witchcraft *58*
  capital/non-capital *98*
  career as a witch *69–78*
  familial connections *55, 62*
  male witches *58, 60*
  "murder by witchcraft" *98*
  tests for witchcraft *137*
  "Thou shalt not suffer a witch to live" *96*
  urban witches *53*
  Warboys witches *140*
  witch bottles *83*
  Witchcraft Act 1563 *60*
  Witchcraft Acts (generally) *91*
  "witch craze" *39, 181*
  witchfinders *31, 184*

witch-hunting *39, 118*

witch "prickers" *57*

"witch's mark" *84, 178*

witch's teat. See *teat: witch's teat*

witnesses *121*, *158–160*

   children, liars, etc. as *159*

wizards *72*, *205*

   "common wizard" *97*

women *60*, *141*

   as prosecutors *52*

   women victims *62*

writings *24*

Wurttemberg *181*

Wurzburg *39*, *125*

Y

Yorkshire (examples) *30*, *52*, *60*, *79*, *134*, *194*

   West Riding Quarter Sessions *133*

Z

zealots *63*, *167*

Fields, Fens and Felonies: Crime and Justice in Eighteenth-Century East Anglia
by Gregory J Durston

It was a time of highwaymen, footpads and desperate petty offenders, draconian penalties, extremes of wealth and poverty, corruption and rough and emerging forms of justice. The contents include justices of the peace, policing, crimes, courts and judges as well as summary trial, jury trial, execution (and reprieve), a variety of offences including murder, violence and sexual offences, smuggling, poaching, property crimes, riots and disturbances. The book also looks at the hierarchies that existed whether social, legal, judicial, religious, military or otherwise to exert social controls at a time of relative lawlessness. A fascinating and statistically absorbing account of crimes, responses and penal outcomes of the era.

Paperback & Ebook | ISBN 978-1-909976-11-5 | 2016 | 736 pages

www.WatersidePress.co.uk

Whores and Highwaymen: Crime and Justice in the Eighteenth-Century Metropolis
by Gregory J Durston

The 'whores' and 'highwaymen' of Gregory Durston's title are just some of the dubious characters met with in this absorbing work. They include thief-takers, trading justices, an upstart legal profession whose lower orders developed ways to line their own pockets and court officials who did the same.

'A very-well-researched and readable book… a bit of a romp'
The Law Society Gazette

Paperback, Hardback & Ebook | ISBN 978-1-909976-39-9 | 2016 | 672 pages

www.WatersidePress.co.uk

A History of Criminal Justice in England and Wales
by John Hostettler

Charts all the main developments of criminal justice, from Anglo-Saxon dooms to the Common Law, struggles for political, legislative and judicial ascendency and the formation of the modern-day Criminal Justice System. Among a wealth of topics the book looks at the Rule of Law, the development of the criminal courts, police forces, the jury, judges and justices of the peace and individual crimes and punishments. It locates all the iconic events of criminal justice history within a wider context—demonstrating a wealth and depth of knowledge.

'Every student entering law school should have a copy and read it'
Criminal Law and Justice Weekly

'Highly recommended'
Choice

Paperback & Ebook | ISBN 978-1-904380-51-1 | 2009 | 352 pages

www.WatersidePress.co.uk